A World of Beliefs

To access the eBook

Simply…

1. Go to **folensonline.ie/redeem**

2. Register or sign in

3. Once signed in follow the onscreen instructions

4. Scratch the foil below to reveal your unique licence code

MYVW-IZFJ

Teachers please go to FolensOnline.ie

Shuna Hutchinson-Edgar   Mary-Deirdre Kinsella

First published in 2019 by Folens Publishers

Hibernian Industrial Estate, Greenhills Road, Tallaght, Dublin 24

© Shuna Hutchinson-Edgar and Mary-Deirdre Kinsella, 2019

Illustrations: Nigel Dobbyn/Beehive Illustration, Neal@KJA-artists, David Russell

ISBN: 978-1-78927-993-1

Copyright and Image Acknowledgements

The authors and publisher wish to thank the following for permission to reproduce extracts:

Extract from *The Lion, the Witch and the Wardrobe* by C. S. Lewis copyright © C. S. Lewis Pte Ltd 1950 reprinted by permission; extract from 'Global warming must not exceed 1.5°C, warns landmark UN report' by Jonathan Watts, *The Guardian* (8 October 2018) © Guardian News & Media Ltd 2018.

The authors and publisher wish to thank the following for permission to reproduce images:

Alamy, Cartoonstock.com, The Catholic Society, Central Statistics Office, Getty Images, ICAN (International Campaign to Abolish Nuclear Weapons), iStockphoto, PA Photos, Shutterstock, Sportsfile, Simon Community, Society of St Vincent de Paul, United Nations, The Global Goals for Sustainable Development icon grid by Project Everyone (project-everyone.org); photo of Desmond Doss courtesy of the Doss Council; signing of the UN Refugee Convention, 1951, and 'Education is a basic right' poster, both courtesy of UNHCR; extract from flyer 'Healing Racism Series: Muslim Mythbusters', courtesy of Arizona State University; photo of morning prayers on opening day of the Global Christian Forum in Bogotá, Colombia, 24–27 April 2018 under the theme of 'Let mutual love continue' © Albin Hillert/WCC; photo of Diverse City FC from Sport Against Racism Ireland's (SARI) 'Hijabs and Hat-tricks' programme © Mark Henderson; logo and photos courtesy of the Glencree Centre for Peace and Reconciliation; leaflet 'For a Greener Jewish World' courtesy of the Jewish Federations of North America; photo of UN Faith in the Future Meeting, Bristol, UK, © ARC/Katia Marsh; photo of sculpture *The Prodigal Son* by Margaret Adams Parker (www.margaretadamsparker.com) © Dwayne E. Huebner; photo of winter solstice, Newgrange burial chamber, by Alan Betson (*Irish Times*, 21 Dec. 2016); cover of *Exploring the Book of Kells* by George Otto Simms, published by O'Brien Press; photo by Jeffrey Vaughn Sr of *Crucifixion – Haiti 1999*, acrylic and collage on wood, MOCRA collection, Saint Louis University, by Helen David Brancato IHM (b. 1944); logos of Bóthar, Faith and Belief Forum, International Committee of the Red Cross, International Federation of Red Cross and Red Crescent Societies, Irish Cancer Society, Irish Hospice Foundation, Islamic Relief, Pax Christi, Save the Children, Society of St Vincent de Paul, Trócaire.

The publisher has made every effort to contact all copyright holders but if any have been overlooked, we will be pleased to make any necessary arrangements.

Any links or references to external websites or third-party publications should not be construed as an endorsement by Folens of the content or views of these websites or publications.

Contents

Introduction

Welcome to *A World of Beliefs*, a textbook for Junior Cycle Religious Education. This book covers all you need to know and do for the new RE course. This new subject aims to develop your knowledge, understanding, skills, attitudes and values so that you can come to an 'understanding of religion and its relevance to life, relationships, society and the wider world.' In this book, you will find the information needed to achieve that aim. We have tried to cover everything that is necessary to understand religion, and the content – especially the exercises that involve 'Enquiry', 'Exploration', and 'Reflection and Action' – will help you to develop the skills associated with understanding religion and its relevance to the world today.

Each of the **learning outcomes** of the subject specification are covered in the book. Each chapter has a learning outcome at its heart, to help you have the confidence that what you are learning will form part of your overall assessment in Religious Education. The chapters are colour-coded depending on which strand they are connected to, making it easy for you to work your way through the textbook and to note which outcome belongs to which strand.

For your benefit, at the start of each chapter there is a list of **learning intentions** to identify what you need to know or be able to do by the end of the chapter. This breaks down the learning outcome into something you can clearly understand and measure. At the end of each chapter, you can refer back to these learning intentions to check if you fully understand what was covered. You will have an opportunity here to let your teacher know if you are confident that you know all you need to about this outcome or if you need more time and help with it.

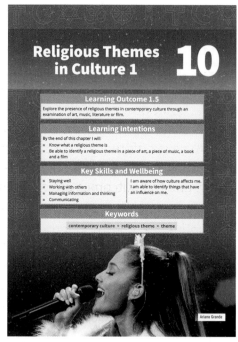

This book gives you an opportunity to explore the world view of members of **all five major world religions and humanism**. The course is broad and inclusive, and you will have a good opportunity to find out more about world views other than your own. There is no emphasis on one world view as being more important or better, and all are viewed as equally valuable. This is part of you learning to live in a world that includes people of many different religious beliefs or world views. You can, of course, learn more about a world view with which you identify closely, while at the same time you can learn to understand more about other world views and how important it is to be respectful of other people's beliefs.

The course has three strands: **Expressing Beliefs**, **Exploring Questions** and **Living Our Values**.

Strand 1 (Expressing Beliefs) is broken down into **12 learning outcomes**. This section should help you to understand, respect and appreciate how people's beliefs have been expressed in the past and continue to be expressed today, and to see how people live out their beliefs, focusing on understanding and appreciating that there is diversity within religions. Strand 1 is coloured pink, and the outcomes are covered in Chapters 1, 2, 3, 4, 10, 11, 12, 13, 15, 21, 23, 24 and 31.

In this strand you will study the major world religions and humanism, the religious communities in your area, the impact of Christianity on Irish culture, the importance of non-religious rituals for people, the expression of religious belief in rituals, places and prayer, the use of religious themes in film, art, music and literature, and the development of a sacred writing. Each relevant chapter has questions to assess your learning and understanding, exercises that will develop your skills, and suggestions for projects or further learning.

Strand 2 (Exploring Questions) is broken down into **10 learning outcomes**. This strand will give you a chance to look into the big questions of life and how people search for meaning. This could be described as the *philosophical section* – it sets out ideas on how to reflect on questions and explores how people with different religious beliefs and other interpretations of life respond to these questions. Strand 2 is coloured blue, and the outcomes are covered in Chapters 5, 6, 14, 16, 17, 22, 25, 26 and 32.

In this strand you will learn about how people have expressed their search for meaning in art, architecture and archaeology, how people have tried to answer the big questions about life, how people have made sense of the world and how it began through story, how people understand God, the life story of a founder of a major world religion, a timeline of a major world religion, the impact people can have on others through their commitment to their beliefs and how a person's faith can change. There are many tasks set to help you learn about and understand these topics.

Strand 3 (Living Our Values) is broken down into **nine learning outcomes**. This strand focuses on helping you to understand more about how a person's values affect their actions, how moral decision-making occurs and how to discuss moral issues, communicating with others in a respectful way. This section is all about *morals*, how people have different ideas of right and wrong and where those ideas come from. There is a lot of emphasis on discussion and debate in this strand. Strand 3 is coloured green, and the outcomes are covered in Chapters 7, 8, 9, 18, 19, 20, 27, 28, 29 and 30.

In this strand you will think about what it means to be moral, explore moral codes and their influence, think about the different ways people try to live a good life, debate moral issues, examine a moral decision-making process, examine the sources of values, research compassion, justice, peace and reconciliation, and explain how caring for the earth is important in one major world religion. Again, you will have lots of exercises to help you learn and reflect on your learning, and suggested actions for you to carry out.

We decided that two topics/learning outcomes needed three chapters each so that you can revisit them each year and, as your understanding develops, study them in greater detail and with an increasing maturity. **Learning outcome 3.6** asks you to 'debate a moral issue and consider what influences different points of view on the issue'. All three chapters on this topic offer you a great chance to express your opinions and ideas and to contribute to the class.

Learning outcome 1.5 asks you to 'explore the presence of religious themes in contemporary culture through an examination of art, music, literature or film'. If you like film, music, art and literature, you will really enjoy the chapters devoted to this topic.

Throughout the book, we have highlighted important words that you will need to understand in order to study this subject. They are like the building blocks for learning about the major world religions. These words are defined throughout the book, and we have also put them in the **glossary**. The glossary will be useful for you to check your understanding and as a quick reference.

Religious Education links to other subjects you do in school, including History, English, CSPE, SPHE and Geography. There are also connections with subjects not always studied in school but that we encounter in our lives, such as philosophy, morality and cultural studies. If you have opinions on current political situations, if you care about the environment, if you think it is important to respect other world religions and contribute to mutual respect and understanding between differing cultures and people, then there is plenty for you here. Bring in your own ideas and question everything! We share this world, this country and each of our communities with other people. We need to be open-minded and respectful. All of this starts with an understanding and knowledge of each other and our different beliefs.

We hope you enjoy reading this book and studying this subject as much as we enjoyed writing it. We aimed to make the book as modern and relevant as possible. There are topics as far-ranging as the history of Judaism, the serious issue of climate change, the plight of refugees, the meaning of life and the celebration of birthdays! The subject is open to all, and no one should feel they cannot do this subject or that it is not relevant.

Remember, there is 'A World of Beliefs' for you to engage with.

Shuna Hutchinson-Edgar and Mary-Deirdre Kinsella
March 2019

Help with the Classroom-Based Assessments

Part of the new Junior Cycle includes carrying out two Classroom-Based Assessments (CBAs). These will form part of your Junior Cycle Profile of Achievement (JCPA). These should help you to engage in 'Enquiry', 'Exploration', and 'Reflection and Action', which are the three elements underpinning the new course. These are the skills and approach you will need to take as you work through the course and as you carry out your CBAs.

To help you prepare for either CBA, study closely the chapters directly related to them. We have outlined them below. They provide guidance and clarity for this assessment.

- **CBA 1** asks you to, over a specified time, research and present on a person whose religious beliefs or world view have had a positive impact on the world around them, past or present. The chapter most associated with this is **Chapter 22**, which is on learning outcome 2.8 ('present stories of individuals or of groups in the history of two major world religions that have had a positive impact on the lives of people because of their commitment to living out their beliefs'). This CBA will take place during your Second Year.

- **CBA 2** asks you to, over a specified time, explore artistic **or** architectural **or** archaeological evidence that shows ways in which people have engaged in religious belief/the human search for meaning and purpose in life. The chapter most associated with this is **Chapter 32**, which is on learning outcome 2.1 ('research artistic, architectural or archaeological evidence that shows ways in which people have searched for meaning and purpose in life'). This CBA will take place in your Third Year.

- CBA2 also provides the subject matter for your **Written Assessment Task**, which also takes place towards the end of Third Year. The assessment task is worth 10% of your marks in the Junior Cycle. You will be assessed on how well you reflect on your new knowledge or understanding following the CBA, and on the skills, attitudes and values you have developed and how you will be able to apply these in the future.

Icons Used in This Textbook

 Icebreaker

An exercise to set the scene for the concepts being covered.

 Action Verb Focus

Explains the action verb contained in the learning outcome related to that chapter.

 What Does This Mean?

An explanation of key concepts or phrases.

 Did You Know?

An interesting piece of information on a theme or topic.

 Review and Reflect

Section review questions.

 Over to You

An opportunity for students to engage with the topic being covered. These relate specifically to the three elements of the course:

1. Enquiry   **2.** Exploration   **3.** Reflection and Action

 The Note Box feature highlights in more detail certain key concepts.

 Encourages communication and dialogue on an activity or topic.

 Pair work (Working with Others)

 Shows the links between chapters on certain learning outcomes.

 Group work (Working with Others)

Junior Cycle Key Skills icons

The following icons highlight where Junior Cycle key skills are covered within this book. They feature in Key Skill exercise boxes, as well as in Over to You exercises and Review and Reflect exercises.

 Communicating

 Managing Information and Thinking

 Managing Myself

 Working with Others

 Staying Well

 Being Creative

 Being Numerate

 Being Literate

Dedications

I would like to dedicate this to my father Frank Hutchinson – he was the coolest, smartest and kindest dad. I know he would be very proud.

Shuna Hutchinson-Edgar

I would like to dedicate this to my mam, Catherine Kinsella, the most kind, supportive and heroic mother. You are an incredible role model and I am blessed to have you.

Mary-Deirdre Kinsella

. . .

Acknowledgements

Finally, I would like to thank some people for their help and encouragement in writing this book. Friends who have given me words of encouragement every step of the way, my students in the High School Dublin, who keep me up to date and who are always teaching me, and my fellow teachers, who give great advice and chocolate. All in Folens who have worked tirelessly on this book, especially Adam, Priscilla, Ciara and Kate. Seriously, you were very committed to the production of this book and I really appreciate it. My co-author, Dee, you were fantastic to work with. Most of all my husband, David, I would never have completed any of this without him, not only all his practical help, reading, proofreading and checking everything countless times, but the confidence he shows in me without which I never would have even considered writing this book, and my two children, Nathan and Tirzah, you were great at coming up with ideas and just keeping me sane throughout this process. Finally, my family, especially my Mum, Nadya and Natasha, who have always supported me and who have made me who I am.

Shuna Hutchinson-Edgar

I would like to acknowledge so many people for their support and encouragement. The wonderful staff and students of St Angela's Secondary School, Waterford (especially the RE department), you are amazing and inspirational, and I am so grateful to be part of this community. All our team at Folens, thank you most sincerely for your dedication and hard work. My co-author, Shuna, you are a rock I could not have done without. My past teachers Eugene Broderick and Martina Kavanagh, whose passion for education made a lasting impression on me and set the bar very high. All my dear friends, how you had the patience for me during all this I'll never know! My truly excellent siblings, Morgan, Neil, Louise, John and Aoife, for spurring me on and all the kind words! You guys are just the best! And to Tom, who is solely responsible for keeping me sane.

Mary-Deirdre Kinsella

Beliefs of the Major World Religions

1

Introduction

There are many different religions around the world. The five big world religions are Hinduism, Judaism, Buddhism, Christianity and Islam. There are people belonging to all of these major world religions living in Ireland today. Other people do not belong to any religious group. Some people identify themselves as atheists and do not believe in the existence of a God or Gods. Others identify themselves as humanists, believing that people can find meaning in their own lives without belonging to a religion. Others still choose not to be members of any particular group.

In this chapter, we will explore the main **beliefs** of these five major world religions.

What Does This Mean?

Belief: To hold a strong opinion or viewpoint on something.

Icebreaker

The items or symbols shown in the pictures below all belong to one of the five major world religions. Can you match each image with the correct religion?

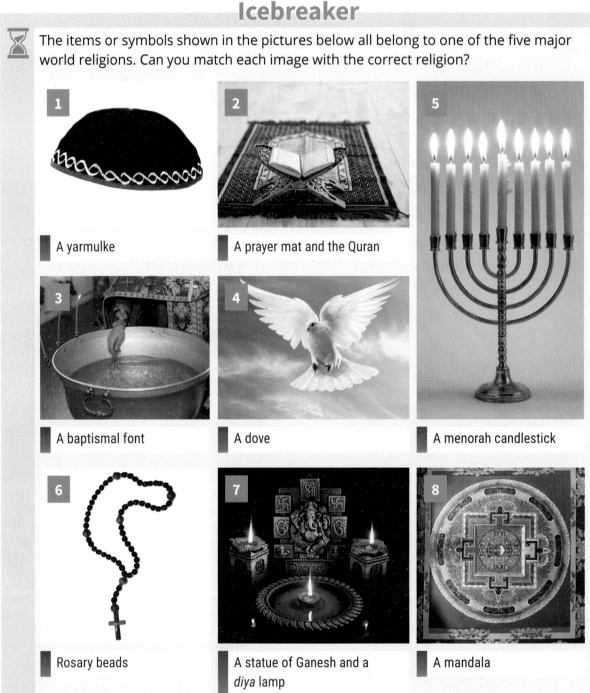

1	2	5
A yarmulke	A prayer mat and the Quran	A menorah candlestick

3	4	
A baptismal font	A dove	

6	7	8
Rosary beads	A statue of Ganesh and a *diya* lamp	A mandala

Where in the World?

Key

1 🕉 Hinduism (near modern-day Pakistan)   3 ☸ Buddhism (north-east India)   5 ☪ Islam (Saudi Arabia)

2 ✡ Judaism (Israel-Palestine)   4 ✝ Christianity (Israel-Palestine)

This map shows where the five major world religions started.
Today, followers of each religion can be found on every continent.

Timeline of Major World Religions

This timeline of the five major world religions gives the approximate date of origin for each religion and the name of the person who founded it (if known).

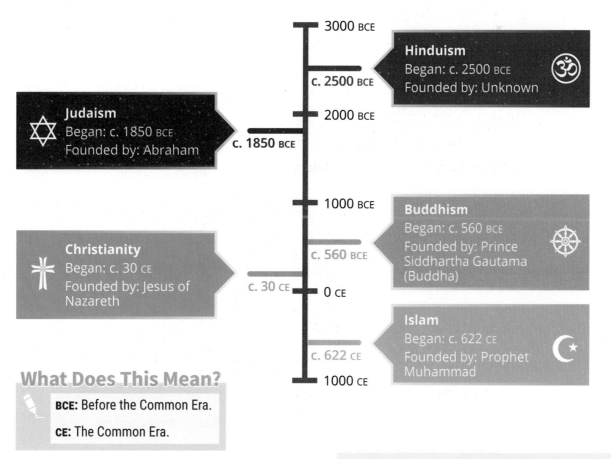

3000 BCE

Hinduism
Began: c. 2500 BCE
Founded by: Unknown

c. 2500 BCE

2000 BCE

Judaism
Began: c. 1850 BCE
Founded by: Abraham

c. 1850 BCE

1000 BCE

Buddhism
Began: c. 560 BCE
Founded by: Prince Siddhartha Gautama (Buddha)

c. 560 BCE

Christianity
Began: c. 30 CE
Founded by: Jesus of Nazareth

c. 30 CE

0 CE

Islam
Began: c. 622 CE
Founded by: Prophet Muhammad

c. 622 CE

1000 CE

What Does This Mean?

BCE: Before the Common Era.

CE: The Common Era.

1. Hinduism

Hinduism is an ancient world religion, most associated with India. Hinduism is a way of life and a way of understanding the world and how people are a part of it. Hinduism started in the Indus Valley, where a civilisation of people lived near the River Indus near what is modern-day Pakistan.

Hinduism is so old that no one knows for sure who started it. Hindus believe it was started about 2500 BCE by a group of unknown wise men or **rishis**. During a time known as the Vedic period, the people who made up the Indus Valley Civilisation composed a group of sacred writings known as the **Vedas**. The language they used was Sanskrit. Sanskrit is still the language of Hinduism.

What Does This Mean?

Polytheism: The belief in many Gods. Hindus are polytheists as they worship many Gods.

The Main Beliefs of Hinduism

- Hindus have many Gods, but they believe in one universal God, **Brahman**, which exists in all life. Belief in many Gods is called **polytheism**.

- Hindus believe in **reincarnation**. This is the belief that when a person dies his or her soul is reborn into a new life in this world. Each life cycle depends upon one's behaviour in a previous life.

- Hindus believe in **dharma** or sacred duty. This means that people have an obligation or duty to do the right thing for whatever stage in life they are in.

- Hindus believe in **karma**, the law of cause and effect. It means that from good comes good, while from bad comes bad. Hindus believe this will affect a person's next life – that how you live has consequences.

- Hindus believe that the ultimate goal in life is to break this cycle of birth, death and rebirth and achieve **moksha** or union back with God.

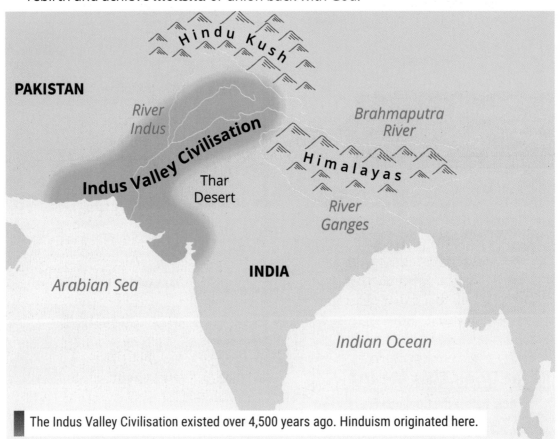

The Indus Valley Civilisation existed over 4,500 years ago. Hinduism originated here.

The Hindu Gods

Hindus have many Gods. The highest God, Brahman, lives in everything and takes many forms: male, female and even animal. Apart from Brahman, there are three main Hindu Gods, known as the **Trimurti**:

- **Brahma**, the source of all creation, is known as the creator.
- **Vishnu**, who keeps all good things on earth and brings harmony when needed, is known as the preserver.
- **Shiva** helps to create new things. As some things have to end for others to begin, Shiva is known as the destroyer.

Shiva is known as the destroyer God.

Did You Know?

According to Hindu tradition, the God Vishnu has descended to earth nine times in the past and will descend once more in the future. Each time he has appeared on earth in the past, he has taken a different form, or incarnation. He has taken the form of:

- Animals, such as a turtle and a boar
- The Hindu Gods **Lord Krishna** and **Prince Rama**
- The Buddha

Vishnu is usually shown riding a sacred bird-like creature called Garuda.

Vishnu sometimes takes the form of Lord Krishna.

Review and Reflect

1. Recall **three** of the main beliefs of Hinduism.
2. Define the following words:
   - Brahman
   - reincarnation
   - *Dharma*
   - *Karma*
   - *Moksha*

Vishnu sometimes takes the form of Prince Rama.

2. Judaism

Judaism began around 1850 BCE and is the oldest religion in the world to believe in one God. Belief in one God is known as **monotheism**. Judaism is the oldest monotheistic religion. Judaism has had a very big influence on the world and it is very closely related to Christianity and Islam.

Abraham was the person who started this belief in one God. Abraham came from Ur, and later lived in Haran in Mesopotamia, a place in modern-day Iraq. Abraham is believed to have had a **revelation** from God telling him to go to a promised land and that he was to be the father of a great nation. The land he was promised was called Canaan.

Abraham had started a **covenant** or agreement with God: the people would worship one God and, in return, God would take care of them. This agreement has been important to Judaism ever since. Abraham had a son Isaac and a grandson Jacob. These three men – Abraham, Isaac and Jacob – are said to be the founding fathers or **patriarchs** of Judaism.

What Does This Mean?

Monotheism: The belief in one God. Judaism, Christianity and Islam are monotheistic religions.

Revelation: When God (or Gods) make something known to people.

Covenant: An agreement. In Judaism, the covenant is an agreement or promise between God and the people. It was first made by Abraham.

Patriarch: 'Founding father', the male leader of a group of people. In Judaism, the patriarchs are Abraham, Isaac and Jacob.

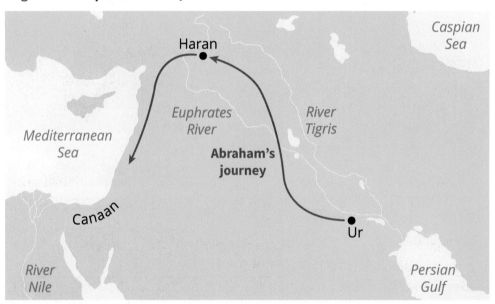

Abraham's journey took him from Ur to the Promised Land of Canaan. Why do you think he went so far north to go south again and not just straight across?

The Main Beliefs of Judaism

- Jews are monotheistic. They believe in one God. This belief is summed up in the words of the **Shema**: 'Hear O Israel, the Lord our God is one.'
- Jews believe in the covenant or agreement between the people and God.
- Jews believe in the Torah – 'law' or 'instruction' – which was given to them by God through Moses.
- Jews believe in God's revelation to the people through the prophets. The story of that revelation is told in the sacred texts (writings) of Judaism.
- Jews believe in and follow the Ten Commandments.

Did You Know?

? The **Shema** is a statement of faith that sums up the central belief in Judaism of 'One God'. It is very important. It is written on a piece of paper and placed in the **mezuzah**, a small box found on the doorposts of Jewish homes, as well as in a little box sometimes worn by Jewish people when they pray.

Jewish Writings

The story of Judaism is found in the Jewish sacred texts or writings known as the **Tanakh**. In Judaism the Tanakh is divided into three parts:

1. The **Torah** or law, which is the first five books of the Tanakh.
2. The **Nevi'im** or Prophets.
3. The **Ketuvim** or writings that include the proverbs and psalms.

The Jewish writings are a mix of history, poetry, wise sayings, letters, songs, psalms and stories.

Jewish people use a special stick called a *yad* to follow the text of the Torah, as they do not wish to mark the scrolls.

The Torah

The Torah or the Law of Moses is considered the most important part of the Jewish sacred writings. A copy of the Torah is found in all synagogues, where it is kept in a special location known as the 'Ark'. It is taken out during services and read from.

Jewish writings are in Hebrew. This was the language of ancient Judaism and it is still used today. Hebrew text is read from right to left.

The Torah gives guidance on every aspect of life, including family, work, personal hygiene and diet. A unit of law is called a **mitzvah** (the plural is **mitzvot**). This Hebrew word can mean either a commandment or good deed. There are 613 *mitzvot* in the Torah.

Other writings found in Judaism are called the **Mishnah** and the **Talmud**. These writings discuss and interpret how the commandments of the Torah should be applied.

Review and Reflect

1. What does monotheism mean?
2. Who made the covenant with God?
3. What does Torah mean?
4. How many commandments are there?
5. What is the name of the sacred writings of Judaism?

3. Buddhism

Buddhism began around 560 BCE in the north-east of India. It was started by **Prince Siddhartha Gautama**. The basic idea of Buddhism is that individuals need to achieve their own personal **enlightenment** – that is, to realise the truth about life.

The Story of the Buddha

Prince Siddhartha Gautama, later to become the Buddha, was born into a very wealthy family. When Siddhartha was born, a holy man foretold that he would either be a great political leader or a great holy man. Siddhartha's father wanted him to be a great political leader like himself, so he tried to protect Siddhartha from suffering of any kind. Siddhartha had an ideal life in the palace.

Siddhartha married and had a son. However, Siddhartha was not at peace and in his twenties he left the palace for the first time. On that day, he saw signs of suffering, which he had never seen before. The four sights he saw unsettled him. They were a sick man, an old man and a dead body, as well as a holy man, who had very few possessions but was smiling and seemed happy and at peace.

Soon afterwards, on his 29th birthday, Siddhartha left the palace for good and went in search of a deeper meaning to life.

Enlightenment

At first, Siddhartha tried the life of a wandering monk. He practised **asceticism** – a life of hardship and eating very little – and he studied with Hindu holy men. In the end, Siddhartha decided that this severe lifestyle made him feel nothing except unwell and he started to eat again.

From then on, he believed in a middle way: neither luxury nor poverty. Alone and searching he went to a place called **Bodh Gaya**. Here, he meditated for seven days under a Bodhi tree. His meditation was deep and on a night of a full moon he achieved enlightenment (known as **nirvana**). He became the Buddha or enlightened one.

What Does This Mean?

Asceticism: Practising self-discipline and the denial of any pleasure. Often associated with trying to achieve a spiritual goal. It can be a way of devoting yourself to God or religion through hardship.

Nirvana: The state of enlightenment that Buddhists are trying to reach.

The Buddha reached enlightenment under a Bodhi tree.

The Main Beliefs of Buddhism

- Buddhists see the Buddha as the 'enlightened one' and they follow his example in order to reach enlightenment (*nirvana*). They do not worship him as a God. They believe each person can reach a state of enlightenment.
- Buddhists believe in the cycle of birth, life, death and rebirth, known as **samsara**.
- Buddhists believe in the **Four Noble Truths**, which refer to suffering and how it can be overcome.
- Buddhists follow the **Noble Eightfold Path** to overcome suffering and to reach a state of enlightenment.
- Buddhists follow five rules called the **Five Precepts**. These are to help Buddhists live a good life.

Did You Know?

? The sacred texts of Buddhism are known as the **Pali Canon** or Three Baskets.

 ## Action Verb Focus: Present

Present: To show something for others to examine.

You can present in different ways: you can use PowerPoint presentations, hand-outs, dramatisations or give a talk. You can present an account of the life of someone, or you can present your argument for or against something.

You may be asked to present something to your class. This will involve doing research and then presenting your findings to the others. You can use tools to help you to make your presentation, such as drawings, notes, video clips or diagrams.

When you have presented something, others will usually have an opportunity to ask you questions about your presentation. Giving a presentation allows you to develop your research, communication and creativity skills.

Key Skill: Being Creative

The eight-spoked *dharma* wheel, or **dharmachakra**, is one of the oldest symbols of Buddhism. It represents Buddhism in the same way that a cross represents Christianity or a Star of David represents Judaism. It is also known to Buddhists as the Wheel of Life.

- Find out what makes up the eight steps of the Noble Eightfold Path.
- Draw an eight-spoked wheel and put the main word of each step into it.
- Present your wheel to the class.
- What does the *dharma* wheel represent?

4. Christianity

Christianity is based on the teachings of Jesus of Nazareth, who lived about 2,000 years ago. Most Christians see Jesus as the Son of God, **Messiah** or God's anointed or chosen one.

Jesus was born in Bethlehem in Judea, and he grew up in Nazareth in Galilee. Both Judea and Galilee were provinces of the Roman Empire at this time. As an adult, Jesus was baptised and became a teacher. He taught people about God and God's kingdom, and he is believed to have performed miracles. Jesus was an inspiring teacher and large crowds gathered to hear him speak. He had a small group of close followers, called disciples.

Roman Rule

At the time, the Romans ruled this area. Jesus, who was Jewish, became known to them as a troublemaker. The Romans convicted Jesus of treason (acting against the government) and he was executed. After his death, Jesus' followers believed he had been **resurrected** – that God had raised him from the dead – and he had then ascended into heaven. The disciples continued his teaching and the religion spread.

Today, Christianity is the biggest religion in the world, with over 2 billion followers. It has three main traditions: Orthodox, Roman Catholic and Protestant.

The Roman provinces of Galilee, Samaria and Judea are all places connected with the life story of Jesus.

Did You Know?

? The Christian holy book or sacred text is called the **Bible**. Bible means 'books'. The Christian Bible is made up of lots of books. It was first written in Hebrew and Greek. It has two parts: the Old Testament, which contains the texts of the Jewish Tanakh, and the New Testament, which contains the writings of the early Christians.

The Main Beliefs of Christianity

- Christians believe in one God.
- Christians believe that Jesus was the Messiah or chosen one, God's son, and that he died to save the whole world.
- Christians believe in Jesus' teaching of love of God and love of one's neighbour.
- Christians follow the Ten Commandments.
- Christians believe in life after death and that they will be judged for how they lived their life.

Review and Reflect

Do you remember which other religion has one God?

What Is the Trinity?

The **Trinity** refers to the idea of God as Father, Son and Holy Spirit. This does not mean Christians believe in three separate Gods. Christians believe that God took human form as Jesus and that God is present today through the work of the Holy Spirit.

One Religion, Many Branches

People talk about different branches or denominations in Christianity; these include the Orthodox, Roman Catholic and Protestant traditions. The word 'Protestant' is actually a general name for many different churches that are considered to be reformed and do not accept the pope's authority. In Ireland, there are many different types of Protestant, including members of the Church of Ireland and the Salvation Army, Methodists, Presbyterians, Baptists and Quakers. Although these people belong to the different churches and have different ways of doing things, they all belong to the same religion: Christianity.

In Ireland, people often use the shamrock as a way to explain the idea of the Trinity. Do you know the saint who is associated with this?

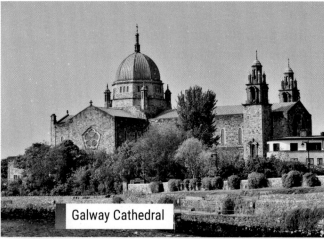

Galway Cathedral

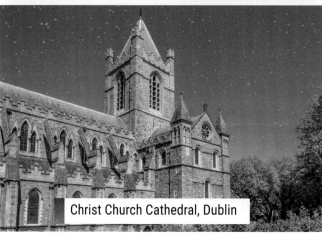

Christ Church Cathedral, Dublin

St Basil's Cathedral, Moscow, Russia

These three cathedrals are all Christian. Each one is used by a different branch of Christianity. Find out which branch each cathedral is associated with.

Over to You

In pairs, make a list of **five** true or false questions about Christianity. Share your list with the class.

5. Islam

The word '**Islam**' means 'peace' through submission to Allah (the Muslim name for God). A Muslim is one who submits to Allah's will.

Islam was founded by a man called Muhammad, who Muslims believe was the great **prophet** (messenger). He was born in a town called Mecca in Saudi Arabia in 570 CE. Muhammad had a difficult early life. His parents had both died by the time he was six and he was raised by his uncle. When he grew up, Muhammad married a woman called Khadijah and they had four daughters and two sons.

The Prophet and His Revelations

Muslims believe that Muhammad received his first revelation from Allah in 610 CE in a cave in Mount Hira outside Mecca. In this revelation, an angel of Allah told Muhammad that he was to be Allah's prophet. With support from his wife Khadijah, Muhammad tried to preach the message to the people that there is only one God, Allah. Muhammad was forced to flee Mecca in 622 CE and went to the town of Medina. This journey is called the **Hijrah** (migration). This event is so important for Muslims that the Islamic calendar starts from 622 CE. In 630 CE, Muhammad returned to Mecca with a group of followers. He became the ruler of Mecca and he dedicated the building known as the Kaaba to Allah. Throughout his life, Muhammad continued to receive revelations from Allah. The words that he heard were recorded and have become the sacred text of Islam: the **Quran**. Muhammad died in 632 CE.

Muslims believe that Muhammad is **the seal of the prophets**. He is the final prophet and his message is the final message from God. When Muslims say the name of the Prophet Muhammad, they add the phrase, 'Peace be upon him'.

One of Muhammad's most famous speeches was about the direction in which prayers should be offered to God. It has led to the important Muslim practice of always praying in the direction of Mecca.

What Does This Mean?

Prophet: A messenger of God, someone who brings God's message to people.

We have seen you turning your face towards heaven. We shall surely turn you in a direction that shall satisfy you. So turn your face towards the Sacred Mosque (built by Abraham); wherever you are, turn your faces to it.

From the Quran Sura 2

The Kaaba is in Mecca. This building is the house of God, which was built by the Prophet Ibrahim and his son Ismail. It is the direction towards which Muslims pray every day.

The Main Beliefs of Islam

- Muslims believe that there is only one God, Allah.
- Muslims believe that Muhammad is the prophet of Allah.
- Muslims believe that the Kaaba is the house of God and the direction towards which to pray.
- Muslims believe in following the **Five Pillars of Islam**.
- Muslims believe that the Quran is the revealed word of God.

Expressing Beliefs

What Does This Mean?

The Five Pillars of Islam: A guide to living as a Muslim. They are the foundation for any Muslim in living out their faith. These are: the statement of faith **(Shahadah)**; pray five times a day **(salat)**; give to charity **(zakat)**; fast during the holy month of Ramadan **(sawm)** and go on pilgrimage to Mecca **(Hajj)**.

Key Skill: Managing Information and Thinking

- Draw a picture of each of the Five Pillars of Islam.
- Write a brief description of each pillar and display them in your classroom.

Revision Questions

Enquiry

1. Name the **five** major world religions.
2. List **two** of the central beliefs of each of the five religions.
3. Are these religions monotheistic or polytheistic?

Exploration

1. What did you know about each of the major world religions before reading this chapter?
2. What did you learn?
3. What was your favourite religion to learn about?
4. What belief from each of the five religions do you find the most interesting?
5. How might the beliefs of followers affect their daily life?
6. Do you think it is important to know about other people's beliefs? Explain why or why not.
7. Do you think it is good to have something you believe in? Explain why or why not.

Reflection and Action

- Pick **one** of the five major world religions.
- Create a poster outlining its founding story and key beliefs.
- Present your poster to the class.

2 Faith Communities in Your Locality

Learning Outcome 1.2

Investigate two communities of faith that have a significant presence in their locality/region.

Learning Intentions

By the end of this chapter I will:

- Understand what community and locality means
- Learn and understand how to investigate a topic of interest
- Understand what a community of faith is
- Be able to identify the communities of faith present in my locality
- Appreciate the diversity of Irish society

Key Skills and Wellbeing

- Managing information and thinking
- Working with others
- Being literate

I am aware that I am part of the community in my locality. I have a responsibility to be aware of the religious diversity within my community and to be tolerant of everyone, regardless of religious differences.

Keywords

census ▪ community ▪ diversity ▪ faith community ▪ locality

Introduction

Modern Ireland is a diverse place. People who live here are lucky to be able to experience many different cultures and different ways of life on their doorstep. In 2016, the Central Statistics Office did a huge survey, asking every person in Ireland about themselves and their lives. This national survey is called a **census.** This census contains lots of information about the country we live in. It tells us about the age, gender, countries of origin, religious belief, employment, education and much more of every person living in Ireland at the time the census was taken. Below is an infograph from the Central Statistics Office website, which gives us a profile of religious belief in Ireland in 2016.

 An Phríomh-Oifig Staidrimh — Central Statistics Office

CENSUS 2016
Religion & Ethnicity in Ireland

 census 2016 RESULTS www.cso.ie

Religion in Numbers

Religion	Population	Average Age
Roman Catholics	3,729,115 ⬇ by -3.4	38.2
No religion	468,421 ⬆ by 73.6	34
Church of Ireland	126,414 ⬇ by -2.0	40.3
Muslim (Islamic)	63,443 ⬆ by 28.9	26
Orthodox	62,187 ⬆ by 37.5	30.2

Roman Catholic

88.6%
Offaly has the highest % of Catholics

69.9%
Dún Laoghaire – Rathdown has the lowest % of Catholics

No Religion

Dublin –
41.5 % of all persons with no religion 199,602

Longford
0.4% of all persons with no religion with 1,904

Students
had largest response to no religion at 15.3% ⬆ from 9.4 % in 2011

Church of Ireland

14,379
Church of Ireland primary school-going (5-12 year olds)
⬆ by 2,738 between 2006 and 2016

Secondary school age children (13-18 year olds) rose by 764 to 9,291.

Muslim

63,443
Irelands Muslim community
⬆ from 32,539 in 2006

Orthodox

Romanians largest group among Orthodox Christians
33.5% of total

Icebreaker

 True or False?

Study the infograph and decide whether the following statements are true or false.

1. Roman Catholicism has the highest number of believers.
2. The average age of a Muslim person is higher than that of an Orthodox Christian.
3. The Muslim **community** in Ireland has nearly doubled since 2011.
4. Most of the people in Dún Laoghaire – Rathdown are Catholic.
5. Neary 200,000 people who live in Dublin do not believe in any religion.
6. Romanians are the largest group among Roman Catholic Christians.
7. The number of people who are in the Church of Ireland has risen since 2011.

Action Verb Focus: Investigate

Investigate: To observe, study or make a detailed and systematic examination, in order to establish facts and to provide supporting evidence for conclusions.

To investigate something is to gather together lots of different pieces of information or evidence to get a better and truthful overall picture of something. When detectives investigate a crime, they gather all the evidence and witness statements to try to figure out who the criminal is. Doctors investigate patients' symptoms to work out what illness they have.

Key Skill: Managing Information and Thinking

Investigate aspects of your **locality** to find out what communities of faith are present there. To gather all the information, you will need to investigate and do research to find evidence of a **faith community**:

- Talk to and listen to the people in your area.
- Do research using books.
- Investigate what information your local library might have.
- Do research using the internet.

You can then combine your findings into a report.

In your report, you should outline what information you have **researched**, what you have **experienced** and your **findings.**

To get an overall picture of a faith community, you should investigate them under the following headings:

- Leadership and membership
- Main beliefs
- Worship and practice
- Customs and way of life

What Does This Mean?

Locality: An area or a neighbourhood, or the place where something is found or happens.

Faith community: A group of people who share a faith.

Can you identify any features of religious belief in this picture?

Investigation of the Religious Communities of Faith Present in the Locality of Clonskeagh, Dublin 14

Research (internet)

- Clonskeagh has one parish church, Miraculous Medal Church, on Bird Avenue. This church is Roman Catholic and offers Mass every day, and twice on Sundays. From its website I can see it recently held a coffee morning to help raise funds for charity.

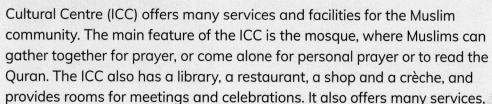

Miraculous Medal Church, Bird Avenue

- Clonskeagh is home to the Islamic Cultural Centre, on Roebuck Road. The Islamic Cultural Centre (ICC) offers many services and facilities for the Muslim community. The main feature of the ICC is the mosque, where Muslims can gather together for prayer, or come alone for personal prayer or to read the Quran. The ICC also has a library, a restaurant, a shop and a crèche, and provides rooms for meetings and celebrations. It also offers many services, including marriage and death services, translation services, a youth group and adult education.

- From searching on the internet I can see that there are four schools in Clonskeagh: Our Lady's National School, Jesus and Mary's College, the Muslim National School and St Killian's German School. Three of these schools have a Christian ethos, and one has a Muslim ethos.

The Islamic Cultural Centre, Roebuck Road

Experience

- I visited the mosque and the ICC. While there, I went on a tour of the centre given by the imam, I watched an informational video and asked questions at the end.

- I visited the church and local school. I spoke to the sacristan of the church and asked her questions.

Findings

- There are two communities of faith, associated with the major world religions, present in my locality: Christian and Muslim.

- Both of these communities are very supportive of their members and offer spaces for worship and social gatherings.

Islamic Cultural Centre

- **Leadership and membership:** The imam leads Friday midday prayer in the mosque. Muslims travel from all over Ireland to make use of the facilities in the ICC and many attend worship on Friday at midday.

Pages of the Quran

- **Main beliefs:** Muslims who attend the mosque for prayer, both personal and communal, have several key beliefs. The creed is the most important belief in Islam: 'There is no God but Allah, and Muhammad is the messenger of Allah.' After the creed, the key beliefs for Muslims are summed up in the 6 Articles of Faith. Muslims also hold the Quran as very special, as it is believed to be the actual word of Allah, given directly to Muhammad by the Angel Gabriel.

- **Worship and practice:** On a daily basis, Muslims practise their faith by adhering to the Five Pillars of Islam: creed, prayer, fasting, pilgrimage and charity. They show their belief in the first pillar, the creed, by reciting it regularly and praying to Allah, and by adding the phrase 'Peace be upon him' after they say Muhammad's name. Worship of Allah can also be seen in the absence of pictures of Allah

Muslims believe communal prayer is more powerful than personal prayer, so they pray together every Friday at midday.

or Muhammad in the mosque. Muslims believe that people may worship the picture representation of Allah instead of worshiping Allah, so this distraction is removed.

- **Customs and way of life:** The restaurant in the ICC serves only **halal** food. *Halal* food is meat that is prepared so it complies with Islamic teachings. The shop in the ICC also sells *halal* food. Beside the ICC is the Muslim National School; students from the school are educated in Islamic teachings and brought to the mosque to pray. Many Muslims who use the facilities in the ICC wear special clothing to show their faith in Allah. Women often wear headscarves, and both men and women sometimes wear long clothing to show their devotion.

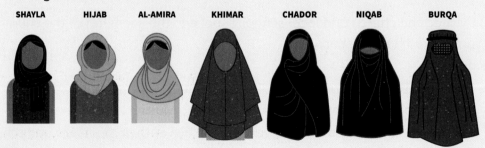

SHAYLA   HIJAB   AL-AMIRA   KHIMAR   CHADOR   NIQAB   BURQA

There are many different types of clothing that women can wear to show religious devotion.

Miraculous Medal Church

- **Leadership and membership:** The church is led by the parish priest. He is aided in the running of the church by the sacristan and many other volunteers. Some Catholics living in the area attend Mass every day, others attend on Sunday and special religious holidays such as Christmas and Easter.

A Roman Catholic priest wearing a full-length, black garment called a cassock

- **Main beliefs:** Roman Catholics believe that God is the one true God and that he was represented on earth in human form through his son, Jesus. They believe that Jesus died on the cross for humanity's sins and rose from the dead three days later. They believe that if you lead a good life full of love for everyone you will be welcomed into the Kingdom of God. Catholics also hold the Ten Commandments as very important.

- **Worship and practice:** Catholics show their faith by attending worship in the church, especially on Sundays. The church is open throughout the day for people to pray whenever they wish. Catholics practise the Ten Commandments in their daily lives and try to treat others as they would like to be treated (the Golden Rule). Giving to charity and looking out for people in need is an important part of a Catholic's life, and so this community ran a coffee morning to help raise money for charity.

A Roman Catholic bishop wearing liturgical vestments. Usually this type of ornate clothing is worn only for celebrations.

- **Customs and way of life:** The parish priest wears distinctive black clothing with a white collar, and puts on special garments for saying Mass called vestments. Churchgoers can wear their own clothes, although it is important to be respectful and dress appropriately for worship. Many significant life events or milestones are celebrated with the rest of their faith community, such as baptisms, weddings and funerals. Many people also ask for the memory of someone who has died to be remembered during Sunday Mass on the anniversary of his or her death.

Review and Reflect

1. What **two** world religions are represented in the locality of Clonskeagh?
2. What places of worship are present in the locality?
3. From the report outline **three** Islamic beliefs.
4. Name **one** way Muslims practise one of the beliefs you have outlined.
5. From the report outline **three** Catholic beliefs.
6. Name **one** way Catholics practise one of the beliefs you have outlined.

Diversity

Ireland is full of **diversity**. There are many different faith and non-religious belief communities present across the country: from the Amish-Mennonite community in Dunmore East, Co. Waterford to the Tibetan Buddhist Retreat Centre on the Beara Peninsula, Co. Cork and the Dublin South Central Humanists, who meet in the Nutgrove Shopping Centre. Ireland has a wide variety of inclusive religious and non-religious groups. You do not have to go far to meet people from different faiths in your locality. Your locality could mean your classroom or school. It could mean your parish or town. Someone just needs to look carefully at the world around them to see the variety of different faiths present in our country.

Atlantic Ocean

NORTHERN IRELAND

Dublin South Central Humanists meet in the Nutgrove Shopping Centre, Dublin

Dublin

Irish Sea

IRELAND

Tibetan Buddhist Retreat Centre on the Beara Peninsula, Co. Cork

Waterford city

Cork city

Amish-Mennonite community in Dunmore East, Co. Waterford

The location of some of the different communities of faith present on our island.

The Tibetan Buddhist Retreat Centre on the Beara Peninsula, Co. Cork. How do you feel when you look at this picture?

Over to You – Exploration

- Which different faith communities are present in your locality?
- Make a list of all the different faith communities you think are represented in your locality, and give an example of how you know that community of faith is present.

Revision Questions

Enquiry

1. What is a locality?
2. What is a faith community?
3. What does diversity mean?
4. What is a census?
5. Who might use the skill of investigation in their work?
6. Write down **two** ways you could investigate a community of faith.
7. What headings could you use to research a community of faith?

Exploration

1. What localities do you belong to?
2. Which **one** of the research headings from the Key Skills exercise on page 16 do you think is the most important? Explain why.
3. When else in your life might you use your new investigation skill?

Reflection and Action

- Individually, in pairs or in groups, investigate a faith community present in your locality.
- You can use the headings in this chapter to guide you in your investigation.

- Put together a presentation outlining your findings. Your presentation could be on a poster, presented using PowerPoint or given orally.

3 Members of Faith Communities

Learning Outcome 1.3

Engage with members of a faith community associated with one of the five major world religions and show an appreciation of how the religious beliefs of the community influence the day-to-day life of its members.

Learning Intentions

By the end of this chapter I will:

- Learn how to appropriately interact with other people in my locality
- Learn about the key beliefs of world religions that are present in my locality
- Understand how these key beliefs make an impact or difference to the day-to-day life of its members
- Realise how religion has a deep effect on people's lives
- Reflect on what key religious or non-religious beliefs influence my own life

Key Skills and Wellbeing

- Communicating
- Managing myself
- Working with others

I am aware of the diversity that exists within my locality and that I can find evidence of this diversity if I examine the evidence of the world around me. I realise that spirituality is a key aspect of life for some people and it is important to respect other people's spirituality as my beliefs should be respected, even if they differ.

Keywords

community ■ diversity ■ engage ■ influence ■ locality ■ tolerance

Introduction

Being part of a **community** is important for everyone. It means you have connections with those around you – you share something. Maybe you share your **locality**. You could share a sport or a hobby, or you could work or go to school in the same place. You share common ground with the people in your community. Because of this, everyone must help to create a positive atmosphere, so all members of the community have equal opportunity to do well and live a good life.

In the diverse society that Ireland is today, **tolerance** is very important. Tolerance is having respect for other people and their beliefs and choices. Even if someone has a different belief to you, you must show respect. Tolerance involves being kind and understanding, and never being intentionally mean or hurting someone.

A school community should be an inclusive and supportive place.

The GAA community share a passion for the world of Gaelic sports.

What Does This Mean?

Tolerance: Being kind and understanding, showing respect for other people and their beliefs. Not intentionally hurting someone or treating them badly.

Icebreaker

How could you encourage tolerance in your community? In pairs, think up **three** ways you could teach others about tolerance or encourage people to be tolerant in a community.

Action Verb Focus: Engage

Engage: To participate or become involved in something, allowing it to occupy your interest or attention.

To engage is to truly try to connect with a person, a place, a symbol or some information. You learn about the subject, and then reflect and think about it on a deeper level. You then become involved by reaching out to another person, by going to visit a place or object, or participating in an event.

In order to engage with members of your community, you must think about how you could reach out to them.

Some ways you could engage with a community of faith in your locality are by:

- Sending a questionnaire by email or post.
- Inviting a speaker in to the school.
- Sending a group of students into the community to conduct an interview.
- Planning a visit to the community for the entire group and having a Q&A session afterwards.

Over to You – Reflection and Action

 The Hot Seat

- Divide into groups and engage in the following activity.
- Select one person to role-play as a person from any community of faith. They sit in the 'hot seat'.
- Together come up with a list of five questions that you would ask that person in a mock interview.
- Everyone can help the person in the hot seat think about how they would answer the questions.
- Group by group, invite each community of faith member up to sit in the hot seat and answer the prepared questions.

Discoveries

Evidence of the **influence** of religious belief is all around us, especially in Ireland. Ireland has a long and rich tradition of Christian belief, and aspects of this belief can still be seen in our culture and society today. For example, Ireland is divided into parishes, and at the centre of each parish is the church and the parish priest. While the church may not be the focal point it once was, and the priest may not hold the same influence he once did, Ireland still holds the community of the parish as significant.

 Chapter 11

What Does This Mean?

Evidence: Any fact, piece of information or physical thing that indicates something.

Influence: The capacity to have an effect on the character, development or behaviour of someone or something.

The Impact of Religion

Religion can have a big influence on people's lives, what they do and the choices they make.

Many Buddhists are vegetarian because of their belief in reincarnation. Reincarnation means that when a person passes away, their spirit does not leave the earth but goes into another body. What that body becomes depends on how they lived their life. A person who has not lived a good life could be reincarnated as an animal, such as a pig. By eating pork you could potentially be eating another person's spirit in animal form! So, Buddhists avoid eating animals. Because of this belief, if a Buddhist decided to open a restaurant it might only serve vegetarian food. In this way, the Buddhist's beliefs have influenced their choice of restaurant to open.

But not all beliefs have such an obvious impact. It could be something less visible, such as a Christian blessing themselves when an ambulance goes past, and saying a quiet prayer for the person who is ill or injured.

Review and Reflect

- Brainstorm: What other evidence of religious belief can you see in your community or locality?
- As a class, write down some of the evidence you can see in your community to suggest that people from different faiths live in your locality.

Many Buddhists adopt a vegetarian diet because of their belief in reincarnation.

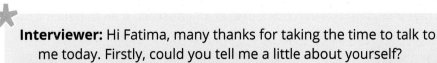

An Interview with Fatima

The following is an example of the type of interview that could take place between a researcher and a member of the Islamic community.

Interviewer: Hi Fatima, many thanks for taking the time to talk to me today. Firstly, could you tell me a little about yourself?

Fatima: Hi, yes of course. My name is Fatima Kundi, I'm 16 years old and currently in Fifth Year. My dad is originally from Pakistan but moved to England when he was a young man. There he met my mother and they moved to Ireland after they were married. I was born here in Galway, and so were my two younger brothers. We are all practising Muslims.

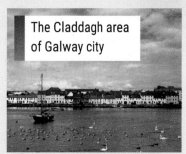

The Claddagh area of Galway city

Interviewer: And have you been practising this faith since childhood?

Fatima: Yes, I have. Faith is very important to our family. My father's family are very strict, my mother's family are less so, and my family are somewhere in the middle of the two!

Interviewer: Could you tell me what beliefs are the most important to you regarding your faith?

Fatima: The most important things for me, and all Muslims, are that Allah is the one true God and that Muhammad is the last and greatest prophet of Allah. This belief is summed up in the *Shahadah*, or creed.

Interviewer: And how do you put this belief into practice?

Fatima: Through all aspects of my life! I try to show my love of Allah through being the best person I can be, and by following the Five Pillars of Islam, and showing respect and kindness to all people.

Interviewer: Can you give me an example?

Fatima: Yes, take for example the third pillar of Islam, *zakat*. This means charity, so my family and I give to charity, but not just money, our time too. We often look in on two of our elderly neighbours to make sure they have everything they need, and when we are celebrating, we always make sure to think of others who are less fortunate than us first.

Interviewer: Is there anywhere special you go to practise your faith?

Fatima: At home we have prayer mats, which we take out and use to pray every day. And for special occasions and at special times of the year we travel to the mosque in Dublin to pray.

Interviewer: Are there any signs of your faith around your home?

Fatima: When my dad came back from *Hajj* in Mecca five years ago, he brought back a framed copy of the *Shahadah*, hand painted in gold lettering. This is hanging on the wall in the sitting room and it reminds me every day to live a good life. There are also other keepsakes that my parents have brought back from *Hajj* over the years. My father has gone on *Hajj* many times, and once my little brothers are a little older, we will all go together. I'm really looking forward to that!

The *Shahadah* – the creed and key belief of Islam

Interviewer: Is there anything in the way you dress that shows your faith?

Fatima: When I'm not at home I wear my headscarf to cover my hair. My parents left the decision to wear it or not up to me when I became a teenager. I choose to wear it, but many Muslim women do not wear a headscarf. It all depends on their beliefs and traditions.

Interviewer: What about in what you eat?

Fatima: We eat only *halal* meat; this is meat that has been prepared in a special way to make it ritually clean to eat. There is a *halal* butcher not too far from where my mother works, so she pops in once or twice a week. When my friends come over for dinner, they always want to try it! But no one has ever noticed a difference.

Sharing a meal together is an important part of family life.

Interviewer: And finally, is there anything you do every day, week, month or year that you only do because you have faith in Islam?

Fatima: There are many things I do for my faith, but an important one is **Ramadan**. Once a year, for a month, my parents and I fast during sunlight hours. My little brothers are still too small to do it, but once they are a little older, they will. We don't eat or drink anything during the day but get up in the middle of the night for a big meal together. It can be hard at times, but it is a sacrifice to Allah, so my faith helps me through it! Next year Ramadan falls on the month of my Leaving Cert so I might not be able to do it then, but I'll have to see closer to the time.

Interviewer: That's great, Fatima, thank you so much for taking the time to answer my questions, and giving me an insight into your life and faith. I really appreciate it.

Over to You

 Carousel

1. Divide into five groups. Take five large sheets of paper and write one of the following onto each sheet:
   - Beliefs
   - Practice
   - Objects and Symbols
   - Food
   - Clothing

2. Each group takes a different coloured marker and sits at a different sheet around the room. You have one minute per sheet of paper to write down everything you learned about Fatima's religion from the interview. When the minute is up, each group moves on to the next sheet.

3. When every group has written something on every sheet, you should be back at your original sheet.

4. Each group selects **three** pieces of information from each sheet that they believe are the most important and writes them on the whiteboard or simply calls them out.

5. As a group, you should explain each piece of information and why you decided to select that one.

Revision Questions

Enquiry

1. What is a locality?
2. What is evidence?
3. Where could you find evidence of a community of faith in your locality?
4. How might someone engage with another person or group? List **three** ways.
5. Explain what diversity means.

Exploration

1. Why is it important to promote tolerance?
2. Give an example of **one** way someone could promote tolerance in his or her locality.
3. What do you think is the best way to engage with someone else? Why do you think this is the best way?
4. Do you think diversity is a good thing? Why or why not?

Reflection and Action

- Using the information you discovered in your mini-project from the Reflection and Action exercise on page 21, select **one** community of faith present in your locality.
- Using **one** of the methods mentioned in this chapter, or **one** of your own, engage with the community of faith you have chosen.
- Give a presentation on how the religious beliefs of the members of this community of faith influence the day-to-day lives of its members.

(This mini-project could be combined with the mini-project from Chapter 2.)

4 Non-Religious Rituals and Celebrations

Learning Outcome 1.7

Discuss the significance of non-religious rituals and celebrations for people's lives.

Learning Intentions

By the end of this chapter I will:

- Understand what a non-religious ritual is
- Realise the significant, non-religious celebration days that are very important for Different people and nations
- Reflect on what non-religious rituals or celebrations I have attended in my life
- Discuss the significance of a non-religious ritual or celebration in people's lives

Key Skills and Wellbeing

- Being creative
- Managing myself
- Managing information and thinking

I am aware of the significance of celebration in my life and in the lives of the people around me. I will strive to celebrate the important moments in my life, to celebrate my achievements and to help others enjoy their accomplishments.

Keywords

celebration ▪ non-religious ▪ ritual ▪ tradition

Introduction

Every country has special days that are celebrated as national holidays. In Ireland, because of our Christian heritage, many of our national holidays are traditionally religious. For example, our most significant national day is St Patrick's Day on 17 March. On this day, not only in Ireland but across the world, people celebrate Irishness. This day originated as a way to celebrate St Patrick and the introduction of Christianity to Ireland. However, there are many national holidays that do not trace their origins back to religion. These days claim their roots from many sources: important people, significant events in history and politics, great moments of joy or sadness. A small sample of some of these days is given below.

Icebreaker

- Think about all the special times you have celebrated with your family or friends. Maybe you went out for the day to an event or stayed at home and celebrated. On the whiteboard or in your copy, list as many of these as you can.
- When you have finished the list, circle the ones that do not have a religious aspect to them. Discuss how these celebrations might be different if they had a religious aspect to them.

Mother's/Father's Day: These days both have religious origins but are now secular holidays. They are celebrated on a Sunday to show the importance of parents in people's lives. Traditionally, children show their appreciation of their parents on these days by giving cards and gifts, sharing a special meal or treating their parents in their own special way.

Independence Day: This day celebrates the independence of the USA from British rule. Traditionally, on this day Americans and their friends celebrate together with special food and fireworks.

Bloom's Day: This day is named after Leopold Bloom, the main character of James Joyce's famous Irish novel *Ulysses*. This book follows Bloom around Dublin on 16 June 1904, and on 16 June every year people get dressed up and follow his path around Dublin.

Kwanzaa: Started in 1966 by Maulana Karenga, Kwanzaa is a festival that celebrates African-American culture and lasts from 26 December to 1 January. During this time, families come together, traditional and colourful African clothes are worn, music is played, and other aspects of African culture are celebrated.

Thanksgiving: Although Thanksgiving has its roots in religious celebration, this traditional American holiday is now a secular celebration of people's appreciation of all the good things in their lives. Family and friends celebrate by coming together and sharing a special thanksgiving meal, during which they tell everyone at the table what they are thankful for. It began in October 1621 when the Pilgrims celebrated the first new harvest in the New World.

Guy Fawkes Day: Also called Bonfire Night, this day commemorates the failed Gunpowder Plot, in which several rebels, including Guy Fawkes, tried to blow up the Houses of Parliament in London, on 5 November 1605. The people of London were so happy that the plot had been foiled and King James I had not been injured that they lit bonfires to celebrate. The British still light bonfires and set off fireworks to celebrate this event.

New Year's Eve: This time is celebrated worldwide. At the turn of the clock from 11.59 p.m. to midnight people come together to celebrate the new year. Firework displays light up the skies and people embrace and celebrate with a kiss.

Over to You – Explanation

- Have you ever celebrated any of these holidays?
- If you have, how did you celebrate them?

Action Verb Focus: Discuss

Discuss: To examine with other people ideas, perspectives or opinions on a topic in order to reach a viewpoint.

We discuss things everyday with the people around us. Discussion is important in the classroom. In order to understand information better, students and teachers must discuss the different concepts, and ask and answer questions to ensure everything is clearly understood. When we want to fully understand something, it can be useful to discuss it with others. We can hear their reasons and opinions and examine their evidence, so that we can come to our own conclusions.

Over to You

Times that Are Important to Me
- Create a collage of times in your life that were or are important to you.
- Write the most important times into your copy, giving each their own bubble. Add to each one: why you celebrated, who celebrated with you, what you did, and what made that time special.
- Discuss why these times were important to you.
- You could bring in a small picture of each event and stick it beside each bubble. (Make sure to ask permission at home first!) Display these in your classroom, so you can see the important moments in each other's lives.

Celebration

When we get good news, the first thing we want to do is to share it with our loved ones! Whether we pass an exam, win a raffle or get the job, we want to share our good feelings with our friends and family. Sometimes we organise a **celebration**, so everyone can feel as good as we do. There are many ways to celebrate. Some are truly Irish, like having a mug of tea, and others are common around the whole world, like eating birthday cake. The important thing is to mark the event by doing something special, no matter how big or small.

Ritual

Do you brush your teeth every morning? Have breakfast? Get dressed? If you do, you are going through the motions of your morning **ritual**. A ritual is any set of actions that is done in a set pattern at a particular time. People engage in rituals for a wide variety of reasons: a family **tradition**, a personal habit or maybe a community event. Rituals can include the following aspects:

- Significant people
- Set actions
- A special place
- Important or symbolic music, clothing or food

Brushing your teeth every day is a very good ritual that we establish from a young age.

Non-Religious Rituals

Birthday

The day we were brought into the world was a special day, full of joy. It is a day we celebrate by commemorating it.

There are many traditional aspects of birthdays. The big ones are giving birthday cards and gifts, singing 'Happy Birthday' and blowing out candles on a birthday cake. The famous song 'Happy Birthday' has been translated into many different languages. According to *The Guinness Book of World Records*, it is the most recognised song in the world!

What Does This Mean?

Celebration: An occasion to be joyful and happy about something.

Ritual: The traditions, habits and actions that are repeated in a family, community or society.

Tradition: A custom or practice that is repeated over a long time. It may be within a small group of people or a large community. It is significant and holds meaning for the people carrying it out.

Birthdays are a great time for family and friends to gather together to celebrate a special person in their lives.

Graduation

Getting a good education takes up the early years of your life. The value placed on education is high and it is compulsory to educate children until they are 16. Most people do this by sending their children to school. Some children are home-schooled. Because our education takes so much time and dedication, when we achieve a key stage we often have a graduation ceremony.

Moving on from one stage of education to another is a big achievement regardless of age.

A graduation ceremony recognises the hard work, effort and diligence the student has put into their education up to this point. It is a moment to shine, be proud and accept congratulations for a job well done. It is a time to celebrate achievement.

- For the ceremony, graduates wear special robes and caps.
- There are speeches and someone who knows the group well and has aided their education talks about their time studying and the future for them.
- Each graduate goes up one by one to collect their graduation certificate or scroll.
- Often the 'Graduation Song' is played, or the students will pick a song that means something to them and play it at the end.
- When the ceremony is over, the graduates traditionally throw their caps in the air in jubilation.
- Photographs are taken and the graduate and their loved ones may go for a meal together.

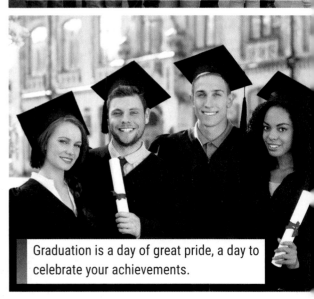
Graduation is a day of great pride, a day to celebrate your achievements.

Wedding

A wedding is a time of happiness and joy but also of huge commitment. Individuals have agreed to stay with their partner for the rest of their life; to be with them and support them in the good times and the bad; to share hopes, dreams and aspirations for the future with them.

The wedding ceremony can take many different forms. In 2016, 35.3 per cent of couples married in Ireland celebrated with either a humanist ceremony or a civil ceremony.

Both types of **non-religious** weddings are very personal to the couple getting married. The couple work closely with their celebrant (the person saying the ceremony) to pick the right rituals, songs, readings and other aspects of the ceremony that suit them as a couple. The basic layout of the ceremony remains the same: the introduction first, followed by readings, rituals and songs, the vows, the giving and receiving of rings, and finally the legal part where the newly married couple, and their witnesses, sign the marriage register. The couple can include as much or as little as they like. For both types of ceremony, the couple may wear whatever they like, but many brides wear the traditional white wedding dress.

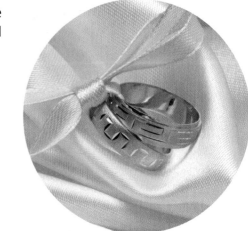

A humanist wedding may take place anywhere as long as it is open to the public, so you can have it on a beach or in a hotel, but not your parent's house. A civil ceremony takes place in a registry office like the one on Lower Grand Canal Street in Dublin or in a location of the couple's choosing. After the ceremony, most couples will invite their guests to share a meal with them and celebrate with music and dancing. The type of food, music and celebrations completely depend on what the couple likes and their budget.

What Does This Mean?

Humanism: A system of thought that attaches prime importance to human rather than divine or supernatural matters.

Did You Know?

- The person who marries the couple in a civil ceremony is called a solemniser.
- For a marriage to be legal in Ireland, there must be two witnesses over the age of 18 to sign the marriage register. These are usually the maid of honour and the best man.

A wedding day can be the most significant moment of a couple's life.

The Unity Sand Ceremony

During the Unity Sand Ceremony, each person is represented by a glass container full of sand. The celebrant explains how two people are joining their lives together. The two containers of sand are poured together into a third container. Now the grains of sand can never be separated, just as the couple's lives are becoming completely intertwined.

The Unity Ceremony: when two lives merge into one

Hand-Fasting Ceremony

This ceremony is one of the oldest wedding rituals. It is where the phrase 'tying the knot' comes from.

- The couple place their right hands together and a cord or ribbon is wrapped around their combined hands.
- The tail of one end is laid under the other.
- When the celebrant says the appropriate words, the couple take a tail each with their left hand and pull while simultaneously slipping the right hand out of the ribbon. A knot is formed in the ribbon signifying the strength of their bond.

The hand-fasting ceremony is not just celebrated in non-religious weddings. It is also a traditional part of Jewish weddings.

Over to You – Explanation

 Copy the following table into your copy and fill in the missing sections.

	Birthday	Graduation	Wedding
Significant people			Celebrant Couple Witnesses and guests
Set actions		Receiving the graduation certificate or scroll Throwing caps into the air	
Special place		School, college or university	
Symbolic music, clothing, food	Birthday cake and the 'Happy Birthday' song		

Revision Questions

Enquiry

1. What is a national holiday?
2. Define the term 'discuss'.
3. What could a student use discussion for?
4. Outline your understanding of a celebration.
5. What is a ritual?
6. List the important aspects of a ritual.
7. List **three** non-religious rituals and explain how **one** of these is celebrated.

Exploration

1. Why is discussion important?
2. Do you think celebration is vital for people? Explain why or why not.
3. What common features do non-religious rituals share?
4. Why do you think graduation ceremonies are a milestone for people?
5. Why do you think humanist weddings are becoming so popular in Ireland?

Reflection and Action

- Individually, in pairs or in groups, pick a significant time or event in a person's life that has not been mentioned in this chapter.
- Plan an event to celebrate that time or event. Outline all the important aspects, including actions, food, music, clothing and the people involved.
- Create an invitation to your event. Share your event with the class.

5 Stories of Origin

Learning Outcome 2.3

Explore how different narratives/stories, religious and non-religious, express an understanding of creation/the natural world, and consider their meaning and relevance for today.

Learning Intentions

By the end of this chapter I will:

- Know the creation stories of two major world religions
- Know how story is used to express belief
- Have compared the two stories, their similarities and differences
- Have thought about the relevance of these stories for believers in these two religions

Key Skills and Wellbeing

- Being creative
- Managing information and thinking
- Communicating

I feel connected to the world.
I appreciate the impact of my actions on the global community.

Keywords

narrative ▪ origins ▪ relevance ▪ story

Imagining where it all came from

Introduction

Before we look at the creation stories of the major world religions, let's think about the following questions:

- What is a **story** or **narrative**?
- Why are stories told?
- How are they remembered?
- Can they mean something even when they are not based on real events?

Icebreaker

1. In pairs, think of a story that you both know.
2. Outline the main points of the story (include three to five points).
3. Explain the meaning of the story.
4. Is there anything this story could teach someone today?

What Does This Mean?

Story/narrative: A description of events that actually happened or that are invented.

Symbols in Stories

Stories have the power to stir up emotions, to get people interested and involved.

Many stories, especially very old ones, are symbolic. Their importance is in the truths that they point to and not in telling about actual events in the past. So, when we look at them we do not simply ask, 'Did this really happen?' but 'What do they stand for? What did they mean for the people who told them? What understanding did they express?'

For example, you can read a story about a person in history that is a legend; all the events may not be true, but it tells something about the person. It is trying to show what type of person he or she was.

Many stories use symbols. These are words, images or actions that have a deeper meaning. They will make us think something. For example, when somebody 'sees red', what does that mean? When a character in a story 'lays down their sword' or 'turns their back', what do these phrases mean?

Stories are used to teach. Are you familiar with the stories behind these images?

Creation Stories

Most ancient cultures had stories about their **origins**, an explanation of how the world was formed and how humans came into being. We sometimes call these 'creation myths'. The word **myth** originates

from the Greek word **mythos**, which means 'story'. These myths or stories developed in ancient civilisations and survived for thousands of years. They are not trying to tell exactly what happened at the beginning of the world, but they are trying to tell people about what they believe and what they think is important. These stories were told and retold over time and passed on from one generation to the next.

Myths

Myths are an ancient story form. They have the power to give people a relationship with the world, their environment and time. They usually contain an important message for a group and an explanation of the way things are. Myths were originally passed on by word of mouth, in what we call 'oral tradition'. As well as to explain the world, myths were used to teach and to entertain.

Here are some questions the ancient creation stories were trying to answer:

- Why was the world made?
- Why are there people in the world?
- What responsibility do people have for the world?
- Why is there suffering in the world?
- Why is there good or bad in the world?

There are many examples of creation stories from around the world, ranging from Australian aboriginal to Maori, Native American and ancient Norse myths.

Action Verb Focus: Explore

Explore: To systematically look into something closely for the purpose of discovery; to scrutinise or probe.

When you explore, you try to find out as much as possible about something. You start with an idea and try to discover more and to ask questions about it. In your history classes, you might be asked to explore the reasons for an event, so you would discover what led up to it, what happened and what caused it to happen. You would explore the topic as much as possible.

Here, you are exploring stories of origin. You are finding out about them and looking into what they had to say and why. You will scrutinise, ask questions and try to understand their function or purpose. You will explore them.

Over to You – Exploration

- Discuss the questions about creation stories above and explore what answers we have for them in the modern world.
- Are some of the questions still difficult to answer?
- Are any of the questions still important questions for people now?

Major World Religion: Hinduism

Hinduism has many creation stories, not just one, because for Hinduism this universe is one of an infinite number of universes. They are linked through an endless cycle of birth, life, death and rebirth. Each universe has its own creation myth. Most Hindu creation stories developed from the sacred texts (the Vedas, **Puranas**, **Upanishads**) and feature Brahma as creator.

The is the symbol of the sacred **Aum** – the sound that began the universe and the sound of deepest meditation.

A Hindu Creation Story

The universe begins as a vast ocean with a serpent floating on the surface of the ocean. In the coil of the snake sleeps the Hindu God Vishnu. Vishnu is very peaceful, he is not afraid and he is not dreaming – he is in a deep sleep. After a long time, a humming sound comes from the ocean. This sound is the sacred sound **Aum**. The sound is full of energy and wakes up the God Vishnu. When Vishnu wakes

The God Vishnu on the snake. Do you think this image captures the story well?

up, he finds a lotus flower coming from his navel (belly button) and on top of the flower is the four-headed Hindu God Brahma. Vishnu tells Brahma that 'it is time' and he is commanded to create the world.

The wind stirs and the ocean begins to toss and turn. Vishnu and the serpent disappear and Brahma sets to work. He calms the sea and then splits the lotus into three parts, making the heavens, the sky and the earth. The earth is bare, so Brahma creates the grass, flowers and trees. He gives these things feelings. He then creates birds, fish and animals and gives them the power to see, hear, touch, smell and move. In this way, Brahma creates the world and all the creatures.

A demon appears and steals the world, throwing it far out into the cosmic ocean. Vishnu returns and changes into animal form so that he can rescue the world from the depths of the ocean. Once the world has been rescued, Brahma continues the process of creation. He produces more species and increases the population of the universe.

Hinduism teaches that one day this universe will, like all others before, be wiped out by the Lord Shiva, the destroyer God. When Shiva grows angry with the evil in the world, he will perform a ferocious dance of destruction, once again leaving nothing except Brahman, the universal soul.

Chapter 1

What Are the Main Ideas in This Story?

- Brahman, the universal soul, is the source of all life and is eternal.
- The world is created and destroyed many times.
- There are many Gods and Goddesses. Each one is a way of showing Brahman.
- The three Gods in the story – Vishnu, Brahma and Shiva – have different roles in the process or cycle of the universe. Brahma creates, Vishnu preserves and Shiva destroys.
- There is a never-ending cycle – the universe goes through continuous cycles of creation, preservation and destruction.

Lord Shiva is the Hindu 'destroyer' God. What is the name of Shiva's weapon?

- Shiva is not bad for destroying; he destroys only when people no longer care for the world or living creatures.

Relevance for Today

Hindus believe in many Gods. The **Trimurti** consists of the three Gods: Brahma, Vishnu and Shiva. They all feature in this story. In Hinduism, they are still considered to be the three agents involved in the processes of creation, preservation and destruction. Hindus believe that people go through a similar process by being reincarnated. So, the story is still relevant when looking at Hindu beliefs.

This story sends an important message about responsibility and duty. People have a duty to care for the universe and living creatures. The God Shiva will destroy the universe when it becomes bad. Hinduism teaches about **dharma**, or sacred duty, for every person. It also teaches that there are consequences for bad action and about the idea of **karma** – from good comes good and from bad comes bad – is a central belief in Hinduism.

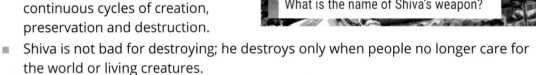

Over to You – Being Creative

- Tell the Hindu creation story in picture form – either as a comic strip with a series of boxes or a poster.
- Write a poem that tells the story.
- Dramatise the story in your class.

Key Skill: Communicating

Discuss the following:

1. What questions was the Hindu creation story trying to answer in ancient times?
2. Are these questions still important today?
3. For Hindus, what important teachings are found in this story?
4. What points in the story do you think have any **relevance**, or meaning, for people today?

Major World Religion: Judaism

The ancient Jewish writings known as the Torah are also the first five books of the Christian Bible. This creation story is therefore part of both Jewish and Christian traditions. The Torah's creation story is found in the Book of Genesis. Genesis means 'origins' and it explores the beginnings of the world. It was written down about 500 BCE. God is the main character of the story. God exists before the world, when there is only a void. Out of the chaos, through a very neat, orderly process, God creates the universe. Genesis begins with the words, 'In the beginning God created the heaven and the earth.'

The creation of the world takes place over seven days. Seven is a symbolic number in the ancient Jewish writings. Each day is a different step towards creation, as the people understood it.

Day one: God creates light, separates the light from the darkness, day from night.

The Contemporary English Version of the Bible presents it as follows:

'In the beginning God created the heaven and the earth. The earth was barren with no form of life; it was under a roaring ocean covered with darkness. But the Spirit of God was moving over the water. God said, 'I command light to shine!' And light started shining. God looked at the light and saw that it was good. He separated light from darkness and named the light 'Day' and darkness 'Night'. Evening came and then morning – that was the first day.'

Day two: God creates the sky, an expanse separating the waters.

Day three: God creates dry ground called 'land', which is separated from the water, which is gathered to form 'seas'. On the land, God creates vegetation.

Day four: God creates the sun, moon and stars to light the earth and to separate night from day. They would also mark the days, seasons and years.

Day five: God creates living creatures to fill the sea and birds to fly in the air. They are blessed to multiply.

Day six: God creates animals for the earth. God then creates 'male and female' humans in God's image to supervise and take care of all the creatures of the earth.

Day seven: God rests and marks this day as a special day of rest.

The natural world is a source of wonder for people.

What Are the Main Ideas in This Story?

In the story, it is repeated five times that God saw everything God had made and 'it was good'. Thus, the creation – the world – was good. Repeating the phrase like this suggests the writer is making a point here.

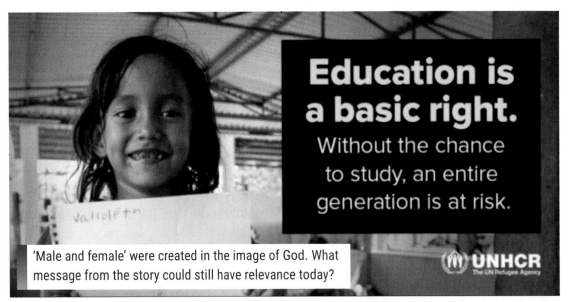

'Male and female' were created in the image of God. What message from the story could still have relevance today?

As a myth or story, the Genesis creation account is trying to answer questions for the ancient people it was written for. Remember, it was written some 2,500 years ago. It answers questions such as where the world came from, why it was created and how people came to be. The story gives a clear answer: everything came from a divine being – God. But it also tells us about what these people believed and what they considered important. We hear in the story that God created everything good, that people were created in the

How much responsibility are people taking for the living world?

image of God and that people had the role of taking care of creation, of the earth and all living things. These were important beliefs for the ancient Jewish people. They are still important for Jewish and Christian people today.

Review and Reflect

1. What does 'Genesis' mean?
2. The Genesis story comes from which collection of sacred writings?
3. How old is this story?
4. How did the creation process start in this story?
5. Mention **three** things that are created during the first five days.
6. What phrase is repeated throughout the story?
7. What questions was the story answering for the ancient people it was written for?
8. In your opinion, what are the main points this story is making?
9. Has this story any messages that are relevant today?

Comparing the Two Creation Stories

What is curious about the two accounts is that they have many similarities. This is particularly interesting considering the clear difference between the two religions: Hinduism has many Gods and Judaism is the oldest monotheistic religion.

- Each story begins at a time when nothing exists except God and a great ocean.
- In the Hindu story, the sea is churning. Genesis mentions a 'roaring ocean'.
- They both begin with a phrase about wind. Genesis talks of the 'spirit of God moving over the water', which can also translate to 'an awesome wind was moving over the water'. In the Hindu story, 'a huge wind gathered'.
- A sound begins the process of creation in both stories. In the Hindu story, it is the *Aum* sound. In Genesis, it is the voice of God.
- In both stories, humans are the final part of the creation process.
- In the Hindu story, the first man and woman are created from the body of a God. In Genesis, God created human beings in God's image.
- In both stories, humans are given responsibility to take care of the world and all living things.

Over to You – Enquiry

Discuss the following:

1. Why do you think people want to understand their world and how it started?
2. If you could ask the authors of either creation story a question, what would you ask them?
3. When people do not know something, they often develop a theory about it. A theory is made from the best knowledge available to the person at a particular time. Do you think either creation story was, for the people who wrote them, a type of theory for their day?
4. We now know a lot more about the natural world. We also know a lot more about the origins of the universe and of human beings. The Big Bang theory and the theory of evolution are widely written about and explained for people to understand. How can these modern theories help us to take care of the world and of living creatures?

How much responsibility do we take for all people?

Revision Questions

Enquiry

1. Write the main points of the **two** creation stories in bullet points.
2. Make a short comparison: list the similarities and differences.
3. What was the purpose of these stories?

Exploration

1. What did you already know about creation myths?
2. What did you learn?
3. When were these stories written? Did people then know as much about the universe as we do today?
4. Why do you think they told these stories?
5. Do these stories have any relevance today?

Reflection and Action

- Explore a modern scientific account of how the world/universe came into existence or how human beings came about.
- Present your findings to the class.
- Discuss the different purpose of these accounts compared with the origin stories of the two world religions.

Action: Design a poster highlighting the problems the world faces today: climate change, extinction of species, pollution of the seas and land. Include a slogan encouraging people to look after the natural world.

A Founder's Biography

Learning Outcome 2.5

Create a biography of a founder or early followers of a major world religion, using religious and historical sources of information.

Learning Intentions

By the end of this chapter I will:

- Know what a founder is
- Understand what a biography is
- Understand the significance of a founder for the origins of a religion
- Know what religious and historical sources of information are

- Understand how to use sources of information to create a full picture of an event
- Use my research skills to create a biography

Key Skills and Wellbeing

- Being creative
- Managing information and thinking
- Managing myself

I have become aware of the significant events in my life that have led me to the path I am on now. I realise how important founding stories are in the origins of religious belief and the origins of the communities I belong to.

Keywords

biography ▪ early follower ▪ evidence ▪ founder ▪ sources

A man is the symbol for Matthew.

A winged lion is the symbol for Mark.

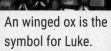

An winged ox is the symbol for Luke.

An eagle is the symbol for John.

Introduction

People who reach the top of their fields in sport, career or ambition have often led interesting lives. They have become important and influential. So people want to read about them.

The **founders** and early followers of the five major world religions are very interesting. This is because their decisions and their spiritual relationships founded and fostered the growth of belief systems that most people still have some belief in today. In order to understand a religion, we must understand its origins, and the origins would be incomplete without a **biography** of the founder and/or early followers.

What Does This Mean?

Biography: An account of a person's life written by someone else. It is similar to an autobiography, which is a person's own account of his or her life.

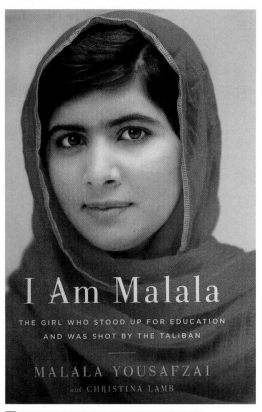

Malala Yousafzai's autobiograhy

Icebreaker

- Have you ever read a biography or watched a biopic? Who was it about?
- Tell your class **three** reasons why the person's life was interesting enough to deserve a biography.

Action Verb Focus: Create

Create: To bring something into existence; to cause something to happen as a result of one's actions.

Humans have always been creative. Art, music, literature, meals, life, the list of what people create goes on and on. Creation adds diversity and beauty to the world; it gives us something new to appreciate and admire.

When you think about how to create something, what pops into your head? An artist painting a masterpiece? A musician composing a symphony? The creation of the world? There are so many ways creation takes place, but they all have one thing in common – they result in something new.

In order to create, we need to have a clear goal. By using our imagination, we can look at the different paths we could take to achieve our goal.

This chapter requires you to become a creator. You will need to draw on your imagination and your knowledge to create a biography of a founder. This should contain all the necessary information, and it should be easily understood and remembered.

Sources of Evidence

In order to create a biography, you need plenty of information about the person. The best place to find this information is from the actual person, but they are not always accessible. A biographer will often need to get the information from other **sources**.

Over to You – Managing Myself

Select some key events from your life that have made a big impact on the person you are today. Create a short autobiography including some of these key events and present it to the class.

Or

Pair up and ask your partner questions about the key moments in his or her life. Select what you want to include and write a short biography of that person. Do not put the name of the author or subject of the biography on the text. Hand them to your teacher, who will read each one aloud. The class has to guess who the biography is about.

Historical Sources

There are two types of historical sources: primary and secondary.

Primary sources are from the time being studied, which means they can be quite difficult to find. This is especially true the further back in history you go. Primary sources from the ancient world have mostly been discovered through the work of archaeologists. Experts who have studied primary sources, such as ancient manuscripts, objects, art, inscriptions and other archaeological finds, often create secondary sources.

Secondary sources are books, documentaries and academic papers created by people who did not witness the event first-hand. They can be found in libraries or online. When studying history, including the foundations of the major world religions, people usually study these secondary sources.

Historical sources, whether primary or secondary, may be biased. Being biased means having an unbalanced opinion; people tend to prefer some things or people over others. In some cases, sources show the **bias** of the people who wrote them. The authors are not objectively giving the facts, and their opinion is coming through the source. We need to examine who created the sources and what their opinion or bias might be.

What Does This Mean?

Source: Anything that gives us information about something or someone. It is where the information comes from about the thing we are studying or trying to find out about.

Primary sources: Sources from the time being studied, e.g. artefacts, manuscripts, diaries, official documents or ruins.

Secondary sources: Sources created about an event after it has happened, e.g. books, documentaries, reconstructions, drawings or diagrams produced later.

A Celtic brooch from the Iron Age is a primary source, whereas a drawing of that brooch created in 2018 is a secondary source.

Biography of a Founder: Christianity

Historical Sources

The man Jesus, a carpenter from Nazareth in Galilee, appears in several historical sources. These sources do not try to outline Jesus' divinity to encourage people to believe in Christianity. They simply include accounts of Jesus and aspects of his life as a matter of record.

Pliny the Younger

The first historical source for Jesus we will look at is that of Pliny the Younger. Pliny was the Roman governor of an area in Asia Minor. He wrote to Emperor Trajan around 112 CE asking for advice on how to deal with the Christians in his area who, at the time, were considered criminals:

Pliny the Younger was an indecisive governor. He wrote many letters to the emperor asking for advice.

They were in the habit of meeting on a certain fixed day before it was light, when they sang in alternate verses a hymn to Christ, as to a god, and bound themselves by a solemn oath, not to any wicked deeds, but never to commit any fraud, theft or adultery, never to falsify their word, nor deny a trust when they should be called upon to deliver it up; after which it was their custom to separate, and then reassemble to partake of food – but food of an ordinary and innocent kind.

What Does This Mean?

Founder: A person or a group of people who have started something. In religion, there is a founder, or founders, who began a particular belief system or way of life. The founder of Christianity was Jesus of Nazareth; the founder of Islam was the Prophet Muhammad.

Early Christians

When we are presented with a piece of historical **evidence**, we need to sift through it to pick out the information we need. In the extract from Pliny's letter, we learn the following about the **early followers** of Christianity:

- Early Christians met together, early in the morning, to celebrate their faith.
- They sang hymns to Christ as a God.
- They promised not to do wrong, including lying, stealing or cheating.
- They came together to eat a humble meal.

Flavius Josephus

The second historical source we will look at is that of Flavius Josephus, a Jewish historian. Josephus wrote mainly about the history of the Jews from their origins to the Jewish revolt of 66–70 CE. He was a Pharisee and later became leader of the Jewish forces in Galilee and a Roman citizen. Pharisees were a group within Judaism during the Second Temple period. They emphasised the importance of following the Jewish law, or Torah.

Josephus was a very busy man, and belonged to many different groups, but one thing is clear – he was not a Christian.

There is a bit of confusion about some of Josephus's work. Some people even believe it may have been tampered with. The following quote is from Josephus's record of Jewish history found in a tenth-century Arabic manuscript:

What Does This Mean?

Evidence: Any fact, piece of information or physical thing that indicates something.

Early followers: People who early on become part of a religion. They are the first followers of a particular founder or belief system.

Josephus is a valuable source of information about Jewish life under the Roman Empire in the first century.

> At that time, a wise man called Jesus, admirable in his conduct, was renowned for his virtue. Many Jews and other peoples were his disciples. Pilate condemned him to death by crucifixion. But those who had become his disciples did not renounce their discipleship and told of how he appeared to them alive three days after the crucifixion, and that because of this, he could be the Messiah of whom the prophets had said such marvellous things.

Review and Reflect

1. What type of person did Josephus say Jesus was?
2. What did Josephus call Jesus' followers?
3. Who sentenced Jesus to death?
4. How was Jesus put to death?
5. What did his disciples say happened three days after Jesus' death?
6. According to Josephus, why was this significant?

Religious Sources

The Bible

The Bible is the biggest religious source of evidence for Jesus, especially the New Testament, which contains the four **gospels**, the Acts of the Apostles, letters (including the Letters of Saint Paul) and the Book of Revelation.

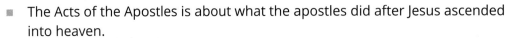
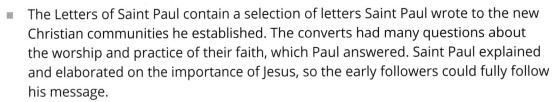

The opening of John's gospel

- The gospels tell us about the life, death and resurrection of Jesus. They were written by the four gospel writers: Matthew, Mark, Luke and John.

- The Acts of the Apostles is about what the apostles did after Jesus ascended into heaven.

- The Letters of Saint Paul contain a selection of letters Saint Paul wrote to the new Christian communities he established. The converts had many questions about the worship and practice of their faith, which Paul answered. Saint Paul explained and elaborated on the importance of Jesus, so the early followers could fully follow his message.

The Gospels: A Religious Source for Jesus

The word 'gospel' means 'good news'. The gospels were written to spread the good news of Jesus Christ. The four gospel writers each had a unique background and wrote for a particular group of Christians. They each wanted to outline a specific side of Jesus that would connect their audience to Jesus and his message. From the gospels, we can find out a lot of information about Jesus and what he preached about the Kingdom of God.

Did You Know?

? A gospel writer is known as an evangelist.

Over to You – Explanation

1. What did Pliny say about Christians in a letter to the Emperor Trajan in 112 CE?
2. What books are contained in the New Testament?
3. What do the gospels tell us?
4. Who are the four gospel writers?
5. What name is given to the gospel writers?
6. What book tells us about what the apostles did after Jesus ascended into heaven?
7. Who did Saint Paul write to?
8. Why did he write his letters?
9. What does the word 'gospel' mean?
10. Who did the gospel writers write for?

How to Find a Bible Reference

A Bible reference contains three parts, a word followed by two numbers, or sets of numbers. The first word in the reference refers to the book of the Bible you will be looking in. There are 66 books in the Bible, though many Catholic editions have 73, as they include the Apocrypha. The books in the Bible are all listed in order in the contents page at the front. The first number in the reference refers to the chapter in that book, and the last number or numbers refer to the verse of that chapter. For example, John 4: 2–5 refers to the second to fifth verses, of the fourth chapter of John's gospel.

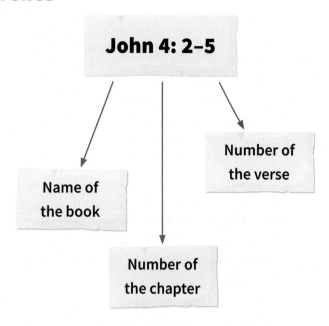

John 4: 2–5

Name of the book

Number of the chapter

Number of the verse

Over to You – Exploration

 Look up the following Bible passages and answer the questions for each of them.

Luke 2: 1–16; Matthew 5: 1–9; Mark 5: 21–42; Luke 22: 14–38; John 20: 11–18

1. Who appears in this passage?
2. What did Jesus say in this passage?
3. What did Jesus do in this passage?
4. What is Jesus' message in the passage?
5. From what you have read, in your opinion, what type of person was Jesus?

Synoptic Gospels

The gospels of Matthew, Mark and Luke are known as the Synoptic Gospels. The word 'synoptic' means 'similar'. These three gospels include many of the same stories, written in a similar way, in the same sequence. It is believed that Matthew and Luke used Mark as a source and also shared another source of information, a document, known as the 'Q' document. John's gospel does not have as much in common as the others do, so it is believed that John did not use or have access to the 'Q' document.

Over to You – Explanation

 Take all the information from the historical and religious sources of Jesus to write a short biography of his life. Use the bullet points to help you include all the important information.

- Jesus' birth and family
- Jesus' characteristics
- Jesus' teachings about the Kingdom of God
- Jesus' followers
- Jesus' death and resurrection

Revision Questions

Enquiry

1. What is a biography?
2. What is the difference between a biography and an autobiography?
3. What is a source?
4. What is a historical source?
5. What is the difference between a primary source and a secondary source?
6. Give an example of a primary source and a secondary source.
7. Give an example of an early religious source for Jesus.

Exploration

1. Why are the biographies of the founders of different religions interesting?
2. Why do we need sources to create a biography?
3. Historical sources can be biased. What does bias mean? Explain the importance of asking about bias when looking for sources about a person in history.
4. What do each of the parts of a Bible reference refer to?

Reflection and Action

- Research the historical and religious sources of evidence for another founder or early follower of one of the major world religions.
- Write a biography of the person you have chosen. Make sure your biography is creative, interesting and catches your classmates' attention.

What Does It Mean to Be Moral?

Learning Outcome 3.2

Reflect upon and discuss what it means to be moral, why people living in society need to be moral and what are the influences on and sources of authority for a person's moral decision-making.

Learning Intentions

By the end of this chapter I will:
- Know what morality means
- Think about why people being moral benefits society
- List things that influence a person's moral choices

Key Skills and Wellbeing

- Managing myself
- Working with others
- Staying well

I am aware of the influences on the choices I make. I know that I have rights and responsibilities. I need to make the right choices for myself.

Keywords

choice ▪ freedom ▪ law ▪ morality ▪ the Golden Rule

Doing the RIGHT thing ←

Doing the WRONG thing →

Which way to go? If only there was a signpost!

Introduction

This chapter is concerned with what it means to be moral. The word 'moral' is something you may have heard before but perhaps you have not considered what it means.

Icebreaker

In pairs, consider the following statements. Are they right or wrong?

1. All people deserve to be treated equally.
2. People should always tell the truth.
3. There should not be a speed limit on a motorway.
4. The drinking age should be reduced to 16.
5. Children under 10 should not have mobile phones.
6. People should give time or money to charities.
7. People should always vote in elections.
8. People should always recycle their rubbish.

When you have finished, share your thoughts with the class. Reflect on whether you agreed with the others in your class about these as being right or wrong. Discuss why people might have different opinions on these issues.

What Is Morality?

Being moral or saying something or someone is moral is to do with right and wrong. When people talk about something being moral, they mean that an action is right or good. When they say an action is not moral, they are implying that it is wrong or bad.

When you think about it, this means there are many different opinions on being moral and what is right or wrong. Many people see **morality** as personal. What one person considers right someone else might consider wrong. Nevertheless, there are accepted standards of right and wrong within societies. These can change over time and from place to place. Different cultures, political structures (how a country is run) and religions can have different beliefs about what is moral or good.

Is it sometimes difficult to do the right thing?

What Does This Mean?

Morality: Concerned with the principles of right and wrong behaviour.

Action Verb Focus: Reflect

Reflect: To give thoughtful and careful consideration to experiences, beliefs and knowledge in order to gain new insights and make meaning of them.

When you reflect, you look back on something, you think deeply about it and ask questions about it. People reflect all the time: they think about their relationships, their behaviour and the way things work out in life. In this chapter, you are asked to reflect on what it means to be moral. This will involve reflecting on what is right or wrong, and how that is important in society. You will use your reflective skills to think about the questions in this topic and hopefully gain some insights into them.

Over to You – Reflection and Action

1. Write down **three** reasons why a person should be moral, i.e. why they should do the right thing.
2. Write down the benefits to society of people being moral.

Society and Morality

Society works on the basis that people live in a community. They share something in common; they live in the same place, country or state and they co-exist. If people living in society do the right thing – if they are moral – it helps society to work. As people are in society, living alongside others, their actions have consequences that affect other people.

- For example, if a person does not drive carefully, if they smoke in a public place, if they tell lies or drop litter, for many people these actions would be seen as immoral or not moral. These actions affect other people, and they make the society less pleasant for other people to live in. They can be upsetting and even dangerous for other people.

- On the other hand, people who behave morally – who do not lie or cheat, who respect others, who drive carefully and who look after their rubbish – make the world a nicer place for everyone to live in.

What Does This Mean?

Society: People living together in an organised community, sharing laws and customs.

Is the dumping of rubbish in rivers a moral issue?

Review and Reflect

Can you think of laws in society that are in place to protect everyone?

Influences on Morality

Many things **influence** a person's moral **choices**. We will look at the following: family, friends, the media, the **law** and religion.

Family

Your family is a major influence on your ideas of right and wrong. A family is the smallest community a person belongs to. Families teach people many things. As a small child, your family teaches you how to eat, how to talk, how to socialise and how to relate to other people.

How important is family in teaching a person about right and wrong?

Growing up in a family, people learn through many different **situations** what is the right and what is the wrong thing to do. There is a popular phrase 'monkey see, monkey do', which refers to how children mimic their parents, but not always in a good way! So parents need to behave appropriately, as their children are likely to copy them. Through families, people learn what is important. They learn values; this makes a big difference to their morality and how it develops.

Friends

For most people, friends are another important influence. Your friends' opinions affect what you see as right or wrong. The influence of friends increases during adolescence. How friends act or behave in a variety of situations, what they think, say or wear, sends out ideas about what is good or bad. Friends talk about things and share their opinions and their ideas. All of this will influence a person when considering moral issues and making moral choices.

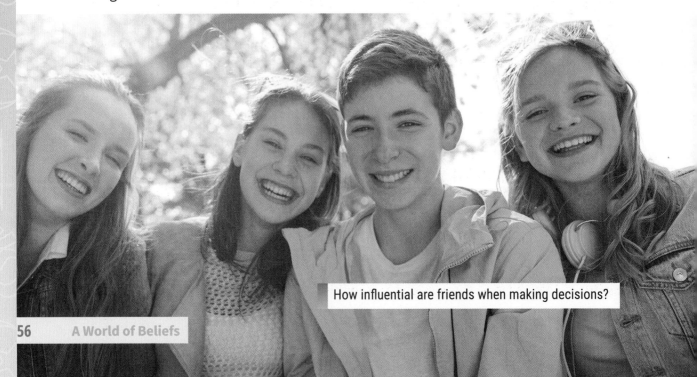

How influential are friends when making decisions?

The Media

Media are the different communication agencies or tools that store or deliver information and data. They include the internet, television, radio, newspapers and magazines. The media give us an almost continuous message of what is right and wrong. The way the media show people, either real or fictional, the way they inform us, the music they play and the images they show are a big influence on what people consider to be good or bad. Most young people spend a lot of time on social media and research shows it affects their development. Social media is influencing morality and moral choices.

How much influence do you think the media has on young people?

The Law

Laws are rules agreed upon by people and governments that regulate the behaviour of members of society. The basic rules that regulate Ireland are found in our constitution, *Bunreacht na hÉireann*. To change any laws in the constitution, we need to have a vote of the people, called a referendum. The European Union also has laws for member states and their citizens.

Do you know when the constitution was first written, when it was last changed and why it was changed?

What Does This Mean?

Law: The rules agreed upon by people and governments that regulate the behaviour of people living in society.

When making moral decisions, people are influenced by the law, because they can be punished if they break it. This then influences what is seen to be right or wrong. For example, it is illegal to drink and drive. This is for everyone's safety. This law also sends out a message about what is the right behaviour. Different countries have different laws, which means that they may have different ideas about what is right and wrong. Laws have changed over time, which shows that ideas of right and wrong can also change.

Religion

Most religions have a lot to say on what is good or bad. Judaism, Christianity and Islam all have versions of the Ten Commandments as a moral code or guide to suggest what is right or wrong. Judaism focuses on the Torah 'law' or 'instruction' as a guide when faced with a moral choice. Christianity has the example and teachings of Jesus. Islam has the example of the Prophet Muhammad. In Hinduism, the sacred writings contain stories that teach what is right. Duty, love, loyalty and honesty are some of the values they promote. In Buddhism, the teachings of the Buddha, especially the Noble Eightfold Path, have a moral vision for Buddhists to follow.

Over to You – Enquiry

1. Write a sentence that includes the word 'influence'.
2. From the list of influences on morality above, which do you think is the biggest influence on you?
3. Do you think laws are important?
4. Do you think laws can ever be wrong?
5. Write a speech on the importance of laws for society.

The writing on the bench means 'Not for Jews'. In Germany, before and during the Second World War, this was law, but was it moral?

Over to You – Exploration

In 1955 when Rosa Parks refused to give up her seat to a white passenger on a bus in Montgomery, Alabama, she was breaking a law. This led to her arrest and trial and was a spark that led to one of the biggest civil rights protests in American history. Research the Montgomery Bus Boycott and how it led to a change in the law.

THE BUS STOP
The Montgomery Bus Boycott

At the stop on this site on December 1, 1955, Mrs. Rosa Parks boarded the bus which would transport her name into history. Returning home after a long day working as a seamstress for Montgomery Fair department store, she refused the bus driver's order to give up her seat to boarding whites. Her arrest, conviction, and fine launched the Montgomery Bus Boycott. The Boycott began December 5, the day of Parks's trial, as a protest by African-Americans for unequal treatment they received on the bus line. Refusing to ride the buses, they maintained the Boycott until the U.S. Supreme Court ordered integration of public transportation one year later. Dr. Martin Luther King, Jr. led the Boycott, the beginning of the modern Civil Rights Movement.

SPONSORED BY ALPHA KAPPA ALPHA SORORITY, INCORPORATED DURING ITS CENTENNIAL SALUTE

The Golden Rule

The Golden Rule is a religious code that is found across all the major world religions. It is found in Judaism, Christianity, Islam, Hinduism and Buddhism. It is the idea that people should treat others in a way that they would like to be treated. This means that if you do not want to be lied to, to be hurt or to be excluded, then you do not do these things to other people. It is sometimes called the 'rule of reciprocity'. Reciprocity is when two people or groups help each other.

There are many versions of the Golden Rule – here are some of them:

'In everything, do to others as you would have them do to you; for this is the law and the prophets.' (Christianity – Jesus, Matthew 7.12)

'What is hateful to you, do not to your neighbour. This is the whole Torah; all the rest is commentary.' (Judaism – Hillel, Talmud, Shabbat 31a)

'Treat not others in ways that you yourself would find hurtful.' (Buddhism – The Buddha)

'This is the sum of duty: do not do to others what would cause pain if done to you.' (Hinduism – Mahabharata 5:1517)

'Not one of you truly believes until you wish for others what you wish for yourself.' (Islam – The Prophet Muhammad, Hadith)

'We are as much alive as we keep the earth alive.' (Native Spirituality – Chief Dan George)

'Treat other people as you would want to be treated in their situation; don't do things you wouldn't want to have done to you.' (British Humanist Association, 1999)

What Does This Mean?

The Golden Rule: A code for how to behave found in the major world religions. It is rooted in the belief that everyone should treat other people the way that they would like to be treated by others.

Over to You – Reflection and Action

Choose your favourite version of the Golden Rule. Design a poster for it.

Morality and Choice

Being moral involves choice. In fact, in order for something to be moral or not, it needs to involve a choice. When making moral choices, people are constantly influenced by many different sources. However, in the end people have to develop their own ideas of right and wrong and make their own decisions. People have a choice as to how they act, what they say and what they do.

What Does This Mean?

Choice: An act of making a decision when faced with two or more possibilities.

Freedom: The power or right to act, speak or think as one wants.

Morality and Freedom

Finally, to make moral choices a person must be free. **Freedom** involves having control over your own choices and the right to live without fear of unfair treatment or punishment. The law should protect this right. It is part of the United Nations Declaration of Human Rights to have freedom of thought, religion and conscience. With freedom comes responsibility: the responsibility to respect other people's freedom and to think about everyone's wellbeing.

Anne Frank said, 'Our lives are fashioned by our choices. First, we make our choices, then our choices make us.'

Nelson Mandela wrote in his autobiography:

For to be free is not merely to cast off one's chains, but to live in a way that respects and enhances the freedom of others.

'It is our choices that show what we truly are, far more than our abilities.' Professor Albus Dumbledore (from *Harry Potter and the Chamber of Secrets* by J. K. Rowling)

Key Skill: Working with Others

- Divide into groups. Each group has to create a list of **three** moral choices.
- One member from each group asks all the other groups to decide what is the right thing to do in these situations.
- When everyone has visited all the groups, each group discusses the responses from the other groups.

Revision Questions

Enquiry

1. What is morality?
2. How does a person being moral help society?
3. List **three** influences on a person's moral choices.
4. What are laws and how do they influence a person's moral choice?
5. What is the Golden Rule?

Exploration

1. Think about what influences your moral choices. What are the most important influences?
2. What do you think are the benefits to society of people behaving morally?

Reflection and Action

- On your own or in a group, carry out a survey of what influences moral choices in your class or year group.
- Try to survey as many people as possible.
- Record your findings.
- Using charts or tables, present or display your findings in your class or school.
- Think about the results of your survey and reflect on the main influences on the people in your class.

8 Making Moral Decisions

Learning Outcome 3.5

Examine how a moral decision-making process can help a person decide what is right and wrong in an everyday life situation.

Learning Intentions

By the end of this chapter I will:

- Know what moral decision-making processes are
- Have a deep knowledge and understanding of at least one moral decision-making process
- Be able to apply this moral decision-making process to everyday life situations
- Realise the value of using a moral decision-making process when making decisions
- Use these decision-making processes in my everyday life

Key Skills and Wellbeing

- Managing myself
- Being numerate
- Communicating

I am aware of the steps I need to take in order to make good decisions for myself. I understand the significance of taking time to stop and think about events that happen in my life before I act.

Keywords

decision-making process ▪ empathy ▪ moral

Introduction

As we get older, we become more aware of the impact of our **moral** choices, and we start to rely less on our parents for guidance on what is right and wrong. We need to be able make our own decisions. Something that can help us make a decision is a moral **decision-making process**. These processes provide a path to follow when we are unsure about what to do, whether the decision is big or small. The most important thing to remember when we are making decisions is to be honest, to be tolerant and to have **empathy**.

What Does This Mean?

Moral: Whether something is considered right or wrong.

Empathy: Being able to imagine and understand how other people might feel.

Icebreaker

Read the following scenarios and, using what you have already learned about morality, decide, in pairs, what you would do.

Scenario one

Your friend is copying her homework from another girl's work in your classroom at lunchtime. The other girl knows she is doing it and does not mind. What do you do?

Scenario two

Your friend is copying her homework from your work in your classroom at lunchtime. She has not asked permission, but you are good friends, so she thinks you will not mind. What do you do?

Scenario three

Your friend is copying her homework from your work in your classroom at lunchtime. She asked if it was OK. You did not want to share your work, but she is a good friend and you did not want her to get into trouble for not doing her homework, so you agreed. Another teacher walks in and sees her copying your work. She takes both copies and says both of you will be disciplined for this. What do you do?

1. Discuss what the right thing for each person to do was in each scenario.
2. How did you decide what was right for each person?
3. Share your thoughts with the class.

The Moral Decision-Making Process

STAR Method

The STAR method is used for making moral decisions. It is easy to remember and can be used for any scenario. It is useful when you are trying to lay the foundations of good decision-making. This method relies on four steps:

S TOP: First, you need to stop before you do anything. Take a step back. In some cases, it might be necessary to cool off for a moment.

T HINK: The second step requires you to take in all the information. Think about the scenario from all angles, not just from your own viewpoint. Get all the facts. Imagine how other people might feel or what they might want. Think about the consequences – both positive and negative. What could happen based on the different decisions you make?

A CT: The third step is to make a decision. Have the confidence that the decision you made took everything into account. Act upon your decision. Take ownership and responsibility for your actions, but be open to making mistakes and learning from them.

R EFLECT: The fourth step is time to reflect. Think deeply about what you have done and how you came to that decision. Did it work in the end? Are you happy with the outcome? If you had the chance, would you do anything differently? If things did not work out so well this time, learn from this experience. Use this new knowledge when faced with a similar situation in the future.

Next time you face a sticky moral dilemma, apply each step of the STAR method to help you make a decision.

What Does This Mean?

 Decision-making process: A step-by-step process that provides a person with a framework for making a moral decision.

Action Verb Focus: Examine

Examine: To look closely at an argument or concept in a way that uncovers its origins, assumptions and relationships.

When you examine something, you look at it carefully and consider it fully. You might examine an idea or proposal to see how it stands up to scrutiny or questioning. Examining a plan, an idea or an event means you study it in detail so that you can discover as much as possible about it.

Over to You – Exploration

1. In pairs, read the following scenarios. Discuss how you might feel in each one.
   - You have won two tickets to see your favourite singer in concert. You want to go with your best friend. But when your mum finds out, she wants to go for a special night out with you, even though she does not like the singer.
   - You begged your parents for a puppy and they have finally agreed, with the understanding that you are responsible for it. One day, your dad says your brother was playing with the puppy in the garden, but he left it there and it dug up the flowerbeds. Your dad says you have to pay for the new flowers and replant them this weekend, instead of hanging out with your friends.
   - You and your friend have fallen out. You are both on a swimming team and at the weekend were going to the beach to train by swimming from pier to pier. You tell her it is not a good idea because the weather is supposed to be miserable, and you do not like going out in the rain. You hear no more about it and assume it has not gone ahead. Then she posts a snap on Instagram of her and another team member after their swim.

2. Using the STAR method, identify what you would do in each scenario above.

3. Think of a moral decision a person might have to make. Then examine how the STAR method would help that person to make the moral decision.

Revision Questions

Enquiry

1. What is a moral decision-making process?
2. What is empathy?
3. What do the letters in STAR stand for?
4. Write a note on each step in the STAR method, in your own words.

Exploration

1. Why would someone use a moral decision-making process?
2. Why would a moral decision-making process help someone to make a decision?
3. Why is empathy important?
4. Which step do you think is the most important in the STAR method? Explain your choice.

Reflection and Action

- Outline a scenario in which you had to make a difficult moral decision. It can be real or made up. If it is real, change the names and some details to protect the identity of the people involved.
- Apply the STAR method to the scenario. Write a paragraph on each step, in relation to this scenario.

Debating a Moral Issue 1

9

Introduction

A **moral issue** can arise in many different ways or at different times. Moral issues involve a choice and different options. When a person makes a moral decision, they are deciding what is right in a particular situation. They may hear different opinions or **points of view** from different people and think about these.

Different viewpoints can be **influenced** by many things: the age of the individuals, their experiences, culture and traditions, background, country, religion and education.

When individuals make their decision on a moral issue, they also consider the consequences of their decision. Consequences are the results of an action or choice.

What Does This Mean?

Moral issue: An issue that has the potential to affect ourselves and others, for good or bad.

Point of view: A way of considering something or an opinion.

Icebreaker

Look at the following topic for a debate and then examine the different viewpoints and what influences them.

 Statement

Schools should not be allowed to make pupils wear uniforms.

The phrase 'should not' implies it is wrong to allow schools to insist that pupils wear a uniform. This could therefore be described as a moral issue. There is a right and wrong being debated.

Now let us look at two different points of view on this issue.

Student A agrees with the statement. Student B disagrees with the statement. What are their points?

Agrees ✓	Disagrees ✗
Uniforms do not allow people to be individuals.	Uniforms give people a sense of community and belonging.
Uniforms are too expensive.	Uniforms are good value for money.
Uniforms are not nice to wear.	Uniforms are practical.
Uniforms are old-fashioned.	Uniforms stop competition and people following fashions.
Uniforms teach children to conform, obey rules and not to question.	Uniforms train people for working life when they may have to wear a uniform.

Looking Deeper

Why does Student A agree with the statement? What has influenced the student's viewpoint?

- ☑ This may be a young student who has to wear a uniform, and does not like it.
- ☑ Friends' opinions of uniforms may influence the student.
- ☑ The fashion industry may influence the student through magazines and advertisements.
- ☑ Older brothers or sisters, who do not like uniforms, may influence the student.
- ☑ Parents may influence the student, because they are stressed by the expense of buying the uniform and, as a result, they dislike it.
- ☑ The media may influence the student: films, television or social media showing a negative image of school uniforms.

Why does Student B disagree with the statement? What has influenced their viewpoint?

- ☒ This student is young and has recently joined a school. He or she likes wearing the uniform, as it helps the student to fit in and there is less pressure to find clothes to wear.
- ☒ Parents may influence the student, because they tell him or her the uniform looks good.
- ☒ Friends, brothers and sisters may have an influence, because they have worn a uniform.
- ☒ The media may influence the student, through films and television showing positive images of uniforms, such as in the *Harry Potter* films.
- ☒ The culture of wearing uniforms may influence the student, because uniforms are worn by Gardaí, firefighters, pilots, and healthcare professionals. These are people who are respected.
- ☒ Someone who dislikes the fashion industry may influence the student.

Does a uniform help you to fit in?

How influential is the fashion industry?

What jobs require people to wear uniforms?

Action Verb Focus: Debate

Debate: To set out a viewpoint or argument on a subject on which people have different views, supporting one's stance with evidence.

When people debate, they take different sides to a motion. The motion is the statement they are debating. They will either be for or against the motion. To debate is to argue but not in the sense of having a row or disagreement. It is putting forward a carefully thought-out point of view on the topic or motion and aiming to convince people to agree with your points. People debate in many different situations, but they don't always call it having a debate, for example, when they are discussing a choice and what they think should happen. Some people, such as politicians or barristers, need to have good debating skills in their profession or job.

Key Skill: Working with Others

Arrange to debate this issue in class. You can have either:

1. A walking debate
     Or
2. A formal debate

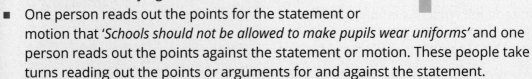

Walking Debate

- For the walking debate, use Student A's points for and Student B's against.
- Put up two signs at opposite sides of the classroom, one saying 'AGREE', the other 'DISAGREE'.
- One person reads out the points for the statement or motion that *'Schools should not be allowed to make pupils wear uniforms'* and one person reads out the points against the statement or motion. These people take turns reading out the points or arguments for and against the statement.
- After each point is made, the rest of the class walk to either the 'AGREE' or 'DISAGREE' sign depending on their viewpoint. A person can stop in the middle or close to but not entirely at one of the signs, depending on how strongly they agree or disagree.
- After each point, three people should be asked to explain why they stopped where they did.
- At the end, someone reads out the motion statement again *'Schools should not be allowed to make pupils wear uniforms'* and everyone chooses which side overall they are on.

Formal Debate

- For the formal debate, students must write their own points.
- Choose three people to be for the motion and three people to be against the motion.
- They are now a team and should work together to write their points or arguments.
- Other people in the class prepare questions to ask during the debate.
- One person acts as the chairperson for the debate.
- The chairperson introduces the debate motion and the teams, and invites each speaker to speak on the motion.

- The chairperson will also make sure that people have time to ask questions and that speakers have time to answer.
- One person acts as the timekeeper, allowing speakers a set amount of time for their speeches.
- Start with one person for the motion. This side of the argument is known as the proposition. They propose the motion that *Schools should not be allowed to make pupils wear uniforms*.
- The next speaker is against the motion. This side of the argument is known as the opposition.
- As this team are against the motion, they are arguing that schools should be allowed to make pupils wear uniforms.
- The chairperson allows the six speakers, three proposing and three opposing the motion, to take it in turns to speak.

Everyone Participates!

After the speakers have made their speeches, the chairperson allows questions from the audience. Each speaker can answer a number of questions.

At the end of the debate, the chairperson can take two votes.

- Vote one is on the debate. Which team do you think won the argument, was more convincing and made better points?
- Vote two is on the motion itself. The chairperson reads out the motion and asks people to vote by putting up their hands if they are in favour of the statement (agree), and then asks those who are against the statement (disagree) to raise their hands.

Suggestions for further debates:

1. Video games are too violent.
2. The drinking age should be reduced to 16.
3. Parents should be charged if their children commit a crime.

 You will have more debates in Second and Third Year. Chapters 20 and 30 cover more debate topics and look in more detail at influences on moral issues.

Revision Questions

Enquiry

1. Define the following terms:
   - Moral issue
   - Influence
   - Choice
   - Point of view
   - Agreeing with/in favour of
   - Disagreeing with/against
2. Write a sentence using each of the terms.

Exploration

1. How often do you make choices?
2. What influences your choices?
3. Who do you listen to most when making choices?

Reflection and Action

- In pairs, think of a moral issue you would like to debate. Try to make it relevant to your class, school or the country.
- Present your ideas to the class and have a vote on which topic or topics you will debate.
- Have another debate!

Religious Themes in Culture 1

10

Learning Outcome 1.5

Explore the presence of religious themes in contemporary culture through an examination of art, music, literature or film.

Learning Intentions

By the end of this chapter I will:

- Know what a religious theme is
- Be able to identify a religious theme in a piece of art, a piece of music, a book and a film

Key Skills and Wellbeing

- Staying well
- Working with others
- Managing information and thinking
- Communicating

I am aware of how culture affects me. I am able to identify things that have an influence on me.

Keywords

contemporary culture ■ religious theme ■ theme

Ariana Grande

Introduction

A **theme** is a subject running through a piece of writing, a film or an exhibition. It is an idea in a work of literature or art. So a theme in *Harry Potter* might be friendship, loyalty or fear. The *Star Wars* films **explore** themes such as love, evil, good, friendship and power. These are not the only themes running through these works, but they are ones you can identify easily. For example, the friendship between Harry, Ron and Hermione runs throughout the *Harry Potter* novels and the evil of the 'dark side' is present throughout the *Star Wars* series.

Which themes can you identify in the *Harry Potter* films?

What Does This Mean?

Theme: An idea that recurs in a film, a work of art, a piece of music or literature.

Explore: To systematically look into something closely for the purpose of discovery; to scrutinise or probe.

Religious Themes

Some themes are considered to be religious. They might include references to the following:

- God or Gods
- Death and the afterlife
- Questions of meaning – people looking for a purpose in life
- Love
- Prayer and meditation
- Morality or good and evil
- Stories from a major world religion, including famous figures from that religion
- Places associated with a religion

Icebreaker

 As a class, brainstorm ideas or themes you would consider to be religious. Remember there are many different religions and different ways of thinking about religion, so you may come up with a long list.

What Is Contemporary Culture?

Contemporary culture exists all around us. We see it on our television screens, on our computers, in advertisements, in music and in books.

Contemporary culture includes the arts: art, music, literature and film; for example, the art created today and which you may see in galleries; the music played on the radio, at concerts and in films. Contemporary literature includes books currently published, found in bookshops and libraries. Contemporary films are movies that you can view in the cinema, on Netflix or on television.

Contemporary culture has themes that we can recognise and some of these themes are religious. Let us look at one example from each of the different cultural expressions – art, music, literature and film – and identify some of the **religious themes** found in them.

 In Chapters 21 and 31, we will explore this subject again and compare more examples and analyse them.

Art

Art is the way people express themselves through painting, sculpture or other forms. It aims to produce something beautiful or powerful. There are various branches of art, including dance, acting, music and other creative processes. In this section, we explore art as the making of objects or images that express feelings, such as paintings, drawings and sculptures.

Finding the Theme in Art

How are themes shown through art?

- What is the subject? Is it a painting of a person, a place, an animal or an object? The subject will affect the theme.
- What is the situation in the painting? Is the subject (the person) doing something? Is the subject in a particular situation that gives a theme to the painting or sculpture?
- What are the colours? Can they mean something? Do they give a feeling to the piece of art?

The tools of the artist. Many artists express themselves through their art.

Art and Religion

During the Renaissance (c. 1300–1600), a period in the Middle Ages, there was a rebirth in interest in ancient Rome and Greece. This led to a flourishing of art. The artists during the Renaissance created a huge amount of art that is still around today, in galleries and other buildings. Some of the most famous have religious themes. Examples include *The Last Supper* by Leonardo da Vinci, the famous paintings on the ceiling of the Sistine Chapel by Michelangelo, and *The Taking of Christ* by Caravaggio.

These examples are a good place to start looking for religious themes. The stories they tell are from the Bible and the Christian tradition.

1. In *The Last Supper*, da Vinci is expressing through art his understanding of the last meal Jesus had with his disciples.

   The painting shows the reaction of the 12 Apostles when Jesus tells them that one of them will betray him.

2. The centre panel of the ceiling of the Sistine Chapel features one of the most famous religious paintings of all time. Here, Michelangelo painted *The Creation of Adam*, telling the story of the creation as imagined by the artist.

3. In *The Taking of Christ*, Caravaggio shows the story of Jesus' betrayal by the disciple Judas.

Over to You

 Can you identify the themes in these famous works of art?

This lamp contains words from the Quran. It is referring to God as the light of the world, a common theme in Islam.

Over to You

Other major world religions have also had an impact on art. Look at works of art from around the world, and see if you can identify religious themes from Hinduism, Judaism, Buddhism or Islam in them.

Did You Know?

? Muslims do not represent Muhammad in pictures or sculptures. This is because they believe that people might be tempted to worship idols.

Religious Themes in Contemporary Art

Two contemporary works of art with religious themes are *Crucifixion – Haiti* (1997) by Helen David Brancato and *Paranirvana* (1999) by Lewis deSoto.

Crucifixion – Haiti

Crucifixion – Haiti was made by artist and art educator Helen Brancato in 2000. She produced this piece for a competition organised in the USA by the *National Catholic Reporter* to find a contemporary image of Jesus. The competition was called 'Jesus 2000'.

Brancato painted it after seeing a photograph in a newspaper of a Haitian woman who had heard that members of her family had died in a ferry sinking in Haiti.

Crucifixion – Haiti by Helen David Brancato

The painting has the themes of suffering and love. It has the image of the woman with her arms outstretched like Jesus being crucified. The boat is in front of her with the people in danger of falling out.

Key Skill: Managing Information and Thinking

1. What feeling do you get from the painting?
2. Do the colours affect the painting?
3. Does the subject affect the overall feeling?
4. What themes can you identify?

Paranirvana

Paranirvana was made by the artist Lewis deSoto. It is a 7.5-metre image of the Buddha made of a nylon skin, inflated with air. It is based on the story of the Buddha staying on earth after his enlightenment to teach others, and dying when he was 80 years old after preaching his final sermon. The *paranirvana* is the physical death of the Buddha when he entered into *nirvana* – a state of perfection. The artist superimposed his own face onto the face of the Buddha.

This piece of art has the themes of death and meaning. It is an interesting way of showing the Buddha and also asking questions about life.

Paranirvana by Lewis deSoto

Over to You – Exploration

Why do you think the artist superimposed his own face onto the figure of the Buddha?

Music

Music expresses many things for people. It is a great way of creating a mood or feeling. The lyrics can communicate ideas, but even by itself music communicates feelings and is shown to have great benefits for a person's wellbeing. Listening to music has the following benefits:

- It improves mood and stress.
- It reduces a person's anxieties.
- It helps people to exercise better.
- It can ease pain and provide comfort.
- It improves memory.

Icebreaker

- As a class, brainstorm the types of music you know.
- Write the list on the board.
- In groups, come up with examples of each of the types of music listed.
- Share your examples with the class. If possible, listen to a few examples.
- Discuss which is your favourite type of music.

Finding the Themes in Music

When you hear a piece of music, you notice how it sounds. This gives it a mood, or a feeling. It might be happy, sad, reflective, loud, angry or surprising. The lyrics of the song are the words put to music. These can tell a story and bring the listener into the artist's world, real or imaginary.

Religious Themes in Music

Sometimes deliberately and sometimes unintentionally, musicians have religious themes in their songs. Some are really obvious: Madonna's 'Like a Prayer', Justin Bieber's 'Pray' and Bob Dylan's 'Knockin' on Heaven's Door' have religious words in

their titles. Some like 'Radioactive' by Kings of Leon or 'Viva la Vida' by Coldplay are maybe less obvious. There are many other songs that people hear but do not realise have religious themes. We might have to look deeper to find the meaning behind the song. Look out for lyrics, themes and ideas in songs that are found in and come from religion.

Making music is often a collaborative process.

Coldplay's song 'Viva la Vida' comes from the album *Viva la Vida or Death and All His Friends*.

Over to You – Reflection and Action

 You Raise Me Up

Find the lyrics to the song 'You Raise Me Up' (lyrics by Brendan Graham and music by Rolf Lovland) online and answer the following questions.

1. The themes of this song are faith, hope, overcoming, strength and God. Can you identify these in the song?
2. Listen to a version of the song and think about the mood. How does the song make you feel?
3. Think of a song out at the moment or a song you like. Can you identify any religious themes in this song (see page 74 for a list of religious themes)? Share your ideas with the class.

Josh Groban and Westlife have covered the song 'You Raise Me Up'. Listen to both versions. Which do you prefer?

Film

There are many genres of film, including action or adventure, drama, romance, comedy, horror, science fiction or fantasy. Regardless of the genre, films can have a variety of themes. Sometimes religion or religious themes are found in films.

Finding the Themes in Films

Themes in a film are shown through the characters and events in the film's plot. A film may have more than one theme. The development of the plot and characters throughout the story may make a theme more detailed as the story goes on.

Some religious themes are obvious in films; others are less so. In the *Star Wars* films, the themes of good and evil are very clear. In interviews, George Lucas, the director of the original films, has said that the Force is connected to a spirituality and that the story relates to issues found in religion.

Religious Themes in Film

The story of Moses is found in the Jewish sacred writings, the Torah, and in the Bible. It has also been made into a number of films. One of the most famous versions is *The Ten Commandments*, made in 1956. There is another version in the 2014 film, *Exodus: Gods and Kings*, starring Christian Bale.

We will look at an animated version made by Steven Spielberg in 1998 called *The Prince of Egypt*. The film tells the story of the Exodus, which is one of the most important stories in Jewish history. It tells of how the Hebrews, as the Jewish people were then called, were enslaved in Egypt and how they were led to freedom by Moses. This story is celebrated in the famous Jewish festival of Passover.

The Prince of Egypt tells the story from the perspective of Moses. It features many songs, with the lyrics in both English and Hebrew. It is a film with a clear and important religious theme. The song 'When You Believe' from the film won the Best Original Song at the Oscars in 1999.

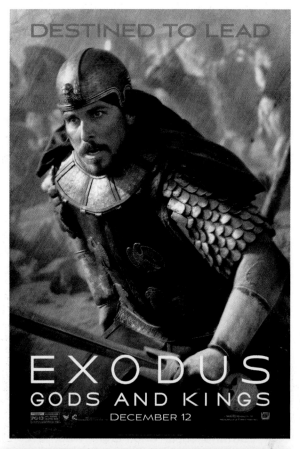

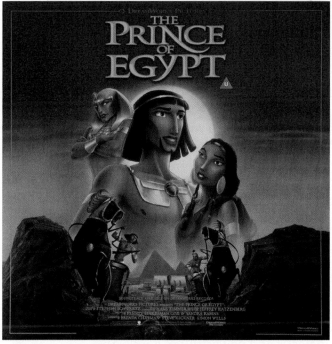

- The subject of the movie is religious: the story of the Exodus.
- The characters are from religion: Moses, his sister Miriam, his brother Aaron and the voice of God.
- The themes are religious: God, hope, faith, love, courage, miracles and belief.

Literature

Written works include poetry, stories, novels and plays. Literature features many different themes, which can be religious. Many poets and storytellers have used religious themes to tell stories and to express ideas. When you read something, it opens you up to other worlds and ideas, but you also bring your own ideas and thoughts to the writing. It is interesting to think whether something means what the author intended it to, or whether it means what the person reading it thinks it does. The answer is, probably, both.

Finding the Theme in Literature

A theme is an idea found throughout a piece of writing. What is the writing about? Who are the characters and how do they behave? As the plot develops, it will help you to identify the themes. The events, the attitudes of the main characters, the words used and the feel of the poem or story combine to give us ideas about the theme or themes in a piece of literature.

Christian Themes in *The Lion, the Witch and the Wardrobe*

The Lion, the Witch and the Wardrobe is a famous children's book by C. S. Lewis. It has been made into a film.

The main characters are four children – Lucy, Edmund, Susan and Peter – who have been sent to the countryside to escape the bombing of British cities during the Second World War. They are staying with an old man called Professor Kirke.

In the story, the children enter a magical world called Narnia through a wardrobe. Narnia, a land filled with talking animals, fauns and dwarves, is under a curse from the White Witch, who makes it always winter but never Christmas. The children, with the help of the great lion Aslan, have to free Narnia from the White Witch and the constant winter. But one of the children, Edmund, betrays the others to the White Witch.

The story is told in a way that presents the figure of Aslan as Christ-like. He is majestic and powerful, yet gentle and kind. His very presence seems to affect the children. He is willing to sacrifice himself for the good of all. The character Edmund betrays his sisters and brother to the White Witch, which is like the betrayal of Jesus by Judas.

 Themes from the story are love, loyalty, good versus evil, betrayal, friendship, courage, hope, temptation and forgiveness.

Over to You – Exploration

 Read this extract in class and then discuss it.

They say Aslan is on the move – perhaps has already landed. And now a very curious thing happened. None of the children knew who Aslan was any more than you do; but the moment the Beaver had spoken these words everyone felt quite different. Perhaps it has sometimes happened to you in a dream that someone says something which you don't understand but in the dream it feels as if it has some enormous meaning – either a terrifying one which turns the whole dream into a nightmare or else a lovely meaning too lovely to put into words, which makes the dream so beautiful that you remember it all your life and are always wishing you could get into that dream again. It was like that now. At the name of Aslan each one of the children felt something jump in its inside. Edmund felt a sensation of mysterious horror. Peter felt suddenly brave and adventurous. Susan felt as if some delicious smell or some delightful strain of music had just floated by her. And Lucy got the feeling you have when you wake up in the morning and realise that it is the beginning of the holidays or the beginning of summer.

An extract from *The Lion, the Witch and the Wardrobe* by C. S. Lewis

1. Why do you think Edmund had the sensation of 'mysterious horror'?
2. Why do you think C. S. Lewis chose a lion to represent Jesus?
3. Do you think the story can be appreciated without knowing the Christian references or themes?
4. Can you think of other stories that have Christian themes?

 Religious themes in art, music, film and literature will be explored further in Chapters 21 and 31. We will make more comparisons and analyse how well the artist, writer or film maker has developed the theme.

Revision Questions

Enquiry

1. What is a religious theme?
2. What is contemporary culture?
3. What were the examples you studied?
4. Which themes did you identify?

Exploration

1. Before you explored religious themes in contemporary culture, were you aware that religious themes were so common?
2. Have you ever noticed religious themes in art, film, literature or music before?
3. Are you surprised by what you have learned? Explain why or why not.

Reflection and Action

- Explore a religious theme found in **one** of the following: art, film, literature or music.
- Make a PowerPoint presentation of your findings.

Or

- Keep a journal for two weeks identifying when you notice religious themes in music or film.

Christianity and Irish Culture

11

What examples of religious belief can be seen in this image?

Introduction

Culture includes beliefs, customs, art and people's way of life. It can be seen in the language, traditions and symbols found in a country. Ireland's culture has been shaped by history and religion. The history of Christianity in Ireland starts in the fifth century. Irish Christianity has developed and changed over more than 1,500 years. How it is practised and expressed has also changed. This is evident through the different cultural expressions of Christianity in Ireland.

This chapter investigates how much Christianity has influenced Irish culture. We will explore architecture, traditions, language, education, legends and symbols to discover the cultural impact of Christianity on Ireland.

Icebreaker

 Investigation of Christianity in Your Community

1. In pairs or groups, walk around your community. Take some paper and a pen and note down any evidence of Christianity you can find. Evidence can come in the form of churches, schools, hospitals, statues, paintings, grottos, graveyards, crosses, sacred spaces, street names and holy wells. When you come back to your class, put all the evidence of Christianity together on the whiteboard.

2. When you encounter these features, do you do anything specific? Explain why or why not.

3. If these things were not present in our communities, do you think it would make a big difference? Explain why or why not.

Ireland: The Island of Saints and Scholars

During the fifth to seventh centuries, Europe was plunged into an era called the Dark Ages. After the fall of the Roman Empire, there was a time of economic and cultural deterioration in Western Europe. During this time, few people kept records, so there is less information about this period than about the preceding and following periods.

During this dark time, Ireland shone. Christianity had arrived in Ireland with **Saint** Patrick and was thriving. The people of Ireland welcomed this monotheistic religion. This was Ireland's Golden Age. Many famous saints lived during this era, including Saint Patrick and Saint Brigid. They dedicated their lives to spreading Christianity throughout Ireland, helping people to move from paganism and to understand their new faith.

How does this Celtic cross show the merging of Christianity and Irish culture?

The Saints

Saint Patrick

Saint Patrick, the **patron saint** of Ireland, was brought to Ireland as a slave from Wales during pagan times in the fifth century. According to legend, Saint Patrick's job was to mind sheep on the mountains of Antrim. It was on these hills that Saint Patrick became a devout Christian. A voice from heaven told him to leave Ireland, and so he did, walking 200 miles to the coast and escaping to Britain, where he was ordained as a priest. He went back to Ireland as a missionary and began converting the Irish people from paganism to Christianity. He cleverly integrated Celtic rituals and symbols into Christian beliefs to help the people transition to Christianity.

Saint Patrick is the patron saint of Ireland.

What Does This Mean?

Patron saint: A heavenly advocate of a country, place, activity, craft, person or family.

In honour of Saint Patrick, every year about one million people from all over the world make a pilgrimage to The Reek, otherwise known as Croagh Patrick. The last Sunday of July is particularly special. This day is known as 'Reek Sunday' and attracts about 25,000 people to Croagh Patrick. At the top, there is a modern chapel where Mass is celebrated, and confession is heard.

Saint Patrick's feast day is 17 March. This is a national holiday in Ireland, and is celebrated all around the world. Many villages, towns and cities hold a Saint Patrick's Day parade. The parade is often made up of all the groups, clubs and societies in the area. It is a wonderful time to appreciate all the great things about our communities and to come together to celebrate the feast day of our patron saint.

Saint Patrick famously used a three-leafed shamrock to explain the Trinity of God the Father, God the Son and God the Holy Spirit in one divine being.

Children dress up to take part in a Saint Patrick's Day Parade.

Saint Brigid

Saint Brigid was born in 451 CE. She was the daughter of a pagan king. Legend has it that when she was a young girl, she prayed that her beauty would be taken away so she would not marry anyone and become a nun instead. Saint Brigid was known for her kindness and care of the poor. She once used the rushes on the floor to make a cross, so she could bless a dying man in his final hours. This tradition is still followed today on her feast day, 1 February.

Saint Brigid is one of Ireland's patron saints.

💡 Key Skill: Being Creative

- Source some rushes from a teacher, family member or friend, or ask an adult to bring you out into nature to collect some. Rushes grow beside water or in bogs.
- Follow the diagram below and create a Saint Brigid's cross.

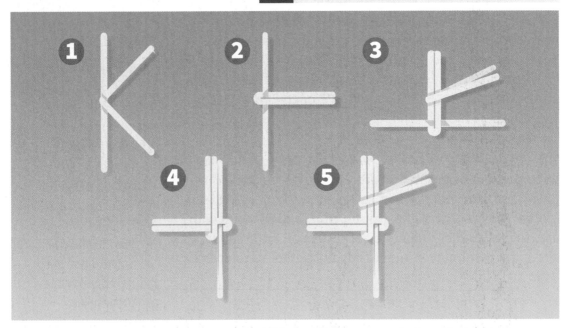

Over to You – Reflection and Action

1. Research the biography of a saint of your choosing. You can pick any saint you want. If you are unsure, below is a list of suggestions:
   - A saint that has the same name as you or as a family member or friend
   - A saint that is from the same place you are
   - The patron saint of your hobby or passion
   - The patron saint of your school
2. Put the biography of the saint in a booklet or on a poster. Include some images and create a classroom display of all the saints you have researched.

How Did Christianity Affect Irish Culture?

These are some of the ways in which Christianity has affected Irish culture:

- Christianity's most obvious impact on Irish culture is with Christian names. In Ireland, the following names are some of the most popular: Patrick, Mary, James, John, Paul, Brigid, Thomas, Stephen and Elizabeth.
- Place names also highlight the close link between Christianity and Irish culture. There are many places named 'Cill' or 'Kill', meaning 'church', e.g. Kildare or Cill Dara, Kilkenny, Kill o' the Grange (and many more).
- Old Celtic festivals became Christian ones, e.g. *Samhain* became Halloween, *Imbolg* became Saint Brigid's Day.
- The first Irish university was opened in 1592. It was named Trinity College, which was a reference to the Christian understanding of God as having three parts.
- The names of schools popular in Ireland also highlight the impact of Christian culture, e.g. St Michael's, St Mark's, St John's, St Mary's and St Joseph's.
- Schools close during Christian festivals, such as Christmas and Easter, and on holy days.
- The Irish for 'Hello' or 'Greeting' is 'Dia duit', which literally means 'God be with you'. The response is 'Dia is Muire duit', which means 'God and Mary be with you'.

Settlement

As Christianity spread throughout Ireland, places of worship and monasteries were built. The monasteries were centres of learning, hostels, hospitals, and sources of food, shelter and work. People settled around them, and over time, they developed into towns. The fact that settlements developed around these sites shows the impact that Christianity had on the whole island of Ireland.

Saint Patrick and other early Christians arrived during Celtic times when Ireland was divided into *tuatha*, or districts, ruled by kings, or *ríthe*. With the arrival of Christianity, bishops ruled over areas called dioceses. Each diocese was then divided into parishes. Irish life became structured around the parish system and still is in many cases. Eventually, each parish came to have a school. After the Reformation in Ireland, many parishes had two schools: one Protestant parish school and one Catholic parish school.

Visitors to Ireland find that many of the tourist sites are religious, such as old monasteries, e.g. Glendalough. Some religious sites are still used for worship, such as Christ Church Cathedral (shown in the photograph), which was founded c. 1028.

Language

Monks in the early monasteries contributed hugely to the development of the Irish language. By placing glosses or explanations in the margins of manuscripts, they translated and explained Latin words in Irish.

Later, in the seventeenth century, some religious leaders promoted the translation of the Bible into Irish. One of these was Bishop William Bedell,

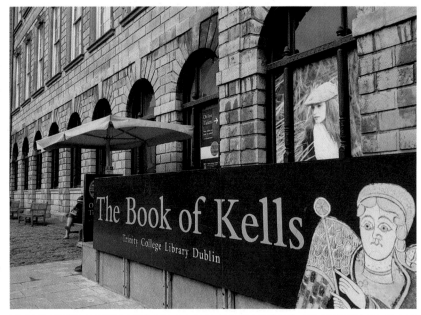

The Book of Kells is a famous early Christian manuscript; it has been on display in the Old Library, Trinity College since the mid-nineteenth century. Today, over 500,000 visitors view it every year.

a **scholar** and Bishop of Kilmore in Co. Cavan. At a meeting of the Church of Ireland in 1634, Bedell proposed translating the Old Testament into Irish to add to the 1602 translation of the New Testament by William O'Donnell. Although Bedell did not live to see it, an Irish translation of the Old Testament was eventually published in 1685.

The Scholars

Along with the introduction of Christianity came formal education. In pre-Christian times, boys and girls were sent to neighbouring families to be educated in animal care, horse riding, sewing and cooking among other things. Reading and writing were not considered important.

Monastic cells on Sceilg Mhichíl

The Christian monks in Ireland were very knowledgeable, especially in Latin, and so many other scholars from all over Europe visited Ireland to study Christianity. The monks lived and worked in monasteries, which soon became centres for learning. People travelled great distances to be educated by the monks. As time went on, education became highly valued, as those who were educated could make a better living for themselves and their family.

What Does This Mean?

Scholar: A person with great knowledge and who is a specialist in a particular branch of study.

Formal Catholic Education

During the harsh Penal Laws of the seventeenth century, the provision of Catholic education was banned. Secret 'hedge schools' were set up to educate Catholic children. Some of the Penal Laws were lifted in the 1790s and formal education of Catholic children began, mainly under the patronage of religious orders. These nuns and brothers taught the children in schools, many of which are still running today. Three of these groups are outlined below.

The Presentation Sisters is a religious congregation founded by Nano Nagle in 1775 to educate the poor and spread Christianity. Today, the sisters are involved in dozens of primary and secondary schools in Ireland and around the world.

The Congregation of Christian Brothers was founded in 1802 by Edmund Rice, a merchant from Waterford. He started this religious community to provide an education to disadvantaged youths. Now the Edmund Rice Schools Trust is responsible for 96 Christian Brother schools in the state.

The Religious Sisters of Mercy was founded by Catherine McAuley in 1831. Its mission was to educate poor young girls in Dublin and provide a shelter for homeless servant girls and women. Today, the order is involved in over 60 pre-schools, primary schools and secondary schools in Ireland and in many more countries around the world.

Over to You – Enquiry

 Is your school under the patronage of a religious order? If so, use the internet, your school library, members of the religious order, or knowledgeable staff members to find out about the history of your school.

The Cultural Impact of Christianity

Have you ever seen people bless themselves as they pass a graveyard or a hearse? Have you heard someone say 'Bless you' when someone has sneezed? Many small gestures and phrases that people use casually every day indicate Ireland's Christian **heritage**. Belief in Christianity was a core part of life in Ireland in the twentieth century. The parish priest was an influential person. If he visited your home, it was a major event. Going to Mass or church was not only a way to worship God but also an opportunity to socialise with your neighbours.

Acting in a Christian manner was important, even if you did not always want to. While modern statistics show that the number of people actively involved in Christianity in Ireland is dropping, religious belief is still a big part of many people's lives in Ireland.

What Does This Mean?

Heritage: The traditions, language and buildings that were created in the past and still have historical importance.

Christian Ethos

Due to the strong Christian **ethos** present in Ireland over hundreds of years, many of the big milestones celebrated in Ireland are traditionally Christian. In Ireland, big events such as births and marriages are usually celebrated in churches, although there are other religious and non-religious groups who offer alternative ways to celebrate these milestones.

What Does This Mean?

Ethos: The set of values associated with a group of people or a particular type of activity.

In 2016, 53 per cent of all marriages took place in a Catholic church, and 73 per cent of all the children born in Ireland in 2015 were baptised. Even though only half of all marriages are Catholic, nearly three-quarters of all babies in Ireland are baptised. This shows that baptism is still an important ritual in the life of an Irish person. The Christian influence in Ireland is still strong.

There are hundreds of churches and graveyards all over Ireland, many of which contain Celtic crosses.

Harvest Festival

Harvest traditions in rural Ireland show the cultural impact of Christianity on people's daily lives. This is particularly the case in Protestant churches, where the foods of the harvest are celebrated by bringing fruit and vegetables to church to celebrate and thank God for the bounty of the earth. This tradition goes back hundreds of years.

Charity

Irish people have a great tradition of donating to charity. Ireland has featured in the top 10 most generous countries in the world for giving to charity, according to surveys carried out by the Charities Aid Foundation. Irish people work and fundraise for charities both at home and abroad. People give most at Christmas.

The idea of giving at Christmas is associated with the presents that the three Magi (the 'Three Wise Men') brought to the infant Jesus in Bethlehem. Giving is also associated with the teaching of Jesus to 'love your neighbour as yourself'.

People often go carol singing at Christmas for different charities. Carols are hymns or songs on the theme of Christmas.

Irish charities are widely supported at this time of the year, from the Irish branch of Christian Aid to Concern and from Bóthar to the Society of St Vincent de Paul, the Simon Community and the Make a Wish Foundation.

Quakers in Ireland

One branch of Christianity that has also influenced Irish culture is the Religious Society of Friends, or Quakers. This is a branch of the Christian church founded in the 1600s in England. The first Irish meeting of the Society of Friends took place in 1654 in the home of William Edmundson in Armagh. Quakers value honesty, equality and integrity, and they are pacifists. This means that they do not believe in fighting or war in any circumstances.

Quaker soup kitchens provided food during the Irish Famine.

The Quakers are famous for their work during the Great Famine of the 1840s. They set up soup kitchens, raised money overseas and gave clothing and food to starving people all over the island of Ireland. Their charity work was an example to others. Quakers believe that serving others is a good way of following the example of Jesus.

In 1812, Quakers founded Bloomfield Care Centre in Dublin to care for the elderly. They have also been involved in education, and there are four Quaker schools in Ireland today: Newtown School, Waterford; Drogheda Grammar School; the Friends' School, Lisburn and Rathgar Junior School.

Sacraments

In Christianity, a **sacrament** is a sacred ritual or ceremony that symbolises God's love. It makes God's invisible love visible through symbolic words and actions. In the Catholic Church, there are seven sacraments that are celebrated at significant moments in people's lives. The seven sacraments are: baptism, penance, the **Eucharist**, confirmation, marriage, holy orders and anointing of the sick. These sacraments are divided into three types:

1. **Initiation** (baptism, the Eucharist, confirmation)
2. Vocation (marriage, holy orders)
3. Healing (penance, anointing of the sick)

What Does This Mean?

Eucharist: The sacrament in which Christians remember the Last Supper, when Jesus gave his disciples bread and wine and commanded them to 'do this in memory of me'.

Most Protestant Churches believe that only baptism and the Eucharist are fundamental sacraments, as these are the two Jesus carried out in the Bible. Some Protestants do not celebrate any sacraments.

Baptism

The birth of a new baby is a special time. A new life has come into the world. Its parents want to celebrate this new life and welcome the baby into the family. The Catholic Church shares the same sentiments; it wants to celebrate new life, as it is a gift from God. It also wants to welcome the child into its religious family, of which God is the Father.

Baptism is the first sacrament, a sacrament of initiation. Most people in Ireland are baptised when they are a few months old, but adult baptism also happens. The baptism ceremony usually takes place during or after Sunday Mass. It has several important aspects to it.

A baby being christened at a baptismal font.

- Traditionally, the baby is dressed in a white christening gown to symbolise purity of faith and cleansing.
- The priest welcomes the child, the parents, the chosen godparents and the rest of the family and friends to the church and asks the parents to give the child's name.
- This name is written on the baptism certificate.
- The baby's christening candle is lit from the Easter Paschal candle and the priest makes the shape of the cross on the baby's forehead and heart with special oil called 'chrism'.

What Does This Mean?

Sacrament: A ritual in the Christian Church involving the use of symbols that represent the loving presence of God.

Initiation: The act of admitting someone into a new group or society.

Baptismal Promises

The parents and godparents bring the baby to the baptismal font. Here, they make a series of promises. After this, the priest pours water from the font onto the baby's forehead three times, while saying the words, 'I baptise you in the name of the Father, Son and Holy Spirit'. Now the child has been initiated into the Catholic Church and is a lifetime member.

Key Skill: Being Creative

Draw a picture of the scene you might expect to see in a Catholic Church during a baptism. Label all the important parts.

Mass Attendance

Years ago, Mass was the focal point of the week for most families. People, regardless of their class or status, would gather at the same place to celebrate the Eucharist. People tried to look their best. Children were scrubbed, hair was brushed, the good clothes were washed and ironed, and shoes were polished. People were on their best behaviour and families enjoyed their Sunday lunch together when Mass was over. Right up to the 1970s, most people living in Ireland attended Mass every Sunday. In 1971, the figure was as high as 91 per cent. However, in recent years, the numbers attending Mass have declined.

The people who attend Mass are called the congregation.

Over to You – Enquiry

1. Why do you think the number of people attending weekly Mass in Ireland has declined over the past 50 years?
2. In pairs, discuss this question and come up with **three** reasons why this may be so.

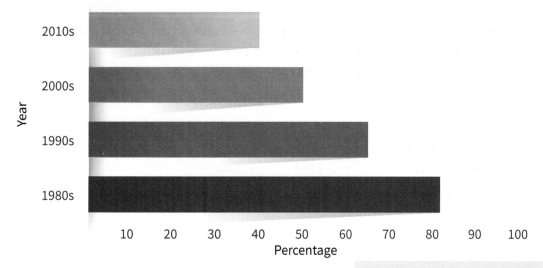

Approximate percentage of the Irish population who attend Mass weekly

Revision Questions

Enquiry

1. What does 'culture' mean?
2. What was the time during the fifth to seventh centuries in Europe known as?
3. What was this time known as in Ireland?
4. Which saint introduced Christianity to Ireland?
5. What was the religion in Ireland before Christianity?
6. What did the saints dedicate their lives to?
7. Why was Saint Patrick brought to Ireland?
8. How did he make the change to Christianity easier for Irish people?
9. How is Saint Patrick celebrated today?
10. What was Saint Brigid known for?
11. What did boys and girls learn in the years before Christianity?
12. Name a religious order that set up schools to educate Catholics.
13. What percentage of the Irish population gets married in a Catholic ceremony?
14. What percentage of Irish babies are baptised?
15. What is a sacrament?
16. How many sacraments are celebrated in the Catholic Church?
17. Name these sacraments.
18. Outline the key moments in a baptism.

Exploration

1. Why do people make crosses from rushes to remember Saint Brigid?
2. Why did people come from other countries to study in Ireland during the golden age?
3. Why do you think the education of Catholic children was banned when the Penal Laws were imposed?
4. Why do you think that the percentage of baptisms in Ireland is higher than the percentage of church marriages?
5. Write a paragraph on how Christianity has contributed to Irish culture and heritage.

Reflection and Action

- Does your school have a Christian heritage? If so, investigate how Christianity has contributed to your school's heritage and culture.
- Put your findings together using a poster presentation or IT and present it to the class.

Expressing Religious Belief 12

Learning Outcome 1.6

Examine and appreciate how people give expression to religious belief in religious rituals, in formal places of worship and other sacred spaces.

Learning Intentions

By the end of this chapter I will:
- Know what ritual is
- Know how to identify religious beliefs in places of worship
- Realise the significance of sacred spaces in the expression of beliefs
- Appreciate the expression of religious belief in places of religious significance that I have visited
- Examine how the religious beliefs of some of the major world religions are shown in rituals I have experienced or witnessed

Key Skills and Wellbeing

- Being creative
- Managing information and thinking
- Managing myself

I am aware of the rituals and special places in my life. I now realise what beliefs are significant to other people through the rituals and places they see as important.

Keywords

pilgrimage ▪ places of worship ▪ religious rituals ▪ sacred spaces

Can you identify which religion this place of worship belongs to?

Introduction

Humans are creatures of habit. We like to follow a pattern, and once we settle into our rhythm it can be hard to break out of it. There are things we do every day which make up our daily rituals. For some, a morning does not start without a mug of coffee, while others do not feel right unless they get a run in before lunch. Rituals can be as common as a handshake and as complex as a healing ceremony.

Over to You – Exploration

 What are your daily rituals?

- In your copy, make a list of the things you do every day.
- Beside each one, write down why you do it.
- Once you have completed the list, choose your favourite ritual and explain why it is your favourite.

Icebreaker

- Think about your bedroom – your personal space. What things in your bedroom are sacred? What pictures and posters decorate the walls? Is there anything from your childhood that you still hold onto, even though it is a bit worn and tattered now?
- Create a list of the most important aspects of your bedroom. Beside each one, write down what makes it so important.
- Now put yourself in someone else's shoes: if a stranger walked into your room, what would they learn about you?
- You have given expression to the things that are important to you by the way you have decorated your room. Religions do this too in places of worship, sacred places and rituals.

A World of Beliefs

Religious Rituals

All religions use rituals to signify important events and key moments. **Religious rituals** tell us about the beliefs of that religion. Rituals give expression to key beliefs through actions and words. They can bring our attention to significant moments in our spiritual journey.

Judaism: Bat Mitzvah and Bar Mitzvah

In Judaism, there are 613 commandments that all Jewish adults must follow. Children are not required to follow all of them, even though they are encouraged to. When a boy turns 13 and a girl turns 12, they are considered adults in Jewish tradition and so they become a *bar* or *bat mitzvah*, which means 'son or daughter of the commandments'. This means that they are now responsible for their actions under religious law and need to make good decisions.

At this age, the young person automatically becomes a *bat* (girl) or *bar* (boy) *mitzvah*. At the first Sabbath after the young person's birthday, a ritual is held to celebrate this coming of age.

He or she marks this rite of passage by reciting sections of the Torah and leading part of the prayer service in the synagogue.

It is also customary for the boy or girl to make a short speech. This speech usually begins with the phrase, 'Today I have become a man/woman. The father also says a blessing.

A family gathered together around a scroll of the Torah during a *bar mitzvah*

This ceremony is then followed by a reception or party where the young person receives gifts and celebrates with friends and family.

This ritual tells us many things about the Jewish faith.

- First, it shows the importance of the commandments in Jewish life. We know this because the time when a person is ready to follow all 613 commandments is marked in a special way.
- Second, it outlines the importance of the Torah, as this sacred text is used in the ceremony.
- Finally, the *bar* or *bat mitzvah* shows how important family is in the Jewish tradition. The father gives a blessing and the ceremony takes place in the heart of the community – the synagogue. The whole family celebrates this ritual with friends and other members of the community.

Review and Reflect

1. What is the difference between a *bar mitzvah* and a *bat mitzvah*?
2. What happens during a *bar* or *bat mitzvah*?
3. How is a *bar* or *bat mitzvah* marked as a special occasion?
4. What key beliefs does this ritual show us?

1. Examine the following religious rituals carefully. When you have finished, select the key beliefs expressed in that ritual.
2. Outline how you know this is a key belief from this religious ritual.

Cremation

When a Hindu dies, his or her body is kept at home for 24 hours before it is cremated. Before the cremation, the body is kept in an open casket. Hymns are sung and mantras are recited, and offerings are made to the Gods. The body is burned and it is believed that the soul is released for reincarnation. The fire releases the soul from the skull. The ashes are then scattered at a sacred body of water or at a place the person found special. After the service, the family usually wear white to symbolise that they are in mourning. Ten days later, a ceremony is held at the home of the deceased person.

Reconciliation

When a Roman Catholic has done wrong, they will seek God's forgiveness in a ritual called 'reconciliation'. There are four parts to a reconciliation service:

1. **Contrition:** The first part requires the person to be aware of what has been done wrong, be truly sorry and intend to sin no more.
2. **Confession:** The person will then openly tell the wrong doings to the priest.
3. **Penance:** The priest will request the person do an act of penance to make up for what they have done, usually in the form of a few short prayers.
4. **Absolution:** The priest grants God's forgiveness and restores the relationship between God and the person.

Places of Worship

A **place of worship** is the heart of any faith community. Not only is it a place where people can pray, it also offers a social aspect to faith, giving people a chance to meet others in their religious community and celebrate together. Often in places of worship, you will find a notice board about social gatherings, daycare facilities and other services.

Expressing Beliefs

What Does This Mean?

Worship: To show devotion or love to a God or deity.

Islam: The Mosque

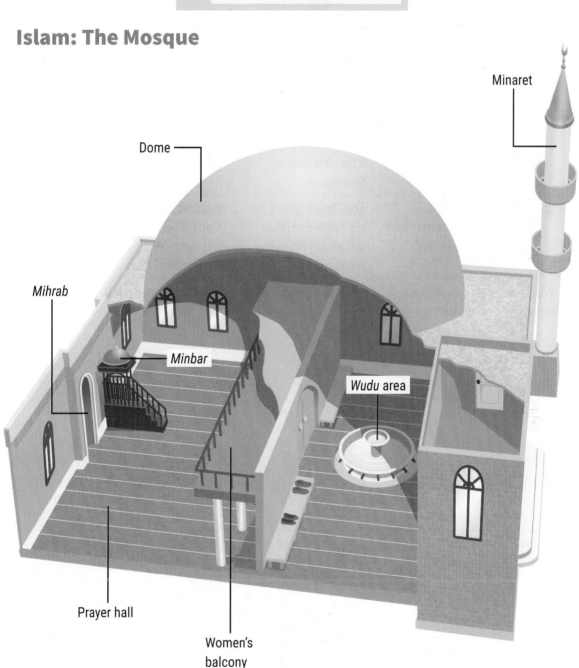

Minaret

Dome

Mihrab

Minbar

Wudu area

Prayer hall

Women's balcony

Did You Know?

? The largest mosque in the world is the Al-Haram Mosque in Mecca. It can hold up to 300,000 people at one time.

For many Muslims, a mosque is not just for worship. It is also a meeting place, somewhere to learn about Islam and to study the Quran. In Ireland, the Islamic Cultural Centre has many vital functions for its community. The most important time for prayer in the Islamic week is midday on Friday. Muslims gather to pray communally. An imam leads prayer. Religious festivals and ceremonies, such as funerals, also take place in a mosque. Mosques have rules about how people should behave inside, such as removing your shoes and not disturbing someone in prayer.

Chapter 2

Features of a Mosque

Feature	Description	Function	Key belief
Mihrab	A semicircular niche in the wall of a mosque	It indicates the **qibla**, the direction of the Kaaba in Mecca.	The Kaaba is the holiest shrine in Islam; because of its significance, Muslims pray towards Mecca.
Minaret	A tall tower	A *muezzin* performs the call to prayer from the top of this tower.	Prayer is one of the Five Pillars of Islam and an important part of daily life for all Muslims.
Minbar	A raised platform in the prayer hall	The imam gives his Friday sermon (*khutbah*) from the minbar.	*Khutbah* is public preaching in Islam. The imam is a learned man and helps other Muslims understand Islamic teachings.
Wudu area	A wash area featuring fountains, taps and sinks	Muslims ritually cleanse themselves before prayer.	Prayer is a sacred time to communicate and show submission to Allah. It is important to come to prayer physically and ritually clean.
Women's balcony	A balcony at the back of the prayer hall	This provides a place for women and children to pray.	Traditionally, men and women separate for prayer.
Dome	A semicircular roof over the main hall	The dome represents the universe Allah created.	Allah's creation of the world is of the utmost importance and the dome offers a reminder of that creation.
Prayer hall	A large hall with no furniture. The carpet may feature very faint straight lines	This is a place where all Muslims can prayer together. The straight lines on the carpet indicate where to stand.	Communal prayer is thought to be better than praying alone. It is important to stand shoulder to shoulder in the prayer hall to show that everyone is equal before Allah.

Over to You – Enquiry

- Imagine you have to give a tour of a mosque to a group of people who have never heard about Islam before.
- Write out the text of the short talk you would give them, while showing them **three** features of the mosque.

Key Skill: Managing Information and Thinking

- Using the knowledge you gained in Chapter 1, look at the images of the places of worship belonging to two world religions below. Each image is labelled with the important features of that place of worship.

- Using your online research skills, look up the features labelled in each image and find out what the function of each feature is.

- Divide into groups. Each group should focus on one of the two places of worship below.

- Study the images and outline which key belief is expressed by **three** features in the image.

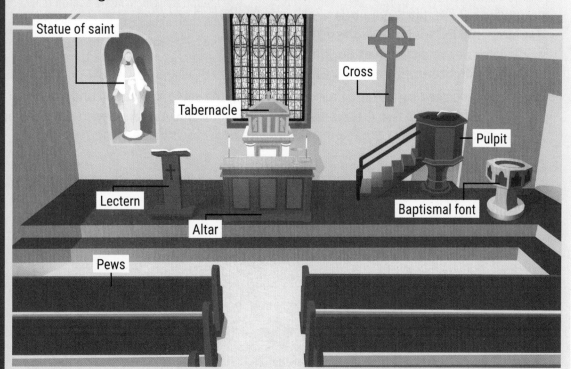

Statue of saint
Tabernacle
Cross
Pulpit
Lectern
Baptismal font
Altar
Pews

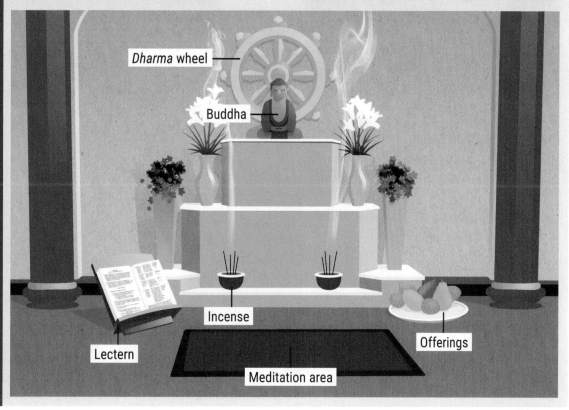

Dharma wheel
Buddha
Incense
Offerings
Lectern
Meditation area

Sacred Spaces

A **sacred space** is a place considered special and holy by a religious community. A sacred space can be a place of pilgrimage for thousands or a personal place of meditation.

Buddhism: Bodh Gaya

The most important sacred spaces for Buddhists are located in India. They are:

- Bodh Gaya
- The Bodhi tree
- The Maha Bodhi temple

Buddhists believe that Siddhartha Gautama, the founder of Buddhism, who would later become known as Buddha, achieved **enlightenment** at Bodh Gaya.

What Does This Mean?

Enlightenment: When a person realises the truth about life. To be freed from the birth-death-rebirth cycle, one must achieve enlightenment.

Bodh Gaya is located in northern India. Here, Siddhartha sat in meditation under a Bodhi tree until he came to realise the truth about life and suffering. A Bodhi tree that is believed to be a direct descendant of that original Bodhi tree still grows in the same spot.

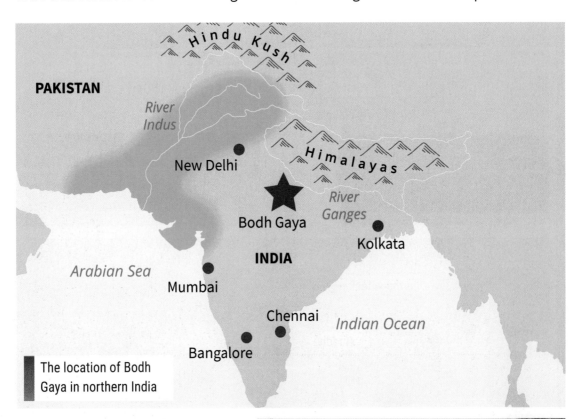

The location of Bodh Gaya in northern India

Did You Know?

In 1989, a huge statue of Buddha was unveiled in Bodh Gaya. The statue is 25 metres tall. That's taller than five double decker buses stacked on top of one another!

The statue of Buddha at Bodh Gaya

Pilgrimage

The place where Buddha achieved enlightenment became a place of **pilgrimage** for millions of Buddhists. About 250 years after Buddha died, the Emperor Ashoka visited the site and built the Maha Bodhi temple. Inside the temple there is a huge image of Buddha sitting as he did when he achieved enlightenment. This image is believed to be 1,700 years old!

Thousands of Buddhists make the pilgrimage to Bodh Gaya each year. They follow in Buddha's footsteps to achieve enlightenment, so meditation under the Bodhi tree is a key feature of this pilgrimage. They visit the Maha Bodhi temple and bow in front of Buddha. Pilgrims pray and present offerings in the temple, and they give gifts to the monks who look after the shrine.

Every Buddhist strives to achieve enlightenment, so that they may break the cycle of **samsara**. The Buddhist belief in *samsara* and motivation to follow the way of life of the 'enlightened one' gives significance to Bodh Gaya.

Buddhist pilgrims pay homage at the Maha Bodhi Temple.

What Does This Mean?

Pilgrimage: A journey to a place of religious importance. The journey may be difficult and is undertaken to show devotion.

Samsara: The process of reincarnation, the endless cycle of life, death and rebirth.

Over to You – Reflection and Action

1. **(a)** Read the following extract and instructions. You need a blank sheet of paper and some coloured pens. The extract is from the blog of a young woman who went on her first pilgrimage to Bodh Gaya when she was 19 years old.

    > Imagine … You're sitting next to the Maha Bodhi temple, only metres away from the very spot where the Buddha gained full enlightenment. You take in a few deep breaths and look up at the beautiful heart-shaped Bodhi tree leaves moving gently in the breeze above you. There is a feeling of wonder and excitement in the air, knowing that this was the place where the Buddha sat in meditation and achieved a great awakening 2,600 years ago.

    (b) Take a moment, close your eyes and imagine you are at Bodh Gaya. You have gone on a pilgrimage to meditate in the same spot Buddha meditated in – the place where he achieved enlightenment. The air is full of peace and calm and deep breaths come easily to you. Your spirit feels at rest. Relax and pause in this place for a few moments.

    (c) When you are ready, draw a picture of how you feel right now. It does not have to be a picture of a scene; it can be something abstract. Allow your feelings to pick the colours and your hand to go wherever it wants.

    (d) When you are finished, reflect on the image you have created and what it means to you.

2. Select **one** of the following sacred spaces. Research what makes that space sacred and what key beliefs are expressed in that sacred space.
    - Judaism – Wailing Wall
    - Hinduism – Varanasi
    - Islam – *Hajj* to Mecca
    - Christianity – Pilgrimage to Knock

People use special places to meditate. These places can instil a sense of calm and unity with nature. If you were going to meditate, where would you choose as your special place?

Revision Questions

Enquiry

1. What is a ritual?
2. What do religious rituals tell us?
3. What is a place of worship?
4. What happens at a place of worship?
5. What is a sacred space?
6. What happened at Bodh Gaya?

Exploration

1. How do rituals or sacred places show us the key beliefs of a religion?
2. What was your favourite part of this chapter? Why?
3. Can you think of any personal sacred spaces that are special to you?
4. Why is Bodh Gaya sacred to Buddhists?

Reflection and Action

- Outline the key beliefs of a world religion of your choice.
- Create a presentation on how these key beliefs are seen in rituals, places of worship and sacred spaces associated with that religion. Your presentation can be in poster form or using IT.

13 Prayer in the Life of a Faithful Person

Learning Outcome 1.8

Describe the role of prayer in the lives of people of faith.

Learning Intentions

By the end of this chapter I will:

- Know what prayer is
- Know what different types of prayer there are
- Understand the different reasons why someone might pray
- Realise the value of prayer for faithful people
- Be aware of the impact of prayer on the life of people of faith

Key Skills and Wellbeing

- Managing information and thinking
- Communicating
- Managing myself

I will reflect on the importance of prayer in my own life. I understand that prayer can be a very special thing for the people in my community. I can be mindful of the significance of prayer to others by showing tolerance and respect while others are in prayer.

Keywords

penitence ■ petition ■ praise ■ prayer ■ thanksgiving

Introduction

Words of **prayer** have become a part of our everyday vocabulary. Snippets of prayer can be heard in ordinary conversation all over Ireland and in the rest of the world. We use simple words of prayer when someone sneezes or to express delight or happiness with an event or piece of news. Prayer has great importance in the lives of people of faith: Muslims pray facing Mecca five times a day, Gautama Siddhartha achieved enlightenment after seven days meditation under a tree.

> Bless you

> Insha Allah

> L'chaim

> Thanks be to God

> Prayer

Icebreaker

1. In your copy book, write down all the words that pop into your head when you think of prayer.
2. Share the words you have written down with the rest of the class and record a common list on the board.
3. Analyse the list and pick the top **five** words that come up most regularly.

📌 Prayer, at its core, is communication – a two-way conversation between humans and the sacred or holy. Saint Teresa of Avila described prayer as 'an intimate friendship, a frequent conversation held with the Beloved'.

Types of Prayer

Prayer comes in many forms across all religions. Different faiths have different understandings of how to pray, or even the best way to pray. Some religions have clear and specific guidelines on how and when to pray, while others allow for more personal interpretation. Some of the categories which are common to many religions are:

- **Communal prayer or prayer said with others:** In Islam prayer is believed to be 25 times more rewarding when done together in the mosque rather than at home, alone.
- **Private prayer or prayer said alone:** Meditation is a form of private prayer where Buddhists spend time in deep reflection, often using beads or a mantra (a repeated phrase) to help them achieve enlightenment.
- **Vocal prayer or prayer said aloud:** The cantor leads the prayers in a Jewish synagogue.
- **Silent prayer or prayer said in the mind:** Saint Teresa of Avila created 'contemplation', a type of prayer that uses no words or thoughts.

Can you identify which religion this woman praying privately belongs to?

A group of Jews in communal prayer

Purpose of Prayer

The purpose of prayer also varies. Someone facing a difficult time might use a prayer to ask God for strength or guidance. Someone feeling guilty who wants to make amends for an act might use a prayer to ask for God's forgiveness.

In Christianity there are four main types of prayer:

1. **Petition:** When asking for something, e.g. help to cope with stress before an exam.
2. **Praise:** When praising or glorifying God, e.g. when realising how beautiful a sunset is.
3. **Penitence:** When asking for God's forgiveness, e.g. if a person hurts someone they love.
4. **Thanksgiving:** When giving thanks to God, e.g. when someone has arrived safely after a journey.

Examples of each of these types of prayer can be seen in the prayer Jesus taught his followers – the 'Our Father'. Below is the Roman Catholic version of this prayer.

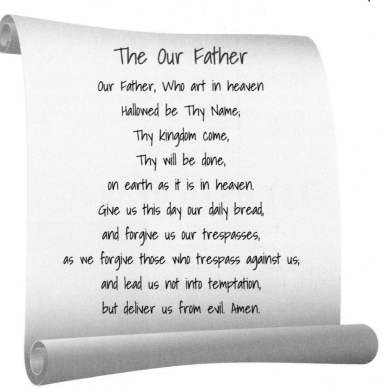

The Our Father

Our Father, Who art in heaven
Hallowed be Thy Name;
Thy kingdom come,
Thy will be done,
on earth as it is in heaven.
Give us this day our daily bread,
and forgive us our trespasses,
as we forgive those who trespass against us;
and lead us not into temptation,
but deliver us from evil. Amen.

Did You Know?

 In the Protestant tradition, the 'Our Father' has an extra line at the end, when people pray: 'For thine is the kingdom, the power and the glory, for ever and ever. Amen.'

Over to You – Enquiry

 In pairs, select an example from the 'Our Father' of:

- Petition
- Praise
- Penitence
- Thanksgiving

Share your findings with the class.

Prayer in the Life of People of Faith

Prayer plays a huge role in the lives of some people. They use prayer to help them come to a conclusion on moral issues, what path to take in life or how to approach an injustice. Prayer offers the person of faith a time to reflect, listen to God's guidance and take strength from God. Let us look at the role prayer played in the life of a person of faith who has faced difficult situations and helped many people across the world.

Malala Yousafzai

Malala was born on 12 July 1997, to Ziauddin and Tor Pekai Yousafzai, in Mingora, Pakistan. Her father ran a chain of private schools in the city. It was through the family's involvement in education that Malala developed her thirst for knowledge. As a very young child, before she could even talk, Malala would toddle into classrooms and pretend to be the teacher.

Life under the Taliban

When Malala was 10 years old, life changed drastically for people living in her community. The Taliban, an extremist group, began to control the area and quickly became the dominant force. Girls were banned from attending school,

What did Malala blog about?

as were everyday social activities like dancing and watching television. A reign of terror had begun, with suicide bombings becoming widespread. By 2008, the Taliban had destroyed some 400 schools.

Malala was determined to get an education and stood up for the rights of all children – girls and boys – to get an education. In 2009, she began to blog anonymously about life under Taliban rule and her desire to go to school. She used social media to campaign publicly for her right to go to school. Over the next few years, Malala and her father became known throughout Pakistan for their determination to give Pakistani girls a free, good-quality education. Malala received many awards for her work for peace, including the International Children's Peace Prize and Pakistan's National Youth Peace Prize.

Attacked by the Taliban

On the morning of 9 October 2012, 15-year-old Malala was sitting on a bus heading home from school. She was talking with her friends about schoolwork when two members of the Taliban stopped the bus. One of the men asked for Malala by name, and then they shot her in the head.

Malala's Success

Miraculously, Malala survived and was airlifted to hospital. From there, she was brought to an intensive care unit in Birmingham, England. She had to undergo several surgeries but had suffered no brain damage.

In March 2013 Malala began to attend school in Birmingham. She continues to campaign for the right of all children to get an education and has published a book, *I Am Malala*, outlining her story. In 2014, aged 17, she became the youngest person ever to receive the Nobel Peace Prize. She has set up the Malala Fund, a foundation that uses education to empower girls to achieve their potential and become strong, confident leaders.

Malala receiving the Nobel Prize for Peace

Prayer to Reflect

Malala used prayer to reflect on the teachings of Islam. Islam teaches equality for all people. According to the Quran, men and women have the same religious and moral duties and responsibilities:

> Never will I suffer to be lost the work of any of you be it male or female: you are members of one another...
>
> (Quran 3: 195)

Speaking in a news interview, Malala said, 'But to me Islam is about equality and calling myself feminist would have no opposition from the religion.'

Malala has used prayer to reflect on the teachings of Islam, and through this she has come to understand the place equality has in everyone's life.

The Healing Power of Prayer

Speaking to the Christian Broadcasting Network, Malala outlined how prayer has helped her to heal from the vicious attack. She states that she is 'getting better day by day just because of the prayers of people. Because all people, men, women, children, all of them, have prayed for me.' It is clear that Malala takes strength from other people's faith as well as from her own.

Using Prayer to Inspire Action

Malala is deeply saddened by the civil war in Syria and the effect this violence has had on the children of the city of Aleppo. Malala explained that she is praying for the children of Aleppo but that prayer is no longer enough. She has been inspired by her prayers to go further and has called for action to help the children of Syria.

Muslims praying communally in a mosque

Action Verb Focus: Describe

Present: To give an account, using words, diagrams or images, of the main points of the topic.

When we describe something, we need to give plenty of details so others can get a clear understanding of the person, place or thing. When we are describing a topic or concept, we should give an account of the main points using words, diagrams or images. We can give a description in writing or in an oral presentation.

Over to You – Enquiry

1. When and where was Malala born?
2. What did her father do?
3. When she was 10 years old, how did Malala's life drastically change?
4. How did Malala feel about the ban on girls attending school?
5. What did she do to show how she felt?
6. What happened to Malala in 2012?
7. In your opinion, why did Malala want every child to get a good education?
8. Outline **three** characteristics Malala has. Explain why you picked each one.
9. Describe **three** ways prayer played a vital role in Malala's life.
10. Do you think Malala is a good role model for young people? Explain why or why not.

Over to You – Explanation

Create an interview for a person you know, asking them about prayer in their life and what impact it has had on their choices (you can use the headings from the Reflection and Action exercise on page 114). Write up the transcript of the interview.

Revision Questions

Enquiry

1. What does prayer mean?
2. List some of the ways a person could pray.
3. Why might someone pray?
4. At what times in their life might a person of faith use the different types of prayer?

Exploration

1. Does prayer play a role in your own life, or in the life of someone you know? Share your thoughts with the rest of your class.
2. Using your own knowledge and understanding, write a reflection or prayer (non-religious or religious) about something that is important to you.

Reflection and Action

Research another person of faith (e.g. Martin Luther King, Gandhi, Sr Stanislaus Kennedy, Fr Peter McVerry or someone you know personally) under the following headings:

- His/Her life
- His/Her religious beliefs
- How he/she has helped others
- How prayer influenced his/her choices or helped him/her

Write a report on the person you have chosen, using the headings above.

Or

Create a poster outlining the key points you found out through your research.

A Timeline of a Major World Religion

14

Learning Outcome 2.6

Construct a timeline of one major world religion, making reference to key people, times of expansion and times of challenge.

Learning Intentions

By the end of this chapter I will:

- Know what a timeline is
- Have explored the timeline of one major world religion
- Know the significant people, events and places on the timeline
- Know when times of expansion and times of challenge took place
- Think about the importance for members of this world religion of the key people and events from the timeline

Key Skills and Wellbeing

- Managing information and thinking
- Communicating
- Working with others
- Staying well

I will show care and respect for others.

Keywords

chronology ■ expansion ■ key people ■ timeline

Introduction

A **timeline** is a graphical or visual representation of a time period on which important events are marked. This chapter asks you to create a timeline of a major world religion. You will research the history of the religion, so that you can find out when to start your timeline. You will also explore how the religion developed and the events that took place, so that you can place the important events in the correct order on your timeline.

 ## Action Verb Focus: Construct

Present: To bring together different elements to form something whole.

We use the word 'construct' when we talk about making something. We construct bridges, buildings and machines from lots of parts. We can also construct something from information, for example a diagram, a chart or a table of contents. To construct something well, we need to pick the correct elements and combine them into something whole that makes sense to us and is understandable to others.

Icebreaker

 My Timeline
Using this diagram to get started, construct a timeline of your own life.

Date of birth

First day at school

Important event

First day at second-level school

Add into your timeline **key people** and events that are important for you.

What Does This Mean?

Key people: Individuals who are considered important in relation to something.

A Historical Timeline of Dublin

Below is an example of a timeline of Dublin, with a **chronology** of the key events noted on it. You can see that it starts with the Vikings settling in Dublin in 841 and ends with the completion of the Spire in 2003. Timelines start with the oldest event. They are marked in the order in which the events happened, ending with the most recent event. You do not have to put everything on a timeline, but you should try to mark in the important events. This chapter will help you to create a timeline of Judaism.

841 – Vikings settle in Dublin

1014 – Battle of Clontarf takes place

1028 – King Sitric founds Christ Church

1172 – Normans under Strongbow in Dublin

1592 – Trinity College is founded

1662 – The Phoenix Park is founded

1759 – Guinness Brewery is founded

1816 – Ha'penny Bridge is opened

1831 – Dublin Zoo is founded

1904 – The Abbey Theatre is opened

1912 – Suffragettes attack the British prime minister on a visit to Dublin

1916 – The Easter Rising takes place

1963 – John F. Kennedy drives in a motorcade down O'Connell Street

2003 – The Spire is completed

A Timeline of Judaism

In order to create a timeline of Judaism, you need to have an outline of Jewish history. The history of the Jewish people goes back to the time of Abraham, in approximately 1850 BCE. The information about Jewish history comes from the sacred texts of Judaism known as the Tanakh, which is a combination of three types of writing: the Torah (law), the Nevi'im (prophets) and the Ketuvim (writings).

The history of Judaism can be divided into different sections or time periods:

1. The story of the Patriarchs – Abraham, Isaac and Jacob
2. The story of the Exodus
3. The story of the Kings
4. The story of the Babylonian Exile
5. The Second Temple Period, Jewish Revolt and Dispersal
6. European Jewish History
7. Modern Judaism

1. The Story of the Patriarchs

Judaism started with a man called Abraham, who believed in one God. Abraham made an agreement with God; this is called a 'covenant'. Abraham left his homeland in Ur in Mesopotamia and travelled to Canaan. He believed that God was bringing him there to a 'promised land'. Abraham had a son Isaac, and Isaac had a son Jacob. These three figures are known as the 'patriarchs', or founding fathers, of Judaism.

Jacob had 12 sons. Joseph was Jacob's favourite son. Jacob's other sons were jealous of Joseph and sold him into slavery. Joseph ended up in Egypt, which was ruled by the **Pharaoh**. While in Egypt, Joseph became very important because he had the ability to interpret dreams. Interpreting a dream of the Pharaoh, Joseph foretold that there would be a time of plenty followed by a famine. He told the Pharaoh to save lots of food during the time of plenty so that they would have enough during the famine. When the famine came, Joseph's brothers in Canaan were also hungry and they came to Egypt looking for help. Here they were reunited with Joseph. The people now stayed in Egypt and were no longer in the promised land of Canaan.

What Does This Mean?

Pharaoh: A king or emperor in Egypt.

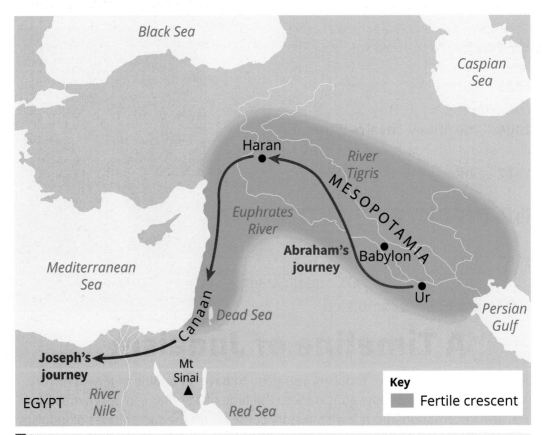

This map shows the journey of Abraham and the journey of Joseph into Egypt. Trace it into your copy book. Include the arrows and the places mentioned in the story.

2. The Story of the Exodus

Around 1250 BCE, hundreds of years after Joseph and his brothers were dead, the ancient Jewish people, called the Hebrews, were still in Egypt. They were being treated badly by the Egyptians. The Pharaoh made them slaves and they had to work on the big building projects of the Egyptians. At one point, the Pharaoh was worried that there were too many of the Hebrews and that they might revolt, so he ordered that the baby boys of the Hebrews be killed. It was at this time that Moses was born. In order to save him, his mother placed him in a basket and hid it among rushes beside the River Nile. Moses was taken from the river by an Egyptian princess and raised as an Egyptian.

The Burning Bush

When he was grown up, Moses encountered God in the form of a burning bush. God told Moses to free the people from slavery in Egypt. When Moses asked the Pharaoh to free the slaves, the Pharaoh refused.

Following 10 plagues, the Pharaoh agreed to let the people leave, but he then changed his mind. He sent his army to pursue the Hebrews as they fled Egypt. They seemed trapped, but Moses then performed a famous miracle – he parted the Red Sea and led the people to safety. When the Pharaoh's army tried to follow them, the sea closed over the soldiers, allowing the Hebrews to escape.

This event is called the Exodus, which means 'departure'. After their escape from Egypt, the Hebrew people spent 40 years in the desert before they entered the 'promised land' of Canaan. During this time, Moses gave the people the Ten Commandments.

Moses is hugely important in Jewish history. He had the honour of encountering God and showing God's power, and he was responsible for giving the Torah to the people.

> Find out where Moses is said to have received the Ten Commandments.

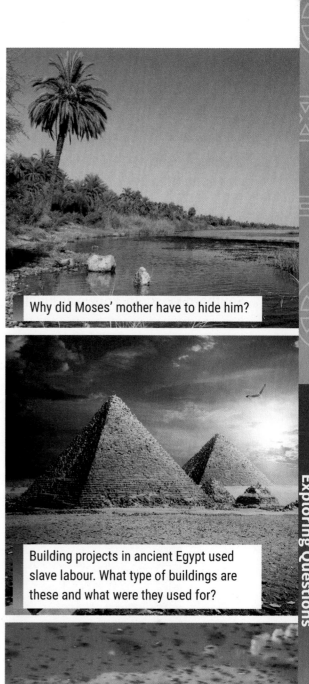

Why did Moses' mother have to hide him?

Building projects in ancient Egypt used slave labour. What type of buildings are these and what were they used for?

A plague of locusts destroys all vegetation in its path. Find out what other plagues are said to have occurred.

Review and Reflect

Read the story of Moses. Draw a picture of **one** part of the story, e.g. the 10 plagues, the burning bush or the parting of the Red Sea.

3. The Story of the Kings

After the people returned to the 'promised land', they were led by tribal leaders called Judges. The Hebrew people were made up of 12 tribes. After some years, they decided they wanted a king to rule over them. They were told by the prophets (messengers of God) that they did not need a king, as God was their ruler. They kept asking, and eventually God agreed to give them a king. The king was anointed with oil to show he was appointed by God.

Their first king was Saul, who was replaced by David, one of the most successful Jewish kings. During David's rule around 1000 BCE, the kingdom was prosperous. David was succeeded by his son, Solomon. Solomon was known as a wise king and was responsible for building the first Jewish Temple in Jerusalem. After Solomon, the kingdom was divided into two parts: the Northern Kingdom, known as Israel, and the Southern Kingdom, known as Judah.

The first Jewish Temple, built by King Solomon, housed the Ark of the Covenant. This was a special wooden box that was said to contain the stone tablets of the Ten Commandments. Outside the temple was the area for rabbis (Jewish religious teachers/leaders) to wash and the altar for them to offer sacrifices to God.

Over to You – Reflection and Action

1. Discuss why you think the people would have wanted a king. Why did the prophets think they did not need one?
2. What would be the advantages and disadvantages of having a king?
3. Find out more about the three kings: Saul, David and Solomon. Write a short paragraph about each.
4. Which king do you think was the best ruler?

4. The Story of the Babylonian Exile

Division had made the kingdoms weak and vulnerable. The Northern Kingdom of Israel was taken over by the Assyrians in 722 BCE and came to an end. The Southern Kingdom of Judah was taken over by the Babylonians in 586 BCE. The first Jewish Temple was destroyed. The Babylonians also forced the people out of Judah and brought them to Babylon in an event known as the 'Babylonian exile'. The people, now known as the Jews (because they were 'from Judah'), were outside of their homeland, the 'promised land'.

Over to You – Exploration

- Find out where Babylon was.
- On a modern map of the world, which countries would the Babylonian empire include today?

5. The Second Temple Period, Jewish Revolt and Dispersal

The people spent almost 40 years in Babylon until 539 BCE, when the Persians took over. The leader of the Persians, Cyrus, issued an order in 537 BCE allowing the people to return to Judah. They went back but were deeply affected by their time in exile.

The era known as the Second Temple period lasted about six centuries from around 530 BCE to 70 CE. During this time, the Jews lived under a series of empires: the Persians, the Greeks and the Romans.

The people had a temple in Jerusalem, local synagogues and rabbis, and they tried to follow the Torah, or Jewish law. The Temple in Jerusalem was very important to the Jewish people during this time. They had to fight to get it back in 167 BCE when a Greek king, Antiochus IV Epiphanes, tried to impose his belief in many Gods onto the people. This event is called the Maccabean Revolt and is remembered during the Jewish festival of **Hanukkah**.

The Second Temple period ended in 70 CE when the Jewish people revolted against the Romans. In response, the Romans destroyed the Second Temple. There was another Jewish revolt in 135 CE, after which the Romans forced the people out of Israel. The Jewish people were dispersed throughout Europe, Asia and North Africa.

A **Hanukkah** menorah candlestick, used when celebrating this festival. The story tells how when the Maccabees took back the Temple, they rededicated it to God by lighting a candle. This required oil, but they only had enough for one day, and it would take eight days for new oil to arrive. However, the oil miraculously lasted the full eight days, allowing the candle to remain lit. As a result, Hanukkah came to be known as the Festival of Lights.

6. European Jewish History

Without a temple or homeland, the Jewish people focused on the law and the teachings found in their writings. At this time, they added to their writings: the Talmud, a collection of writings on Jewish law and traditions was put together between approximately the third and sixth centuries CE.

Large Jewish communities settled in the area around the River Rhine in Western Germany and northern France; these were the Ashkenazi Jews. They later moved further east into central and eastern Europe. A large Jewish community also settled in Spain, known as the Sephardic Jewish community. They were expelled from Spain in 1492.

The Jewish communities in Europe and elsewhere were often treated very badly by the majority populations because of **anti-Semitism**. During the Middle Ages, Jewish people were often **segregated** from the rest of the population.

In Italy, Jewish people were forced to live in separate areas of towns, called ghettos. They were often forced to change religion and to deny their beliefs. If they refused, they could face torture and sometimes death.

Later in Russia during the 1800s, Jewish people were again treated very badly and forced to flee. Some came to Ireland at that time. Others went to the USA and the UK.

What Does This Mean?

Anti-Semitism: Disliking Jewish people and showing hostility towards them.

Segregated: When some people are forced to live separately from others.

The interior of the Spanish Synagogue in Venice, founded by Jews expelled from Spain in the 1490s. Like many other synagogues in the Jewish ghetto in Venice, it was only permitted if it was hidden within a building that from the outside did not look like a place of worship.

Over to You

- Research the Jewish leader Moses Mendelssohn, and find out what he did.
- Where would he go on the timeline?
- Add his name when making your timeline.

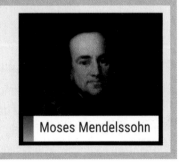

Moses Mendelssohn

The surrender of people at the end of the Warsaw Ghetto uprising.
What kinds of people are surrendering to the well-armed Nazi soldiers?

The Shoah (Holocaust)

The Nazi period in Germany, 1933–45, was when Jewish people suffered the most. Under the rule of Adolf Hitler, the Nazis were extremely anti-Semitic. The Nazis carried out one of the biggest humanitarian crimes in history.

In Germany and other countries the Nazis took over, Jewish people were singled out, labelled and denied the same rights as other people.

- They were not allowed to do certain jobs, or to go to public places like theatres and cinemas.
- They were forced to live in separate areas.
- They were sent to concentration camps and, after 1942, the Nazi leadership planned to kill all the Jews. This is known as the Holocaust or Shoah.

Children who were found at the end of the war by the Allies in the concentration camps often had no family left alive to take care of them.

The Shoah reduced the Jewish population of Europe to only one-third of what it had been before. The Nazis had murdered over 6 million Jewish people and destroyed their homes, synagogues and communities. Following this period, many Jewish people who managed to survive found it difficult to go home. Many emigrated to the USA, Israel, Canada, South Africa and Australia.

7. Modern Judaism

Today, the largest population of Jewish people is found in Israel, followed by the USA, then France, Canada, the UK and Russia. The state of Israel was founded in 1948. There is a small Jewish population in Ireland, mostly based in Dublin.

Modern Judaism has different branches, which include:

- Orthodox
- Conservative
- Reconstructionist

The difference between the groups within Judaism is how they interpret the Torah. This affects the lifestyle of followers, from food laws to what they wear and how they work and live their lives. It is about how people understand the law in terms of morality and religious ceremonies.

Jewish children celebrate the end of the Passover in a village in Israel.

Some people identify culturally and ethnically with Judaism, though they do not follow the Torah or share the same beliefs. We can refer to these people as secular or non-religious Jews.

Review and Reflect

- Looking back over the outline of Jewish history, list the good, prosperous times and list the difficult times.
- When were times of **expansion** and when were times of challenge?
- Share your ideas with the class.

What Does This Mean?

Expansion: When something develops or gets bigger.

Over to You – Reflection and Action

Constructing a Timeline of Judaism

- Working in groups, construct a timeline of Jewish history.
- Give it the heading: 'A Timeline of Judaism'.
- It should start in 1850 BCE and end today.
- Mark along the timeline the following:
    - The names and dates of key events
    - The names and dates of key people
    - The names of key places
- Use photos and illustrations where you feel they are appropriate.

Revision Questions

Enquiry

1. What is a timeline?
2. How are timelines constructed?
3. When does the Jewish history timeline begin?
4. Name **three** important people in the Jewish history timeline.
5. Where can information for constructing a Jewish history timeline be found?

Exploration

1. Have you come across a timeline before?
2. Now that you have studied a timeline from **one** major world religion, do you think it has furthered your understanding of that religion?
3. Do you know the timeline of any other major world religion? Would you like to?

Reflection and Action

Construct a timeline of your school.

- Include the year it was opened.
- Add the names of important people in the history of your school.
- Add important moments during the history of your school.
- Include times the school might have expanded.
- Finally, add when your class joined the school.

15 The Development of Sacred Texts

Learning Outcome 1.9

Explain what was involved in the development of a particular sacred text within a major world religion and consider its continued significance for the lives of believers.

Learning Intentions

By the end of this chapter I will:

- Know what the Bible contains
- Know how and when the Bible came to be written
- Reflect on how important sacred writings are for a religious community

Key Skills and Wellbeing

- Managing information and thinking
- Communicating
- Staying well

I am aware of the need to show respect for others. I feel listened to and valued.

Keywords

foundational ▪ **gospels** ▪ **Old and New Testaments** ▪ **prophets** ▪ **sacred texts** ▪ **significance**

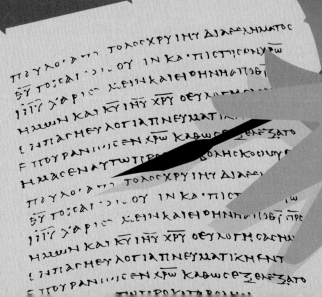

Icebreaker

1. What important writings do countries, schools and businesses have?
2. What role do these documents or writings have?
3. Discuss the importance of writings in society.

Introduction

All major world religions have their **sacred texts**. They are viewed as very important by that religion. They are important for preserving stories and traditions. They can be used as a source of guidance and as a reference when thinking about a moral issue. The writings usually contain the teachings of a founder. Writings have a function during worship or rituals, when they are taken out and read. For example, during Christmas people read the story of Jesus' birth in churches and other places. This story is found in the Bible, the sacred text for Christianity.

Why Are Sacred Writings Foundational?

- **Foundational** writings contain the story of the origins (beginnings) of the religious community.
- The writings have the story of the founder's life.
- The writings outline the relationship between the community and their God or Gods.
- The writings are considered a significant source of knowledge or wisdom for the community.
- The events, traditions and rituals of the community are built from the sacred writings.

What Does This Mean?

Foundational: Forming the base from which everything else develops.

Significance: To have importance in relation to something.

Significance of Sacred Texts for Members of Religious Communities

The **significance** of sacred texts for members include that:

1. They give guidance on morality.
2. They give a sense of belonging.
3. They are used in worship.
4. They are kept in a special place.
5. They teach the community about God(s).

In Judaism, reading from the sacred texts is important in becoming *bar/bat mitzvah*.

Action Verb Focus: Explain

Explain: To make something clear and to give the reasons for the facts or ideas.

If you explain something, you show that you understand it. Explaining goes beyond just saying what something is – it tells us how or why something is. For example, you could know that something happened, but you might not be able to explain why. By explaining something, you have a greater understanding of it. In Biology, you could learn about human digestion, so you might be asked to explain how it occurs. This would involve outlining how the food is broken down at different stages in its digestion. In History, you might be asked to explain why the Second World War broke out. This would require you to explain or give reasons for the outbreak of the war. To give an explanation requires you to have a good understanding of the topic.

Over to You – Explanation

Discuss: Do you think it is important for a religion to have sacred texts? Explain why or why not.

The Bible: A Foundational Text

The Bible is the sacred text in Christianity. The word 'Bible' is from the Greek word *biblia*, which means 'books'. The Bible is divided into two main sections: the **Old Testament** and the **New Testament**.

- In Christian understanding, the Old Testament tells about the relationship between the people and God before the life of Jesus.
- The New Testament tells the story of Jesus and the beginning of the new Christian Church.

The word 'testament' means 'covenant or agreement'. For Christians, the life, death and resurrection of Jesus mark the division between the old agreement and the new agreement.

The Bible: A User's Guide

The Bible has so many books and pages that it can be difficult to find a passage, a phrase or an event. In ancient times when the Bible was first written, people just wrote continuously, so it must have been difficult to find where a story or phrase began or ended.

Today, the Bible is divided into the name of each book and each book is divided into chapters and then verses. This makes it much easier to navigate. A Bible reference always has the name of the book first, then the number of the chapter and then the verse.

For example, Luke 15:1 takes you to the book called Luke, to chapter 15 and to verse 1. This is the beginning of a story called the 'Parable of the Lost Sheep'. To find this, check the contents page of a Bible

Page 51

to get the page number of the book you are looking for (in this case Luke), then look for the chapter number, which is usually in a bigger font at the top of the page. So in this example, 'Luke 15' will be at the top of the page. The verses are small numbers scattered throughout the text.

Old Testament	New Testament
Contains the Jewish sacred writings	Contains the stories of Jesus and the first Christians
First written in Hebrew	First written in Greek
Consists of laws, history, wise sayings, poetry and prophecy	Consists of **gospels**, letters, history and revelations
Written by many people over a period of 700 to 800 years	Written by many people over about 70 years

Over to You – Enquiry

- Look at the contents page of a Bible and find the following books: Deuteronomy, Ruth, Amos, Isaiah, Daniel, Psalms, Matthew, Romans, and Revelation.
- Notice how many have people's names and how many have place names.

Section One: The Old Testament

The Old Testament is the first part of the Christian Bible. This is the same as the Jewish sacred writings called the 'Tanakh'. In Judaism, the Tanakh is divided into three parts, the Torah, Nevi'im and Ketuvim, or the law, the prophets and the writings. They are put together with the New Testament because, for Christians, they form the beginning of the story of God's relationship with the people.

What Does This Mean?

Old Testament and New Testament: The two sections of the Christian Bible.

Gospel: Meaning 'good news'. The Gospels contain stories about the life of Jesus. The Bible contains four Gospels: these are Mark, Matthew, Luke and John.

The Old Testament contains stories, history, legends, myths, customs, laws, poetry, wise sayings and prophecy from over approximately 800 years. It was not put together in one go, and it includes the words of many writers. The Old Testament was written in Hebrew.

The Dead Sea Scrolls are the oldest manuscripts of the Old Testament ever found. They were found in caves near the Dead Sea in 1947. They had been left hidden there in clay jars for nearly 2,000 years.

The Old Testament will have a minimum of 39 books. Some versions have more, as they include a section of books called the 'Apocrypha'. The Apocrypha was found in the Greek version of the Old Testament and is accepted as part of the Bible by the Roman Catholic and Orthodox Churches. Protestant Churches do not include it because it was not in the original Hebrew version.

Stories in the Old Testament

The Old Testament tells the story of creation, the call of Abraham and the beginnings of the **covenant**. It includes the story of Moses and the Exodus, and the story of the kings, Saul, David and Solomon. It has long poems, hundreds of laws, wise sayings called proverbs; psalms, which are hymns; and many other stories. The oldest parts of the Old Testament were written down from approximately 850 BCE and the newest parts from approximately 150 BCE.

Oral Tradition

Some of the songs, laws and stories come from long before they were written down. There was a time when they were passed on by oral or spoken tradition from generation to generation. Over time, the Jewish people collected the writings and divided them into three parts:

1. The **Law** is the first five books: Genesis, Exodus, Leviticus, Numbers and Deuteronomy. This section tells the early history of Judaism and contains the instruction or law that the people were to follow. For Jewish people, this is the most important section of their writings.

2. The **Prophets** are stories about people believed to have been messengers of God. There were the earlier prophets such as Amos and Hosea and later prophets like Jeremiah. They warned people at times when they were not being true to their religion and to God.

3. The **Writings** are made up of songs and poems like the psalms or praises to God, the proverbs or wise sayings and the stories that were used to teach people, e.g. the stories of Ruth and Job.

Over to You – Reflection and Action

1. Why do you think the ancient Jewish people started to write down stories and laws?
2. Why did they divide them into different types of writing?

Section Two: The New Testament

The New Testament is the most important section of the Bible for Christians, as it tells the story of Jesus' life and death. It is made up of the following:

- The Letters, also called 'epistles', were written by the early Christian leaders to new Christian communities, giving advice and explaining teachings.

- The Gospels are stories of the life of Jesus, written by the evangelists Matthew, Mark, Luke and John.

- The Acts of the Apostles tells the story of the spread of Christianity and the new Church after Jesus had died.

- The Book of Revelation tells of a cosmic battle of good versus evil.

Many movies, such as *The 4 Horsemen of the Apocalypse*, have been based on the writings contained in the Book of Revelation.

The Letters

Christians place a lot of importance on the gospels as these tell the stories of Jesus' life and contain his teachings. However, some of the letters found in the New Testament are older than the gospels. The letters were written by leaders of the first Christians, people like Paul who wanted to give advice and leadership to the earliest Christian communities. Paul, who was Jewish, became one of the most important leaders of the early Christian community. Paul wrote 13 letters. His letters show the issues early Christians were concerned with. They are a very important source about the Roman world that this new religion started in.

The ruins of the ancient city of Corinth in Greece. Paul wrote several letters giving advice to the early Christian community that lived here.

The Gospels

In the Bible, there are four gospels: Matthew, Mark, Luke and John. However, in history, there is evidence that there were other gospels – a gospel of Thomas, a gospel of Mary and a gospel of Philip. The gospels are the basic stories about the life of Jesus.

Information about Jesus started out as oral tradition. It was passed on by word of mouth, as most people could not read or write. After a while, the witnesses to Jesus' life were growing old and people were worried that the stories would be forgotten. They wanted to preserve this information, so the gospels came to be written. They were also written to use in Christian worship and rituals, e.g. the sharing of the bread and wine in what is now called the Eucharist.

The first Christians were familiar with the Jewish sacred texts and had them to read from. The writings of the New Testament put down the main ideas and teachings of Christianity. They explained what it was all about. By the fourth century, the four gospels – Matthew, Mark, Luke and John – had become accepted, along with the Letters, Acts and Revelation, as the New Testament.

Order of the Gospels

| Mark – **64 CE** | Matthew and Luke – **80 CE** | John – **90 CE** |

The gospels were written mostly in Greek with the occasional word in Aramaic or Hebrew. This was because Greek was the official language of the region. Hebrew was the language of Judaism; Jesus was Jewish and his followers were too. Aramaic was the spoken language of many people at the time, so there are some phrases and words that occur in that language.

Throughout the gospels of Luke and Matthew are sayings of Jesus that are believed to have come from the same source. We call that source the Q document, from the German word *Quelle*, which means 'source'.

What They Wrote With

The gospel writers did not have pens and paper like we do. They had to write on either animal skins, such as vellum, or on papyrus. Papyrus was made from the papyrus plant that grows in water. The plant was cut and arranged in strips over each other and dried. Instead of a pen, the gospel writers used a 'stylus', and ink was made from minerals or plant extracts.

Making papyrus reeds into paper

What Each Gospel Contains

Name of the Gospel	Who They Wrote For	Ideas and Purpose
Mark 64 CE Also used as a source for Matthew and Luke	Persecuted Christians	■ Theme of suffering important ■ Gives hope and encouragement 'For those who want to save their life will lose it, and those who lose their life for my sake, and for the sake of the gospel, will save it.'
Matthew 80 CE	Jewish Christians	■ Explains Jesus as the fulfilment of the Jewish scriptures ■ Contains sayings of Jesus and evidence from Mark 'Love the Lord your God with all your heart and with all your soul and with all your mind.'
Luke 80 CE A doctor	Non-Jewish Christians	■ Also wrote the Acts of the Apostles ■ Tells how Christianity spread from Jerusalem to Rome ■ Contains sayings of Jesus and evidence from Mark 'Blessed are you who are poor, for yours is the kingdom of God.'
John 90 CE	The last of the gospels	■ Explains Jesus as coming from above ■ Talks of Jesus as the Son of God 'I am the good shepherd. The good shepherd lays down his life for his sheep.'

How the Gospels Came to Be Written

STAGE 1:
Jesus is alive, teaching and living in Galilee and Judea

STAGE 2:
Jesus dies and his followers tell the story by oral tradition

STAGE 3:
The gospels are written to preserve the story of Jesus

The oldest surviving New Testament manuscript in the world is a fragment of John's gospel kept in the John Rylands Library in Manchester. The biggest collection of early New Testament papyri (the plural of papyrus) is kept in the Chester Beatty Library in Dublin. The oldest complete copy of the New Testament is called the *Codex Sinaiticus*, which is kept in the British Library in London.

The Chester Beatty Library in Dublin is home to some of the oldest and most important biblical manuscripts in the world.

Review and Reflect

1. What does 'Testament' mean?
2. What are the **four** types of writing found in the New Testament?
3. What do they contain?
4. What does 'gospel' mean? Why did people call the stories of Jesus that?
5. How did information about Jesus first get told?

The Bible: Significance for Christians Today

Eventually all the books from the Old Testament, the Jewish sacred writings and the New Testament were put together into one volume: the Bible. Over hundreds of years it went from first being written in Hebrew and Greek to just Greek, then Latin and eventually into the spoken languages of people throughout the world.

The Bible has sold billions of copies and has been translated into hundreds of languages. So, why it is important to Christians today? What relevance has it for the lives of Christians in the modern world?

For many Christians, the Bible is an important source of guidance.

The Bible is important as a document of faith for Christians. It helps Christians to understand God and their relationship with God. They use it for the following:

- Worship – during acts of worship the Bible is usually read from. Sometimes, the people reading are called 'Ministers of the Word'.
- Moral guidance – when making moral decisions, Christians sometimes read the Bible for guidance.
- Community – a community is a group of people with something in common. Different religions are referred to as communities of faith. The Christian community is made up of many churches or branches. The Bible is the foundational writing for the Christian community.

Revision Questions

Enquiry

1. What is a sacred text?
2. Name the sacred text of Christianity.
3. What does it contain?
4. Outline **three** steps in how this sacred text developed.

Exploration

1. Think about the importance of a sacred text for a religious community.
2. Think about when the sacred text might be used.
3. How do people treat their sacred writings? Why do you think they do this?
4. How do you think other people should talk about another religion's sacred writings?

Reflection and Action

- In groups, research the Quran and how it came to be written.
- Find out how important the Quran is for followers of Islam.

16 Religious Teachings and an Issue of Concern

Learning Outcome 2.7

Explore how the religious teachings of a major world religion address an issue of concern for the world today.

Learning Intentions

By the end of this chapter I will:

- Know about an issue of concern in the world today
- Know one major world religion's teachings that relate to this issue
- Think about how this encourages followers to do something about this issue
- Think about and reflect on the relevance of a religious teaching

Key Skills and Wellbeing

- Working with others
- Communicating
- Being creative

I feel connected to the wider world.
I take action to protect the wellbeing of others.

Keywords

Hadith ▪ **Quran** ▪ **Ramadan** ▪ **Sunnah** ▪ **world hunger** ▪ **zakat**

A welcome meal following a day of fasting

Introduction

In this chapter, we will explore how the religious teachings of a major world religion address an issue of concern for the world today. We will look at the Sustainable Development Goals of the United Nations to identify some of the issues. We will then take an issue to see how a religion responds to it. We will refer to the teachings of the religion that relate to this issue. This will show whether this religion can address contemporary world issues.

Icebreaker

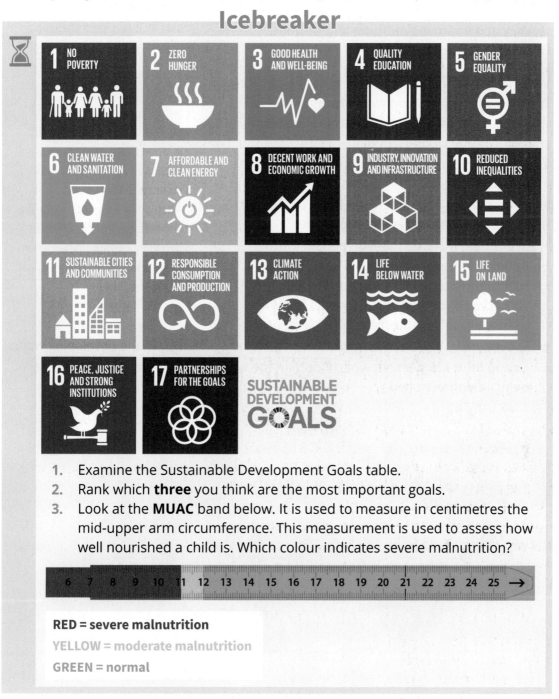

1. Examine the Sustainable Development Goals table.
2. Rank which **three** you think are the most important goals.
3. Look at the **MUAC** band below. It is used to measure in centimetres the mid-upper arm circumference. This measurement is used to assess how well nourished a child is. Which colour indicates severe malnutrition?

RED = severe malnutrition

YELLOW = moderate malnutrition

GREEN = normal

What Does This Mean?

MUAC: Mid-upper arm circumference – remember these bands measure the upper arm.

An Issue of Concern: World Hunger

In 2015, the United Nations General Assembly adopted the 2030 Agenda for Sustainable Development. It included 17 Sustainable Development Goals. Goal number two is zero hunger. This goal is to 'End hunger, achieve food security and improved nutrition and promote sustainable agriculture'.

Why Is Zero Hunger a Goal?

The following statistics on **world hunger** are shocking. According to the United Nations Food and Agricultural Organisation:

- Globally, 825 million people today are undernourished.
- In developing countries, more than one-eighth of the population are undernourished.
- In Southern Asia, 281 million people are undernourished.
- Half of the deaths of children under five are caused by poor nutrition. Some 3.1 million children each year die from poor nutrition.
- Sixty-six million primary school children go to school hungry in the developing world.
- One in four – 25 per cent – of children in the world have stunted growth due to being undernourished.

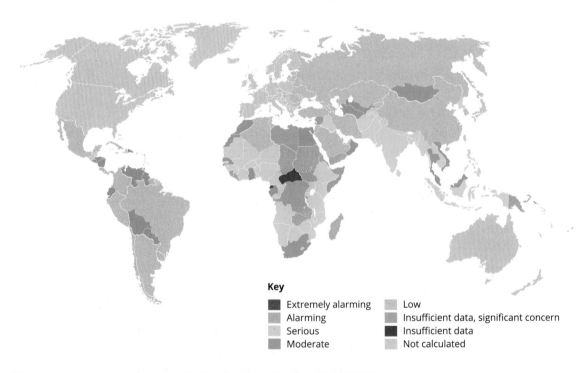

Key

- Extremely alarming
- Alarming
- Serious
- Moderate
- Low
- Insufficient data, significant concern
- Insufficient data
- Not calculated

> Name **three** countries where hunger is at an alarming level, **three** where it is a serious problem and **three** where it is moderate.
> Why do you think hunger is not calculated in some countries?

What Are the Causes of World Hunger?

According to Concern in 2018, the following are the main causes of hunger in the world today:

- **Poverty:** People have no money to buy food or to buy important equipment to help produce food.
- **Food shortages:** If a harvest is bad, people can run out of food before the next harvest. This is called a 'hungry season'.
- **War and conflict:** People are displaced, fields are abandoned, and food is out of reach.
- **Climate change:** This causes droughts and floods that destroy crops and homes.
- **Poor nutrition:** The food people have to eat lacks the nutrients necessary for good health and development.
- **Policy:** These are the ideas and plans of the government of a country.
- **Economy:** This is the state of a country in terms of how it produces goods and services and the supply of money.
- **Food waste:** According to the World Food Programme, one-third of all food produced is not consumed.
- **Gender inequality:** Women farmers, who grow the majority of food in developing countries, are not represented when important decisions are made.

Addressing World Hunger

There are many organisations, individuals and charities around the world trying to tackle the issue of world hunger.

The Food and Agriculture Organisation is a specialised agency of the United Nations that leads international efforts to defeat hunger. Charities around the world are also involved. You may have heard of some of the following that work towards helping people with hunger and other issues: Concern, Oxfam, the Red Cross, Christian Aid, Muslim Aid, MAZON, Goal, Bóthar, Save the Children and Trócaire.

Many charities are working towards reducing world hunger.

Over to You – Reflection and Action

1. Read the list of causes of world hunger. Check you understand the link between the cause and how it affects hunger in the world.
2. Find out about **two** of the charities that deal with the issue of world hunger listed above, and see how they are addressing the issue. Look up one of their recent campaigns.

Islam and World Hunger

How does the major world religion of Islam address the issue of world hunger? For Muslims, there is much guidance on any moral issue. The main sources for guidance are:

1. The **Quran**, which is the revealed word of Allah (God) given to the Prophet Muhammad. These are the sacred writings of Islam.
2. The **Hadith**, meaning 'report' or 'narrative'. This reveals the words and deeds of the Prophet Muhammad; it is an important part of Islamic tradition.
3. The **Sunnah** are the practices, customs and traditions of the Prophet Muhammad. These are seen as the perfect example for Muslims to follow.

The Quran, the Hadith and the Sunnah instruct Muslims to help with the issue of world hunger. For example in Chapter 76 of the Quran it says 'and they feed, for the love of Him, the poor and the orphan', and in Chapter 107 it says one who denies his religion 'does not encourage feeding the poor'.

Islam commands Muslims to give to the poor.

According to Islamic tradition, the Prophet was particularly concerned with how people treated the poor, widows and orphans. To give to charity is important and to show compassion to the less well-off is a way of showing love of Allah.

The Five Pillars of Islam and Charity

The Five Pillars of Islam are the foundations for being a Muslim. To follow Islam a person must:

1. Say the statement of faith, the *Shahadah*
2. Pray five times a day, *salat*
3. Give to charity, *zakat*
4. Fast during Ramadan, *sawm*
5. Try to go on the annual pilgrimage to Mecca, the *Hajj*

Zakat

In addressing world hunger, Muslims have the opportunity to give through *zakat*. *Zakat* is the Third Pillar of Islam. This is an obligation to give 2.5 per cent of your wealth to charity every year. This can be done in a number of ways. One way is to give to organisations that help fight world hunger.

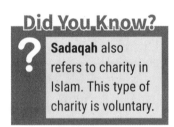

Did You Know?

? **Sadaqah** also refers to charity in Islam. This type of charity is voluntary.

Zakat is mentioned 32 times in the Quran. It means 'purification'. By giving to charity, a Muslim's own wealth is purified. In Islam, giving to charity has many benefits.

- It is a way to obey God.
- It is a way to acknowledge everything came from and belongs to God.
- It is a way of not becoming focused on material things.
- It improves relationships between people and it is good for society.

Ramadan

Fasting during Ramadan also helps Muslims to think about world hunger. Fasting during daylight hours makes Muslims identify with people who feel hungry all the time. The month of Ramadan is a month for prayer, seeking forgiveness and being patient and charitable. It is a month to consider those less fortunate.

Many Muslims use Ramadan as the month to give their charity donations for the year. Charities see a huge rise in fundraising during this month. Many Islamic charities give out free meals for the poor every evening, while many wealthy Muslims give charity bags with basic cooking items (oil, rice, tea etc.) to poorer families at the beginning of the month. The festival at the end of Ramadan – Eid al-Fitr – includes giving to charity.

Did You Know?

? During Ramadan, the meal that Muslims eat after sunset to break their fast is called *iftar*.

WILL YOU
#HONOURHER

Pledge your support to help end violence against women and girls worldwide

TAKE ACTION NOW
IRUK.CO/HONOURHER

What issue is this Islamic Relief campaign highlighting?

Islamic Relief

Islamic Relief is one of the world's largest Islamically inspired humanitarian NGOs working to provide emergency relief and sustainable solutions to global poverty.

Founded in 1984 in Birmingham, UK, the organisation works in over 40 countries, helping local communities irrespective of their race, religion and gender. Islamic Relief aims to challenge the root causes of poverty and inequality in all its forms, including challenging gender-based violence and helping communities become resilient to the effects of climate change.

Over to You – Enquiry

1. Research Islamic Relief and find out about its vision, mission and some of its current projects.
2. Discuss the influence of Islamic values on this organisation and its work.

Islamic Relief was founded in 1984 and works to empower communities, regardless of race, religion or gender.

Revision Questions

Enquiry

1. How many people are undernourished in the world today?
2. What are the main causes of world hunger?
3. List **three** organisations that address this issue.
4. What does Islam teach about this issue?
5. Explain *zakat*.

Exploration

1. Is Islam or any other major world religion able to help followers to address world hunger?
2. Do you think there are other important issues in the world today that religions can address?

Reflection and Action

- What would be the response of the other major world religions to the issue of world hunger?
- How would a humanist respond to this issue?
- In pairs, choose another religion or world view and investigate how it would respond to this issue.
- As a class, see if there is a project you can do to help highlight the issue of world hunger. If possible, fundraise for a suitable charity.

Stages of Faith

Learning Outcome 2.9

Describe how the faith of a believer can change at different stages in life.

Learning Intentions

By the end of this chapter I will:

- Know the three stages of faith
- Understand how faith develops over time
- Know and understand the differences between the stages of faith
- Realise the importance of the stages of faith in the development of a person's personal faith

Key Skills and Wellbeing

- Being creative
- Managing information and thinking

I can see how I will change over time, and that my faith can change also. I will reflect on what faith means to me, and if faith is present in my life I can be mindful of what stage of faith I am at.

Keywords

believers ■ faith ■ mature

Introduction

In many ways, the path of a river is quite similar to the path of life. Just like a river, we have a beginning, small at first but growing every day; a middle, where we are full of life and vitality; and an end, when we are winding down and eventually come to a complete stop. Rivers are full of twists and turns, sudden drops, rough patches and smooth sailing. The older the river is, the calmer it is. Often it is the same with people.

We usually divide life into three main stages: childhood, adolescence and maturity. Throughout these stages, we are changing and growing in many different ways:

- Our bodies are growing and changing. If you look at baby pictures of yourself, can you believe you were ever that small? Can you imagine what you will look like when you are older?

- Our minds grow; we see the world differently as we learn new things at school, from our parents and from the world around us. We strengthen our minds by thinking and forming new opinions.

- Our heart grows, in an emotional sense. We develop our relationships and how our feelings respond to different situations and people.

- Our spirituality grows. For some people, the **faith** that they were raised with becomes deeper. For some, faith can take them in different and new directions. And for others, belief in religion may dwindle, but faith in humanity can grow. Faith can take many different shapes and forms; there is no 'one size fits all'.

When we are young, we look to older members of our family for guidance.

Icebreaker

1. Divide into groups. Each group should draw a picture of a person in one of the three stages of life. Label the diagram with characteristics you think a person in this stage of life would typically have. Present your picture to the class.
2. What is 'faith'?
3. In pairs, discuss this word and write down what you think it means.

Childhood Faith

Early on in life, faith is quite simple, purely because young children listen to their parents. Children are always learning; they absorb new information like human sponges. This is why it is so important to be careful of what we say around them. It is for this reason, we call childhood faith an 'imitative' faith. Children follow the example set by the adults around them. If parents are practising a faith they usually want to raise their children as **believers** in that faith. By being brought to religious services and taught religious values, children will learn the key teachings of that faith.

What Does This Mean?

Faith: To have trust or confidence in someone or something. A strongly held belief that may be based on a spiritual or religious conviction.

Believers: People who have a religious faith and believe in the truth of something.

Children's minds are unable to process very complex concepts, so often adults will break down religious concepts into simple stories to make it easier for them. Bible stories with clear heroes and villains are entertaining regardless of faith, and they are easily remembered. Children's image of God is of a big, all-powerful being, one who is never wrong and can do anything. Often, this is similar to their view of their parents.

Over to You – Exploration

Children's Letters to God

Read the letters below. What do these letters suggest about what the children believe?

Dear God,

Thank you for the little brother that you gave me for Christmas, but I asked for a bike.

Joseph

Dear God,

How do you keep your beard so white?

All my love,
Caoimhe

Dear God,

Why did you put all the clouds so far up in the sky?

From
Oísin

Adolescent Faith

Adolescence can be an exciting but also difficult time. Young people, like you, begin to step out from under the watch of their parents and are given more responsibility and freedom. They become aware of some of the values that they personally hold dear. They have the confidence to make decisions that do not necessarily reflect those of their parents. The opinions and actions of friends become important as they strive to fit in with their peers. During adolescence, people begin to think beyond their own selfish needs and start to look at how they can help others. This is a real sign of maturity.

Fitting in with your peers is a very important part of adolescence. Sometimes, it can be hard to break away from what your friends do, think and say.

Due to their inquiring nature, adolescents question the simple beliefs of childhood. They need more evidence and a better explanation of these beliefs. They test their faith and begin to wonder about religion's role in some of the big questions in life, such as why is there suffering? Why are there evil people in the world?

Their image of God may change also. They might change from viewing deities as all-powerful parental figures to one they can have a more personable, friendly relationship with. God is a friend to talk to, one who will never share secrets and can give guidance.

Over to You – Exploration

1. Using your knowledge of childhood and adolescent faith, create an image or a list of characteristics that a person in the childhood and adolescent stages of faith may have of a God, Gods or a deity.

2. In pairs, discuss what you think it means to be an adult. How is being an adult different from being a child or an adolescent? What things does an adult do or say that is different to what a child or adolescent might do or say? Share your thoughts with the class.

Mature Faith

What Does This Mean?

Mature: When someone or something is fully developed or fully grown.

Read the following account of a **mature** person's faith.

> After years of learning about God, different religious teachings and understandings, I am now very confident in my faith. I have a close relationship with God and I feel the presence of God all around. My faith is a personal one; I do not require others to believe the same as me, and I don't need to believe the same as everyone else; but I am very happy to discuss my faith with others if they would like to. I often discuss faith with my grandchildren; they are so full of questions and curiosity. I truly appreciate the wonderful life I have been given, and am grateful for the beautiful world we live in. I try to be a good person; I give to charity and volunteer my time when I can. If I can help at all, I will. I've been very lucky in life and I think some of that good fortune should be spread around to other people.

Over to You – Enquiry

1. Read the above extract carefully. Copy the table below into your copy book and fill it in, using the information from the account.

Relationship with God	
Image of God	
Living her faith	
Attitude to religion	

2. Add two more columns to your table and fill in similar details for a person with childhood faith and a person with adolescent faith.

Revision Questions

Enquiry

1. How do we change as we get older?
2. What does 'faith' mean?
3. Who are believers?
4. At what age is someone an adolescent?
5. At what age does someone become mature?

Exploration

1. Do you think children should believe what their parents believe in? Explain why or why not.
2. Is growing up easy? Explain why or why not.
3. Are all adults mature?
4. Are all adolescents immature?

Reflection and Action

Using your knowledge and understanding of the stages of faith, find one person in each of the three stages outlined in this chapter. Ask him or her to draw an image of the God, Gods or deity present in his or her life. Compare the three images.

Moral Codes and Their Influence

18

Learning Outcome 3.3

Examine a moral code in two of the five major world religions and discuss how each code could influence moral decision-making for believers.

Learning Intentions

By the end of this chapter I will:

- Know what a moral code is
- Know the moral code for each of the five major world religions
- Know a non-religious moral code
- Reflect on the connection between a moral code and making moral decisions

Key Skills and Wellbeing

- Managing information and thinking
- Being creative
- Working with others
- Communicating
- Managing myself

I am aware of the things that influence my decisions. I think through my decisions and I am aware of my values.

Keywords

dharma ▪ Five Pillars of Islam ▪ the Golden Rule ▪ Noble Eightfold Path ▪ Torah

Moral Codes to live by

Introduction

Icebreaker

1. What is a code?
2. Have you heard of the Safe Cross Code?
3. Have you heard of the Outdoor Code?
4. Can you think of any other examples of codes?

Humans make moral decisions every day. They make choices and decide what is right and wrong in a variety of situations. Codes or guidelines on doing the right thing come from many places. Religion is one. State law is another. In school, you probably have a code of conduct. These can all be seen as **sources of morality**.

Moral decisions are influenced by many things: other people, ideas, outlooks and points of view. Individuals have to consider the consequences of their decisions, the outcomes and the effects they may have for themselves and for other people. Managing our choices and owning our decisions are very important skills. Judging whether an influence is good or bad is an important part of moral decision-making.

THE GOLDEN RULE

The Golden Rule can be a measure for deciding how to behave.

In Chapter 1, we looked at the main beliefs of each of the five major world religions. Each religion has a foundation story, a sacred text and important ideas about the world. All of the major world religions offer guidance to their followers about doing the right thing – on how to make moral decisions.

In Chapter 7, we looked at the **Golden Rule**, which is the moral code found across all major world religions. The Ten Commandments are a moral code for Judaism and Christianity. There are moral codes found in every major religion and in non-religious belief systems. There are a set of guidelines to try to live by and to use when faced with a moral choice.

Chapters 1 and 7

For the Junior Cycle course, you must study the moral code of just two major world religions. In this chapter, we will look at the moral code in all five major world religions and in humanism and explore how such codes might influence the moral decision-making of followers. This gives you some choice and an opportunity to compare the moral codes of the different major world religions and humanism. This information is useful for having a full understanding of the different world views.

Hinduism

Hinduism is based on the belief in a universal God called Brahman, and the worship of many Gods, who are the different forms Brahman takes. For Hindus, the ultimate goal in life is to end reincarnation (the cycle of birth, life, death and rebirth) and to reach union with Brahman. This is called *moksha*. This goal is achieved by living a perfect life and may take many lifetimes.

The Vedas

The Hindu writings, the Vedas, feature epic adventures of the Gods and people that teach important moral lessons on things like love, loyalty, friendship, jealousy and truth.

Through the main writings and traditions in Hinduism, followers have an important moral code to live by. This code is twofold: *dharma* and *karma*.

The sacred writings of Hinduism are the Vedas. These teach important moral lessons for Hindus.

Dharma

The first part of the Hindu moral code of Hinduism is *dharma*, which refers to sacred duty. It can be understood as morality. It refers to the power that maintains society. It gives people the opportunity to be good and it is believed to have been revealed in the Vedas. Being good or acting morally is not the same for everyone in Hinduism and a person's obligation or duty differs depending on age, gender and position in society. In Hinduism, people have their own *dharma*.

Karma

The second part of the Hindu moral code is the idea of *karma*, which simply means 'action' in Sanskrit. The law of *karma* teaches that from every action comes a corresponding consequence, so from good comes good, and from bad comes bad. The more bad things individuals do in this life, the further away from Brahman they become, and so they are further away from achieving *moksha*. The more good things they do, the closer they get to achieving *moksha*. To act correctly in Hinduism is to serve God and humankind.

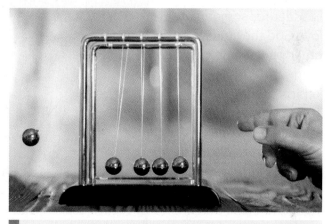

For every action there is an equal and opposite reaction.

Chapters 1 and 7

Hindus also have their own version of the Golden Rule, which we looked at in Chapter 7. It is as follows:

 This is the sum of duty: do not do to others what would cause pain if done to you.

Through the writings, the laws of *dharma* and *karma* and the Golden Rule, Hindus have reference points for making moral decisions.

Review and Reflect

1. What are the considerations a Hindu has to think about when faced with a moral decision?
2. If a Hindu were faced with the following moral decision, what would the response be? 'Should I lie to my parents?'
3. Why would a Hindu come to this conclusion?

Judaism

Judaism is based on the idea of a covenant (agreement) between the people and God. The **Torah** ('law' or 'instruction') provides a detailed moral code for people to live by. In the Torah, there are 613 *mitzvot* or good deeds to follow. For thousands of years, this moral code has given Jewish people an important guideline to follow when making moral decisions.

From very early on, Judaism emphasised that in order for someone to love God they must love other people and treat them well. This is called 'ethical monotheism'. The Ten Commandments are central to the Jewish law. They may be divided into those that refer to a person's relationship with God, and those that are concerned with how people relate to each other.

The Ten Commandments are a central part of the Jewish law or Torah. They are shown here on the silver shield of a Torah book.

Jews also have their own version of the Golden Rule that we looked at in Chapter 7. It is as follows:

Chapters 1 and 7

> ★ What is hateful to you, do not do to your neighbour. This is the whole Torah; all the rest is commentary.

What Does This Mean?

Torah: The Jewish law or instruction.

Through the covenant, the Torah and the Golden Rule, Jewish people have reference points for making moral decisions.

Review and Reflect

1. What are the considerations a Jewish person has to think about when faced with a moral decision?
2. If a Jewish person is faced with the following moral decision, what would the response be? 'Should I lie to my parents?'
3. Why would a Jewish person come to this conclusion?

Buddhism

Based on the teachings of the Buddha, Buddhism emphasises a person's need to reach their own enlightenment. The Buddha taught his followers the **Noble Eightfold Path**. This outlines eight steps a person should follow in order to gain enlightenment:

1. Right vision
2. Right emotion
3. Right speech
4. Right action
5. Right livelihood
6. Right effort
7. Right mindfulness
8. Right meditation

This path involves understanding that life is always changing, but that suffering can be overcome if people let go of the desire to cling to things that are impermanent. Following the path requires commitment and involves thinking about how one

The *dharmachakra* or *dharma* wheel is one of the most important symbols in Buddhism. It represents the teachings of the Buddha.

acts and speaks. The steps of right speech, action and livelihood mean speaking only what is true and helpful, living in a good way and doing work that will not harm others. Considering the world around you and being mindful of others are central to the path.

The Five Precepts

Buddhism has five precepts that all Buddhists undertake to put into practice.

1. Not killing or causing harm to other living beings.
2. Not taking what is not given – avoid taking anything not intended for you.
3. Avoiding sexual misconduct.
4. Avoiding false speech – as well as not lying this covers gossiping or any speech unhelpful to others.
5. Abstaining from drink and drugs that cloud the mind.

Underlying Buddhist moral guidance is that individuals' actions can either harm or help themselves or other people. Buddhism teaches the precepts and the Noble Eightfold Path to help followers act in a way that helps rather than harms. Buddhists also have the three jewels of Buddhism, which help them to try to live as well as possible:

- The Buddha
- The *dharma* (the teachings)
- The *sangha* (community)

Chapters 1 and 7

Buddhists also have their own version of the Golden Rule, which we looked at in Chapter 7. It is as follows:

 Treat not others in ways that you yourself would find hurtful.

Through the Noble Eightfold Path, the Five Precepts and the Golden Rule, Buddhists have reference points for making moral decisions.

Review and Reflect

1. What are the considerations a Buddhist has to think about when faced with a moral decision?
2. If a Buddhist were faced with the following moral decision, what would the response be? 'Should I lie to my parents?'
3. Why would a Buddhist come to this conclusion?

Christianity

Christianity is based on the teachings of Jesus, whom Christians believe is the Messiah or chosen one. Christianity places great importance on each person's own relationship with God. Jesus taught his followers to love God and to love one another. He showed through his words and actions how people needed to live in God's kingdom.

Jesus emphasised treating other people with loving kindness. He always showed this in the way he treated people, especially those whom society treated as outsiders.

Jesus taught about the need to forgive people and to seek forgiveness from God.

The example of Jesus is an important source of morality for Christians. Christians, like Jews, also view the **Ten Commandments** as an important moral code. They also have the Bible, its teachings and stories to guide them when making moral decisions.

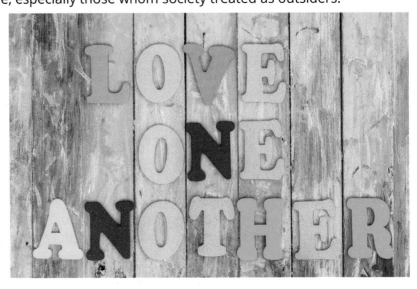

Christian Denominations

The branch (denomination) of Christianity that individuals belong to affects the importance they put on Church teaching and tradition when looking for moral guidance.

The Roman Catholic Church emphasises Church teaching and tradition when thinking about matters of faith or morality. The Church, its leaders and especially

What Does This Mean?

Magisterium: The Teaching Authority of the Roman Catholic Church. It is made up of the Pope and the bishops in union with him.

the Pope are significant sources of authority for Catholics to consider when making moral decisions. This authority is known as the **magisterium** of the Church. For most Protestants, the Bible is the most important source of authority for guidance when making a moral decision.

Christians also have their own version of the Golden Rule that we looked at in Chapter 7. It is as follows:

Chapters 1 and 7

> In everything, do to others as you would have them do to you; for this is the law and the prophets.

Through the example of Jesus, the Ten Commandments, the Bible, Church teaching and the Golden Rule, Christians have reference points for making moral decisions.

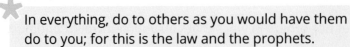

Review and Reflect

1. What are the considerations a Christian has to think about when faced with a moral decision?
2. If a Christian were faced with the following moral decision, what would the response be? 'Should I lie to my parents?'
3. Why would a Christian come to this conclusion?

Islam

Islam is based on the teachings of the Prophet Muhammad, who lived in Mecca in Saudi Arabia during the sixth and seventh centuries. The word 'Islam' means 'peace through submission to the will of Allah'. A follower of Islam is called a Muslim, meaning 'one who submits'.

For Muslims, the main source of guidance is the revealed word of Allah, which is found in the sacred text called the Quran. This writing is believed to have been given to Muhammad over the course of his life when he received many revelations from Allah. In order to submit to the will of Allah, or to do one's duty as a Muslim, a person must follow the **Five Pillars of Islam**.

The Five Pillars of Islam

The Five Pillars are seen as a moral code for Muslims to live by. They are:

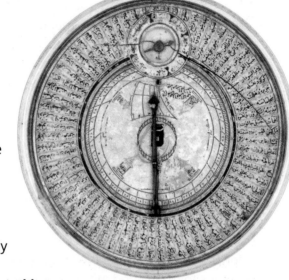

1. *Shahadah:* This involves reciting the statement of faith, 'There is no God but Allah, Muhammad is the messenger of Allah'.

2. *Salat*: Muslims pray five times a day in the direction of the Kaaba in Mecca.

3. *Zakat:* This relates to charity. Each person must typically give 2.5 per cent of his or her wealth to charity each year.

4. *Sawm:* Muslims should fast during the holy month of Ramadan.

5. *Hajj:* This involves going on the pilgrimage to Mecca, which happens every year. A Muslim must make every effort to go at least once in his or her lifetime.

The *qibla* compass shows the direction of the Kaaba in Mecca for prayer five times a day.

 Chapters 1 and 7

As well as the Five Pillars and the Quran, Muslims have traditions about Muhammad known as the **Sunnah**, meaning 'the example of the Prophet', and the **Hadith**, which are traditions about things Muhammad said and did. These act as a moral guide to follow. Muslims follow a version of the Ten Commandments.

Muslims also have their own version of the Golden Rule that we looked at in Chapter 7. It is as follows:

Not one of you truly believes until you wish for others what you wish for yourself.

Through the example of Muhammad, the Quran, the Five Pillars, the Ten Commandments and the Golden Rule, Muslims have reference points for making moral decisions.

Review and Reflect

1. What are the considerations a Muslim has to think about when faced with a moral decision?
2. If a Muslim were faced with the following moral decision, what would the response be? 'Should I lie to my parents?'
3. Why would a Muslim come to this conclusion?

Living Our Values

Humanism

Humanism is a non-religious ethical approach to life. According to the International Humanist and Ethical Union:

> Humanism is a democratic and ethical life stance that affirms that human beings have the right and responsibility to give meaning and shape to their own lives. Humanism stands for the building of a more humane society through an ethics based on human and other natural values in a spirit of reason and free inquiry through human capabilities. Humanism is not theistic, and it does not accept supernatural views of reality.

Some people are atheists, which means they do not believe in a God or Gods. Some people are agnostics, which means they are unsure whether or not a God or Gods exist. Modern humanists tend to be atheists or agnostics, and they reject the idea of knowledge being revealed to humans by Gods or in special writings.

Humanism is a belief in the ability of humans to fulfil their own potential and to find meaning in life. Humanists believe that human experience and rational thinking can provide a source of knowledge and a moral code to live by.

> This emblem used by the International Humanist and Ethical Union shows a human figure happy and reaching out to achieve its full potential. It is known as the 'Happy Human' and it looks like an 'H' for humanism.

Humanism and Morality

Morality is very important in humanism. Humanists believe strongly in the ability of humans to make good moral choices and to act in a way that enhances the human experience. They base morality on reason, knowledge and individual responsibility. Humanists do not depend on divine revelation for knowledge about what to do, and they reject the idea of finding value in being part of a divine plan. They believe humans should take responsibility for themselves and others, value themselves and others, respect the dignity of each person and live life the best way they can, finding their own meaning.

Humanists rely on science for understanding the world and base their actions on that. For humanists, doing what is good is important, not just for this generation, but for future generations. In the UK, there is a group within the Humanist Society called Humanists for a Better World.

 Chapters 1 and 7

Humanists also have their own version of the Golden Rule that we looked at in Chapter 7. It is as follows:

> Treat other people as you would want to be treated in their situation; don't do things you wouldn't want to have done to you.

Through scientific understanding, reason and the Golden Rule, humanists have reference points for making moral decisions.

Review and Reflect

1. What are the considerations a humanist has to think about when faced with a moral decision?
2. If a humanist were faced with the following moral decision, what would the response be? 'Should I lie to my parents?'
3. Why would a humanist come to this conclusion?

The Amsterdam Declaration

At an international humanist congress in Amsterdam in 1952, the basic principles of modern humanism were agreed. This is known as the Amsterdam Declaration. It was updated in 2002 and outlines the main ideas of humanism.

Over to You – Reflection and Action

Hinduism

1. Consider in more detail the idea of *dharma* as found in Hinduism.
   Do you think there are things that people should have a duty to do or that help to maintain society? What duties do parents have? What duties do adolescents have?

2. Discuss the Hindu law of *karma*.
   What actions do you consider to be good that bring good rewards? What actions do you consider to be bad that have bad consequences?

The Ten Commandments (Judaism)

Discuss the Ten Commandments. Explore what each one means, its relevance today and how it translates in the modern world. For example:

1. What are the false idols of today?
2. How do people honour their parents?
3. What types of lies are people telling in the modern world?
4. What types of stealing are there today?
5. Jews, Christians and Muslims all follow versions of the Ten Commandments. Do you think they are an important moral code for the world?

The Noble Eightfold Path (Buddhism)

1. Consider the steps of the Noble Eightfold Path. How would following these steps help a person in their own life and how would it help other people?
2. Do you think living by the Five Precepts would be difficult? Why?
3. To become a Buddhist monk, there are further precepts. Find out what these are.

Christianity

1. Read the parable of the Good Samaritan (Luke 10: 25–37). In response to which question did Jesus tell this story?
2. What was the message of the story?
3. How does this story relate to Jesus' command to love one another and to the Golden Rule in Christianity?

The Five Pillars of Islam

1. Explore in more detail what is involved in committing to Islam and following the Five Pillars.
2. Which of the Five Pillars do you think would be hardest to carry out? Explain why.

Amsterdam Declaration (Humanism)

1. Find out what the points of the Amsterdam Declaration are.
2. Discuss how they may be a moral code for humanists.
3. Which points do you think are most important?
4. Create a poster for the point you find most interesting or important.

The Universal Declaration of Human Rights

If a moral code is a set of guidelines for people to live by, then we could describe the Universal Declaration of Human Rights (UDHR) as a non-religious moral code for the countries of the world. It sets a standard of what is right and wrong. The UDHR was the work of the United Nations Commission on Human Rights. The declaration was adopted at a meeting in Paris on 10 December 1948. Just after the Second World War, the United Nations realised the world needed a universal standard, a code to live by. The UDHR has 30 articles that are for all people and all nations to achieve.

The symbol of the United Nations

Examples of the rights in the UDHR:

🔗 Chapter 27

- All human beings are born free and equal in dignity and rights.
- No one will be held in slavery or servitude.
- Everyone has the right to seek and to enjoy in other countries asylum from persecution.
- Everyone has the right to freedom of thought, conscience and religion.
- Everyone has the right to education.
- Everyone has the right to an adequate standard of living.

Unfortunately, the UDHR is not always followed.

Thinking about Rights

Think about some of the 30 rights, the right to an adequate standard of living, for example. Is this right always fulfilled in Ireland today? Everyone has the right to seek asylum, yet consider what is happening across the world to refugees and asylum seekers.

The UN building in New York

Over to You – Exploration

1. When was the United Nations Declaration of Human Rights agreed upon? Why do you think it comes from that time? Find out more about the origins of this declaration.
2. Find out the 30 rights in the code.
3. Design a poster for the **three** rights you think are most important.
4. Write an essay on the UDHR arguing that it is the most important guideline for what is moral or right in relation to how people are treated.
5. Human Rights Day is on 10 December every year. Do something in school to mark the day.

Revision Questions

Enquiry

1. What is a moral code?
2. In your own words, explain the moral code for the five major world religions.
3. What do humanists believe?
4. What is the UDHR?

Exploration

1. Consider the similarities and differences between the moral codes from the five major world religions and a non-religious code.
2. Do you think people find having moral codes important? Explain why.
3. Discuss why moral codes are good for society.

Reflection and Action

- Create a Venn diagram for moral codes from the different religions and world views.
- Write your own moral code to live by.
- Start by listing your personal values (these are the things you think are important).
- What rules would you include in your moral code?

19 Living a Good Life

Learning Outcome 3.4

Investigate what living a morally good life means with reference to two major world religions and compare with a non-religious world view.

Learning Intentions

By the end of this chapter I will:

- Know what two major world religions see as a good life
- Think about what living a good life means
- Explore a non-religious view on living a good life
- Have an opportunity to compare different ways of living a good life

Key Skills and Wellbeing

- Communicating
- Staying well
- Managing information and thinking
- Being creative
- Working with others

I am aware of the ways in which people live good lives. I am aware of what influences a person choosing to live a good life. I am aware that my actions impact on the wellbeing of myself and others. I show care and respect for others.

Keywords

concern ■ dignity ■ justice ■ respect ■ values

There are many ways of understanding how to live a good life. For some people, finding guidance in sacred writings helps them to understand what that means.

Icebreaker

Brainstorm

1. How does a person live a good life?
2. What is a good life?
3. What **three** things indicate a good life to you?

Introduction

This chapter asks you to investigate what living a morally good life means, and to do so with reference to two major world religions and one other world view. The philosophers of ancient Greece posed this question, and it has been considered by people of different world religions. There are many different opinions on how to live a good life.

We will investigate the teachings and ideas found in the religions of Judaism and Christianity and also the view of humanism. We will explore the values encouraged in these world views. We will also look at how the ideas of living a morally good life find expression in the lifestyle and actions of people who follow these ideas.

Living a Good Life in Judaism

Basic Beliefs

Jewish people believe in one God. They believe in the covenant between the people and God. They believe that God, through Moses, gave the people the Torah, which is referred to as the law, instruction or teaching. It is the first five books of the Hebrew sacred writings.

How to Live a Good Life in Judaism

To live life in accordance with the Torah is to live a good life in Judaism. Acknowledging that people are in a covenant with God and must keep their side of the agreement is key. First and foremost, living a good life in Judaism involves keeping God at the centre of life. Below are some examples of how this is expressed. God is central, so:

1. Jewish people are expected to have a close relationship with God. To develop that relationship involves praying and reading the sacred books.
2. A Jewish home has a *mezuzah*, a small box on the doorpost which contains the words of the *Shema*.
3. People meet in a synagogue to worship God together, setting aside a special day, the **Shabbat** (Sabbath), to focus on their religion and on honouring God.

A *mezuzah* can be found on the doorpost of Jewish homes. It contains the words of the *Shema*, 'Hear, O Israel, the Lord is one'.

A place of worship is important for members of Judaism. Here they can worship God together.

Symbols of Prayer

Symbols of prayer used in Judaism are:

- The skullcap or *yarmulke*
- The *tallit* – a prayer shawl
- The *tefillin* – two small boxes, one for the head and one for the arm, that are attached by leather straps

The *tefillin* are worn to observe the command in Deuteronomy, 'and you shall bind them for a sign upon your hand, and they shall be for ornaments between your eyes'. How these are worn draws attention to the head, the heart and the mind. It reminds people of the covenant and it teaches them to think, feel and act in ways that show their dedication to God.

The *tefillin* are worn to show obedience to the command found in Deuteronomy.

Jewish Food Laws

Jewish food laws are called **kashrut**. How they are interpreted and followed varies within Judaism. **Kosher** refers to food that is fit or clean for consumption. *Kosher* affects how food is selected, prepared and served. Living a good life in Judaism involves keeping a *kosher* home.

This symbol indicates that food is *kosher*. Look out for it on the labels of food you see in the supermarket.

- *Kosher* meat has to be from animals that have cloven hooves and chew the cud. This means that pork is not allowed. Beef and lamb are fine.
- *Kosher* birds include chicken, turkey and domestic fowl but not birds of prey.
- Fish has to have scales and fins to be *kosher*. Shellfish is not kosher.

To prepare *kosher* meat, the animal must have been slaughtered by a ritual slaughterer called a *schochet*. The blood must run out when the animal is slaughtered. Jewish law forbids causing unnecessary pain to the animal. The animal should be made unconscious instantly and death should occur very quickly.

According to *kosher* rules, meat and dairy must not be eaten together, not be stored together and not be prepared with the same utensils. In some Jewish homes, this requires having two sinks, one for dishes used for dairy products and one for dishes used for meat products. Food that is neither meat nor dairy – such as fish, eggs, fruit and vegetables – can be eaten with either dairy or meat.

Traditional Jewish foods include bagels and *challah* bread.

Over to You – Reflection and Action

 Look up some Jewish recipes. Find out how to make them. If possible bring some in to the class to try.

The Sabbath

The Sabbath day is part of the Torah. The Sabbath is a time to honour God and to spend time with family. The Sabbath meal on Friday evening is when families get together to welcome this special day.

Sabbath (or *Shabbat*) is mentioned in the Ten Commandments, where it says clearly that this day is to be kept holy. It is a reminder to keep the covenant with God. As the Sabbath is a day off work and study, Jews see it as a gift from God. People look forward to the Sabbath and try to dress well for it. Everything is prepared in advance, as no work, including housework, should be carried out on the Sabbath. The Sabbath starts at sunset on Friday evening and ends at sunset on Saturday evening. People greet each other with '*Gus Shabbos*' or '*Shabbat Shalom*'.

When Jewish families gather on Friday evening, the mother has the important role of lighting two candles: one to remember *Shabbat* (*sachor*) and the other to observe *Shabbat* (*shamor*). After the candles have been lit, a sweet wine is drunk from a *kiddush* cup. This represents joy and celebration. Another part of the meal is eating *challah*, a type of bread made in the shape of a braid.

The Sabbath in Judaism starts on Friday evening with a family meal. Wine, candles and *challah* bread are an important part of the meal.

Sabbath Prayers

At the beginning of the meal, the following prayer is said: 'Blessed are you, Lord our God, King of the universe, who brings forth bread from the earth'. Another prayer is a blessing for daughters to be like the four matriarchs in the Bible – Sarah, Rebecca, Rachel and Leah – and for sons to be like Ephraim and Manasseh, Joseph's sons, who lived in harmony.

During Sabbath either on Friday evening or Saturday morning, Jewish people visit the synagogue. They sing hymns, say prayers and read from the Torah. The copy of the Torah in a synagogue is very special in Judaism and is treated with great respect. It is kept in a special box or cupboard, known as an ark or *Aron Hakodesh*.

The first three stars in the night sky on Saturday signal the end of the Sabbath and a return to the normal working week.

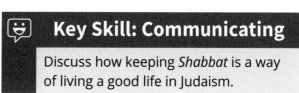

Key Skill: Communicating

Discuss how keeping *Shabbat* is a way of living a good life in Judaism.

Values in Judaism

If something has value it means it is important, useful or worth something. **Values** help us to decide what is important in life and are the basis for standards of behaviour. Our values help us to decide what is good or bad, important or not important. Judaism teaches followers to value some things more than others. For example, Judaism places great importance on family, the community, **justice** and charity, honouring God and caring for the world.

Important Jewish Values

- **Tikkun olam:** This is a Jewish concept that refers to acts of kindness performed to repair the world. It is open to interpretation, but in modern Judaism it has come to refer to social action and improving society. This value implies that living a good life involves **concern** for social justice.

- **Tzedakah:** This refers to justice, fairness, righteousness and charity. In Judaism, charity and justice come together in this idea. Since everything people own really comes from God, we only have it on loan. What God gives to people is given with the condition that they will share with people who have less. Charity is therefore a form of justice in Judaism. Giving to people who are in need is not being generous, it is justice. It is the right thing to do.

- **Teshuva:** This refers to repentance and forgiveness. *Teshuva* translates as 'return', meaning a return to the original situation or state. This idea is most associated with the Jewish festival of Yom Kippur or the Day of Atonement, but can be used any time a person needs forgiveness. Forgiveness can be sought from God or from another person. In relation to God, confessing, expressing regret

In some Jewish homes, people have a *tzedakah* box. They put money into it every Friday just before *Shabbat* or during special Jewish festivals. This money is donated to charity. *Tzedakah* shows that to live a good life in Judaism involves giving to charity.

and promising not to sin again brings atonement. If you have wronged another person, you must right the wrong and complete the three stages of confession, regret and a promise not to repeat the wrong. In Judaism, to live a good life involves seeking forgiveness for wrongdoing and also allowing others to seek forgiveness from you.

What Does This Mean?

Values: Attitudes or ideas that a person or society consider to be important.

Concern: To be worried about or have an interest in someone or something.

Justice: Treating people fairly or equally.

- **Shalom** is Hebrew for 'peace' and is used by Jewish people to say hello or goodbye. *Shalom* means more than peace, as it refers to an absence of war or conflict. It comes from a verb meaning 'to be complete or whole'. As a greeting, it wishes the person true peace, contentment, health, harmony, wellbeing and wholeness. To live a good life in Judaism, a person wishes health, harmony and wellbeing for others.

Learning Religious Values

At home, families teach values. From a young age, Jewish children learn prayers, take part in the Sabbath and enjoy the festivals. They learn about the Torah and the Ten Commandments. From their parents, they understand the value that is placed on these. As they grow and develop, Jewish children learn to understand their religion more and why they do certain things.

Values are passed on in the home in a variety of ways. When children are old enough to understand their faith, they go through a special rite in Judaism, known as *bar* or *bat mitzvah*. This marks children becoming adults in their faith.

The Ten Commandments

Following the Ten Commandments is part of living a good life in Judaism. The commandments are:

A young girl celebrates her *bat mitzvah* with her brother.

1. I am the Lord your God.
2. Have no other Gods and do not worship graven images.
3. Do not take God's name in vain.
4. Keep the Sabbath holy.
5. Honour your father and mother.
6. Do not kill.
7. Do not commit adultery.
8. Do not steal.
9. Do not lie.
10. Do not covet.

Over to You – Exploration

1. Make a list of your own values.
2. With another person, compare your lists. Underline the ones you agree on.
3. Draw a picture to represent the **three** values you think are most important.
4. How do you think a person can help to repair the world?
5. Do you think it is hard to forgive someone? Is it difficult to ask for forgiveness?

Living a Good Life in Christianity

Basic Beliefs

Christians believe in one God. They believe that God became human in the figure of Jesus. They believe that while he was on earth Jesus taught people and healed them, that he was crucified by the Romans and resurrected three days later. Christians believe that Jesus' death on the cross was a sacrifice made by God to save the whole world from sin and death.

How to Live a Good Life in Christianity

The most important part of living a good life in Christianity is having a relationship with Jesus and following his teaching and example. The most important teachings of Jesus are outlined below.

The Kingdom of God

The main theme of Jesus' teaching was the 'Kingdom of God'. It is a way of seeing all the world and every living thing as belonging to God. Jesus spoke about it when he taught people the 'Lord's Prayer' or 'Our Father'. He included the line 'thy kingdom come, thy will be done, on earth as it is in heaven'. This means that earth should be the kingdom of God. It is a very important Christian teaching and affects how Christians should live. In Christianity, to live a good life is to treat people as part of God's kingdom, with loving kindness and **compassion**, with fairness and justice and with **dignity** and **respect**.

What Does This Mean?

Compassion: A strong feeling of sympathy and concern for the suffering of other people. A person with compassion will show care, kindness and a willingness to help other people.

Dignity: The sense of self-worth and respect each person should have.

Respect: To have proper regard for the feelings and rights of other people. When we respect a thing or idea, we consider it important and take care of it.

Illegal dumping is a big problem. Do people take care of the planet?
How are Christians supposed to view the world and live in it?

Parables

To teach about the Kingdom of God, Jesus used parables. A parable is a story with a hidden meaning or message. The parables were a good way of teaching for Jesus, as he could relate them to ordinary life that people could understand. They also required people to think and work out their meaning. This made more of an impact. Some of the parables taught people about God and some about how they needed to live in God's kingdom. Examples include: The Lost Sheep, The Good Samaritan, The Prodigal Son, The Mustard Seed, The Sower, The Talents, and The Wise and Foolish Builders.

How did Jesus use the parable of The Good Samaritan to teach people?

Over to You – Enquiry

1. Choose **one** of the parables mentioned above.
2. Read the parable and think about what it means.
3. Draw a picture to illustrate the parable.
4. Explain how this parable teaches Christians how to live a good life.

The Love Command

Christians, like Jews, have the Ten Commandments to follow. Jesus, who was Jewish, knew and followed the Ten Commandments. When he was asked which was the most important command, he responded with:

> You shall love the Lord your God with all your heart, with all your soul, and with all your mind. This is the first and great commandment. And the second is like it: You shall love your neighbour as yourself. On these two commandments hang all the law and the prophets.
>
> **(Matthew 22: 36)**

Over to You – Enquiry

Living a good life in Christianity means loving God and loving other people. Discuss ways that Christians can show that love in their lives.

What does the **Love Command** teach about how to treat people? Are some people 'outsiders' in the world today?

To live a good life in Christianity, a person must respect and love God and other people. When Jesus talked about your neighbour, he meant anyone – there are no insiders or outsiders in God's kingdom. In the famous parable of The Good Samaritan, Jesus showed how to treat people with loving kindness. He also taught about not judging other people, as there is no room for discrimination in God's kingdom.

The Sacraments and Prayer

Living a good Christian life is to have a close relationship with Jesus. There are many different types of Christian in the world today. They do not all do the same things or carry out the same rituals. There are different ways to be Christian.

In the Roman Catholic Church, people develop a close relationship with Jesus through the sacraments and through prayer. Some Protestant Churches also carry out sacraments, but others do not.

What sacraments are these items associated with?

There are seven sacraments in the Roman Catholic Church. These are:

1. Baptism
2. Reconciliation
3. Eucharist
4. Confirmation
5. Marriage
6. Holy Orders
7. Anointing the sick or dying

In most Protestant denominations, baptism and the Eucharist are the two sacraments that are seen as fundamental to practising Christianity. For Christians, sacraments are a way of experiencing the loving presence of God. Some are carried out regularly; others at important times in individuals' lives, for example, after birth, at marriage and at death. In this way, the sacraments put God at the centre of these important times.

Prayer

Praying is another way of being close to God in Christianity. Prayer is really important to Christians; it is a way of communicating with God. In prayer, people worship God, ask for help for themselves and others, seek forgiveness and look for protection. There are many types of prayer and many ways of praying. Prayer is another aspect of living a good life in Christianity.

Values in Christianity

The Golden Rule in Christianity is to: 'Treat others the way you would like to be treated'. There are many values underlying this rule. Some of the values that shape how Christians live in the world and with other people are justice or fairness, charity, concern, courage, compassion and forgiveness. Examples of this can be seen in the lives of some Christians in history:

- William Wilberforce
- Sophie Scholl
- Dr Martin Luther King Jr
- Oscar Romero
- Mother Teresa
- Nano Nagle

Dr Martin Luther King Jr

Interpreting a Good Christian Life

There are many ways of interpreting how to live a good life in Christianity. Jesus taught about many things. Some Christians look to his teaching about 'turning the other cheek', which taught followers not to accept injustice but not to resort to violence.

Desmond Doss was a conscientious objector.

Others look to Jesus' teaching on looking after the poor or widowed as the best way to live out a good life. In their work with the poor and homeless, Sr Stanislaus Kennedy and Fr Peter McVerry are examples of people who offer themselves in service to others. The founders of many charities were Christians who saw living a good life as helping others.

Many Christians, including Quakers, are pacifists. Quakers refuse to use violence as they believe it is against Christian values to do so.

Desmond Doss, a Seventh Day Adventist, was awarded a Medal of Honour in the Second World War, although as a conscientious objector he refused to even carry a weapon. The movie *Hacksaw Ridge* tells the story of his bravery.

Over to You – Exploration

1. Choose **one** of the people mentioned above to find out more about him or her.
2. Create a presentation about this person and explain how they were, in their understanding, living a good life as a Christian, and what values were important to them.

Living a Good Life in Humanism

Basic Beliefs

Humanism is a belief in the ability of humans to fulfil their own potential and to find their own meaning in life. Humanists believe that human experience and rational thinking provide a source of knowledge and a moral code to live by.

How to Live a Good Life in Humanism

Living a good life in humanism is about finding your own meaning in life. Humanists do so in a way that considers the wellbeing of others and what is good for the whole world. In order to find out what is good for the world, humanism teaches people to gain as much knowledge about the world as possible. They use science and rational thinking to solve problems. Humanism encourages people to think scientifically, but to be careful that science is used in creative not destructive ways.

Scientific discoveries and developments are used in different ways.

Finding Meaning in Humanism

Living a good life in humanism is about finding your own meaning in life. This develops over time through experience and understanding. People are encouraged to be connected to family, their communities and the world. They are to seek happiness for themselves and others. Humanism emphasises the importance of respecting the right of people and all living creatures to live as full a life as possible.

Humanists look to history and to the advances brought about by human endeavour to improve human life. Humanists are encouraged by the ability of humans to discover things in nature and by their own understanding of the world. They wish to celebrate and build on these achievements. Seeking your own meaning in life is key.

Humanists do not believe in an afterlife; they believe that life is meaningful and should be made the most of. They see no evidence for an afterlife, but they do believe a life well lived affects the world and can make it a better place. Being a good humanist is not about gaining a reward after life; it is about doing good for the world and other people here and now.

The Value of Life

Humanists have funerals to celebrate a person's life when he or she dies. In this event, people have an opportunity to remember the deceased. They recognise the sadness that the loss brings to friends and family, and they have an opportunity to share memories of the person. Humanist funerals usually involve readings, music and a moment of silence to remember the loved one.

In Ireland, many people are choosing humanist funerals. There are a number of celebrants available to carry out these ceremonies. Humanism is concerned with the dignity and worth of all people. The humanist celebrant tries to make the ceremony as inclusive as possible.

Over to You – Enquiry

 Research more about humanist ceremonies for birth, marriage and death.

Values in Humanism

Human Dignity

Dignity means to have worth and respect. Humanism emphasises the dignity of individuals regardless of their beliefs, race, ethnicity, background or gender. It is important in humanism that individuals are valued and their rights respected. When a person is treated badly, they

Is this person's dignity respected?

are denied dignity and worth as a human being. These values are expanded further in the International Humanist and Ethical Union's Amsterdam Declaration, which outlines the fundamental principles of humanism.

Concern for Others – Welfare

To live a good life in humanism, a person should be concerned about other people's welfare. The Amsterdam Declaration states: 'Humanists have a duty of care to all of humanity, including future generations'. So living a good life in humanism means caring for people alive today and those in the future. This could be by donating to charity, caring for an elderly friend or relative or by caring for the earth.

Human Rights and Freedom

To live a good life in humanism is to value personal freedom and democracy. The Amsterdam Declaration states: 'democracy and human development are matters of right'. Humanists are concerned with issues of discrimination and situations where people's rights are denied. The Humanist and Ethical Union has consultative status at the United Nations in Geneva and New York. Humanists value the rights of individuals to have freedom of religion, thought and expression. To live a good life in humanism is to be concerned with these issues.

How would a humanist feel about the issue of modern-day slavery? Discuss other issues that humanists might be concerned about.

Human Expression and Fulfilment

To live a good life in humanism is to value the individuality of each person and to allow him or her to express themselves fully in a life lived to the full. The Amsterdam Declaration states: 'Humanism affirms the importance of literature, music, and the visual and performing arts for personal development and fulfilment'.

From a humanist perspective, finding meaning in life is a personal journey and it can be expressed in many different ways. People find meaning in family, friends, music, sport, politics, science and work. The arts are a way of expressing yourself and of developing your talents. Humanists consider this to be a good way of living and encourage people to fulfil their potential.

Over to You – Reflection and Action

1. Create a chart or Venn diagram that shows the similarities between a Jewish, Christian and humanist understanding of how to live a good life.
2. Discuss the impact a world view can have on how a person lives.

Revision Questions

Enquiry

1. Explain the following terms:
   - Values
   - Morally
   - Dignity
   - Justice
2. Give examples of values in Judaism, Christianity and humanism.
3. In Judaism, what is the Torah?
4. In Christianity, what is meant by the 'Kingdom of God'?
5. In humanism, what is the Amsterdam Declaration?

Exploration

1. Reflect on the connection between morality and a person's world view, religious or non-religious.
2. Think about ways in which a person who is a Jewish, Christian or humanist can live a good life and how that affects other people.

Reflection and Action

- As a class, decide on what you value. Choose something you could do to live a good life as members of the school community.
- Put this decision into action.
- This can be a group project or an individual reflection.

Debating a Moral Issue 2

20

Learning Outcome 3.6

Debate a moral issue that arises in their lives and consider what influences two different viewpoints on the issue.

Learning Intentions

By the end of this chapter I will:

- Have learned about a moral issue
- Have heard two different points of view on the issue
- Have learned about what influences different points of view on this issue
- Have participated in a debate

Key Skills and Wellbeing

- Communicating
- Managing myself
- Staying well

I feel listened to and valued. I show care and respect for others.

Keywords

influence ▪ moral issue ▪ point of view

Introduction

Earlier in the course, we looked at what it means to be moral, moral codes and **influences** on morality. In Chapter 9, we debated **moral issues**. That chapter explained that moral issues involve choices, that people have different opinions on moral issues and that many different things influence these **points of view**. In this chapter, we will debate another moral issue: that every country has a moral duty to take refugees.

Icebreaker

Brainstorm
1. What does the word 'moral' mean?
2. What influences a person's point of view?
3. What is the meaning of 'consequences'?

Debate Topic: Every Country Has a Moral Duty to Take Refugees

There are many different opinions on this topic. The rise of far-right parties in many parts of Europe and the actions of US President Trump have shown that some people are hostile to refugees and asylum seekers. Other people campaign tirelessly to help refugees and asylum seekers and believe strongly in the duty of countries and people to care for these people.

These young children have undergone a terrifying journey across the sea to seek safety in Europe. Why is this a moral issue?

While listening to both sides in this debate, it is important to remember that refugees are people who have often gone through very difficult and traumatic events. There are many refugees in Ireland. You might be a refugee yourself, or there may be refugees in your class, school, neighbourhood or amongst your friends and family. Talking about the issue requires you to be sensitive to the feelings of others. You must also be respectful when presenting your opinions and listening to other people's opinions.

The Universal Declaration of Human Rights

Article 14 of the Universal Declaration of Human Rights states:

> Everyone has the right to seek and to enjoy in other countries asylum from persecution.

According to Article 1 of the 1951 UN Refugee Convention, a refugee is defined as:

> A person who owing to well-founded fear of being persecuted for reasons of race, religion, nationality, membership of a particular social group or political opinion, is outside the country of his nationality and is unable or, owing to such fear, is unwilling to avail himself of the protection of that country.

Asylum Seekers and Refugees

Asylum seekers are individuals who are seeking protection as refugees. They are waiting for the authorities to decide whether their claim is valid. Asylum seekers are entitled to stay in the country while their application is being decided and they are entitled to a fair hearing.

Some facts about refugees:

- There are over 65 million displaced people in the world today. Displaced people are forced from their home due to wars, persecution or natural disasters. They can be refugees and forced to leave their home country or they can be displaced within their own country.
- Some 85 per cent are in developing countries, which have less developed economies.
- Approximately half of the refugees in the world are children.
- Refugee children are five times more likely to be out of school than non-refugee children.
- Some 145 countries have signed up to the 1951 Refugee Convention, an international law that protects refugees.
- The top host countries for refugees are Turkey, Lebanon and Pakistan.

Did You Know?

? Michael Marks, who founded the British shop Marks and Spencer along with Thomas Spencer, was a Russian-born Polish refugee.

Review and Reflect

1. What is a refugee?
2. What is an asylum seeker?
3. Name any countries you think refugees are currently fleeing.

Do you think events taking place at the time or shortly before would have influenced the signing of the UN Refugee Convention in 1951? Can history be important for teaching us about the present?

For and Against the Motion

Consider the following points for and against the motion: *'Every country has a moral duty to take refugees'*. These are points often put forward by people discussing this issue. They are not all **facts**; some are **opinions**.

What Does This Mean?

Fact: A thing that is known or proved to be true.

Opinion: A view or judgement formed about something, that is not necessarily based on fact or knowledge.

FOR THE MOTION

- People are entitled under international law to be protected and to seek asylum in another country when they are afraid of being persecuted. This is a human right and countries should fulfil their duty to help people to have that right.

- It is the right thing to do. If we were the ones looking for asylum, we would want to be helped. In the past, thousands of Irish people looked for refuge in other countries.

- It follows the Golden Rule found in all major world religions and followed by humanists: to treat people the way you would want to be treated.

- Refugees contribute a great deal to the countries they make a new home in. They are responsible citizens, they work hard and they bring new skills and ideas. In the long term, refugees help the economy of the country they end up in.

- It is wrong to send people back to a country where they may be tortured or killed. Each country has to take refugees. Very often, poor, neighbouring countries take the majority of refugees, so wealthy countries like Ireland that are in the European Union have a responsibility to help.

AGAINST THE MOTION

- We have enough problems of our own. Looking after Irish people should be a priority. There are many homeless people in Ireland. We have unemployment and economic difficulties of our own. If we take any refugees, we should only do so once we have helped our own people first.

- Refugees use up money and resources. We cannot afford to take them. Where would we house refugees? What jobs would they do? They would end up taking jobs from Irish people.

- There are too many refugees in the world today. The war in Syria has made the problem too big. It is unfortunate for the people involved, but it would only make other countries unstable and create bigger problems. The number of refugees seeking asylum has just gone too far.

- Refugees are different to us. They often do not speak the same language as us. They have different religions and nationalities. They do not fit in and have a bad effect on our neighbourhoods. They will undermine our values and culture and will want to make our country more like theirs.

- Some refugees might cause problems, as they might be criminals. Their background is not checked thoroughly enough. Some of them come from countries where there is a lot of terrorism. How do we know they are not also terrorists?

What problems do refugees face when they move to a new country?

Over to You – Exploration

 Discuss the arguments for and against the motion on page 174.

1. Are they founded on facts or opinion? How do you know?
2. What influences people to have these opinions?
3. Have you heard any of these arguments before?

Debate It!

4. Have a debate. First, do some more research on this topic and find out more about it. You can use and add to the comments made on page 174.

You can have either:

- A walking debate

  Or

- A formal debate

(See pages 70–71 for details on how to hold a debate.)

Suggestions for further debates:

- The use of animals for experimentation should be banned.
- Children under 12 should not have smartphones.
- People should be fined if they do not vote in elections.

> You will have another debate topic in Third Year.

Thinking about Influences

> Discussion helps us to understand viewpoints that are different from our own.

Some important influences on people include their family, friends, the media, their religion and their culture or country of origin.

When discussing any issue, it is really important that you consider why people think the way they do. What has influenced their opinion? People are influenced by many different people and by what they hear in the media. When they hear something, people do not always know whether or not it is true. People often put opinions forward as fact.

What Does This Mean?

Racism: Prejudice and discrimination against people from a different race.

Xenophobia: Dislike and prejudice against people from other countries.

Sometimes irresponsible politicians and commentators put forward their opinion to get support even when it is not true. This can be very dangerous, leading to **racism** and **xenophobia**. This can lead to people being misinformed on an important issue like this one on refugees.

Over to You – Enquiry

 Discuss: How can a person become better informed on issues like this? How can you decide what is fact and what is opinion?

Revision Questions

Enquiry

1. What is the United Nations definition of a refugee?
2. What article of the Declaration of Human Rights refers to the rights of people to seek help as refugees?
3. What is an asylum seeker?
4. How many countries have signed up to the UN Convention on Refugees?
5. How many refugees are there in the world today?

Exploration

1. What are the situations that cause people to become refugees?
2. As well as their homes, what else have refugees lost?
3. What are the challenges individuals face when they arrive in a country as refugees?
4. How can people help refugees to feel welcome?

Reflection and Action

- Research a current situation where there is a refugee crisis, for example, Syria, South Sudan or Myanmar. Find out more on why the people have to flee and seek refuge in another country.
- Find out where they are going and how they are being treated.
- Create a poster to highlight the issue.
- As a class, carry out a project to raise awareness of the issue of refugees in the world today. If possible, have a fundraiser for a charity that helps refugees.

Religious Themes in Culture 2

21

Does this picture remind you of another painting?

Brainstorm

1. What is a theme?
2. What is contemporary culture?
3. How can we identify themes in music, art, literature and film?

Introduction

In Chapter 10, we explored **religious themes** in contemporary culture. We looked at what these **themes** might be and we identified them in a number of works. We listed some religious themes as follows:

- God or Gods
- Death and afterlife
- Questions of meaning – people looking for a purpose in life
- Love
- Prayer and meditation

- Morality, or good and evil
- Stories from a major world religion – including famous figures from that religion
- Places associated with a religion

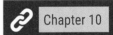
Chapter 10

You may have added to the list. Remind yourself of any other ideas you had for religious themes.

How are religious themes evident in these film titles?

Religious Themes in Music

Like poets, musicians and songwriters put their ideas in verse form. They then put the words to music to create a song. Lyrics are a way to explore themes, such as life and death, the meaning of life, love, hurt, suffering, sorrow, joy, happiness, God or Gods and the unknown.

In some songs, the artist is expressing ideas or questions about having faith and believing in something or someone. Other songs express ideas about being yourself and finding your meaning in life, or about what happens when we die. Sometimes, when we hear a song, we can relate to the lyrics. We may have thought some of the same things, asked similar questions about life, or simply liked the way the song made us feel.

Florence and the Machine

The following songs have lyrics with religious references or themes:

- **Death and loss:** The song 'Tears in Heaven' by Eric Clapton starts with the line, 'Would you know my name, if I saw you in heaven?'
- **Belief and questions:** 'Speed of Sound' by Coldplay contains the lyrics, 'Some things you have to believe, but others are puzzles, puzzling me.'
- **God:** 'One of Us' by Joan Osborne contains the line, 'If God had a face, what would it look like?'
- **Faith:** Florence and the Machine's song 'You've Got the Love' contains the lyrics 'When friends are gone, I know my saviour's love is real'.
- The opening verse of the Bob Dylan song 'Forever Young' is the following prayer or blessing: 'May God bless and keep you always, may your wishes all come true, may you always do for others, and let others do for you.'

Over to You – Exploration

- Think of lyrics from other songs that have religious references or meaning.
- Are these ideas something you can relate to?

Religious Themes in the Music of U2

The Irish band U2 have often used religious themes during their long career in music. Some examples include 'Angel of Harlem', 'One', 'I Still Haven't Found What I'm Looking For' and 'Miss Sarajevo'. Like any piece of art, their song 'When Love Comes to Town' can mean different things to different people. We can see that it repeats the words 'when love comes to town', which makes love the obvious theme. The song was performed by U2 with the American blues singer B.B. King.

The cover of U2's album *Rattle and Hum*

U2 and B.B. King perform together.

Over to You – Enquiry

1. Listen to the song 'When Love Comes to Town' and reflect on the lyrics. What type of love do you think the song is referring to?
2. Explore another song that has religious themes. You can choose **one** mentioned above or a different one.
3. Which words or phrases are connected to religious themes?
4. What is the overall feeling of the song?
5. Are any of the ideas or phrases in the song something you can relate to?

Religious Themes in Film

Like any piece of art, a film is open to interpretation. While some films deliberately start out to express certain themes, sometimes, unintentionally, a different theme emerges. Some films are about finding meaning in life: Why are we here? What is our responsibility in life? Some ask questions of morality: What is good or bad? How do people **redeem** themselves if they have done something bad? Others deal with the issue of God: If there is a God, what is God like?

The famous Christmas movie *It's a Wonderful Life* shows the impact one man's ordinary life has on the people around him. His life has great meaning through the simple act of living in his home town with the love of his family and friends.

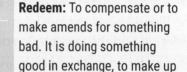

What Does This Mean?

Redeem: To compensate or to make amends for something bad. It is doing something good in exchange, to make up for wrongdoing.

The Italian comedy-drama *Life Is Beautiful* deals with suffering while still being able to find meaning. It shows that love, family and the human spirit are more powerful than the worst that humanity can do. The film is set against the backdrop of the Holocaust and the horrors of a concentration camp. The film is about hope and imagination.

🔗 Chapter 10

In some films, there are images of God. God has been shown in many different ways in film. In *Exodus: Gods and Kings*, God is a small boy. In *Dogma*, God is a woman.

Some famous films tell the story of Jesus, such as *Jesus of Nazareth*, *The Miracle Maker* and *The Passion of the Christ*. Some films have messiah-like figures, like Aslan in *The Lion, the Witch and the Wardrobe*, Harry Potter in *The Deathly Hallows* or *E.T.* The superhero genre typically delves into the area of good versus evil, and some characters are based on the Gods of the ancient world, for example, Thor and Loki.

Did You Know?

? Thor is the God of Thunder and one of the most powerful of the Norse Gods. He is famous for holding a hammer. In Norse mythology, Loki is the trickster God.

A film still from *Life Is Beautiful* starring Roberto Benigni. Benigni won best actor at the Oscars for his role. Benigni's father had been in a Nazi concentration camp.

Religious Themes in E.T.

It can be argued that Steven Spielberg uses religious themes in his movie *E.T. the Extra-Terrestrial*. Spielberg has said that he did not intentionally create a messiah-like figure in his extra-terrestrial character. However, many have noted the parallels:

1. E.T. comes from above and is other-worldly.
2. E.T. has the power to heal.
3. E.T. dies and comes back to life.
4. E.T. is persecuted by the people in power.
5. E.T. ascends back above, telling Elliott 'I will be right here'.

The film also has themes of compassion and acceptance, of kindness, loyalty, pain and suffering and the importance of belonging.

E.T. touches the life of Elliott and his family. He teaches them important moral lessons, leaving them with a stronger sense of who they are and what is important in life.

A still from the movie *E.T.* How does this image make you feel?

Review and Reflect

 Watch the film *E.T. the Extra-Terrestrial* and answer the following questions.

1. Why does E.T. relate to the children?
2. How does E.T. react to violence or suffering?
3. How strong is the connection between E.T. and Elliott? How is this connection shown?
4. What message does the story teach about how people should treat the outsider?
5. Do you think this film has an interesting way of exploring religious themes?

Religious Themes in Contemporary Art

As we learned in Chapter 10, art is the way people express themselves through painting, sculpture or other forms. It is aimed at producing something beautiful, imaginative or inspiring. In this section, we explore art as the making of objects or images that express feelings – in particular photography and paintings.

 **Chapter 10** The major world religions have had an impact on art. The two contemporary artists we will explore are influenced by two different religions: Hinduism and Judaism.

Manjari Sharma is a photographer based in Brooklyn, New York, and Sara Novenson is an artist based in Santa Fe, New Mexico.

Manjari Sharma

Manjari Sharma uses photographs to recreate classical images of Hindu Gods and Goddesses, such as Lakshmi, Shiva, Durga, Ganesh and Vishnu. She uses a stage, props and people to reconstruct traditional pictures before photographing them.

The themes in her photographs come from Hindu stories and traditions. These works of art are created to express devotion.

Manjari Sharma standing in front of her series *Darshan*, showing Hindu Gods

Sara Novenson

Sara Novenson has produced a number of paintings based on stories from the Bible. She completed a set of paintings and wrote a book about them called *Illuminated Visions, Women of the Bible*. These paintings are expressions of her understanding of the stories of the female figures of the Bible, such as Eve, Sarah, Rachael, Rebeccah and Leah. The stories are represented to show the power of the women and to help people today to connect with them.

Over to You – Exploration

 Discuss the following statement: 'Contemporary religious art helps people to relate to the stories that the artist is expressing.'

Religious Themes in Literature

Written works include poetry, stories, novels and plays. Throughout literature, you will find many different themes. These can be religious.

A theme is an idea running through a piece of writing. What is the writing about? Who are the characters and how do they behave?

🔗 Chapter 10

The events, the attitudes of the main characters, the words used and the feel of the story combine to give us ideas about the theme or themes in a piece of literature.

The Book Thief

The Book Thief by Markus Zusak is set in Nazi Germany. It is the story of a young girl, Liesel Meminger. As Liesel is the child of a communist, who was persecuted by the Nazis, she is sent to foster parents Hans and Rosa Hubermann. As the war rages on, Liesel's life becomes increasingly difficult.

Liesel's foster parents also help a Jewish man named Max Vandenburg to hide from the Nazis. Liesel and Max develop a close relationship based on their shared love of words.

The Book Thief is an interesting story, as it is told from the perspective of 'Death'. Death narrates the book but does not explain what happens after life. However, Death describes how he carries a person's soul when he or she dies.

As the book develops, Death appears to take greater care in carrying out this role. Death is troubled by the human capacity to do great evil while at the same time being able to show great love. This highlights the contrast between how humans can be both very good and very bad. Death has a great interest in the life of Liesel and tells her that he is 'haunted by humans'. This story deals with themes of love, sacrifice, morality and compassion, as well as suffering and hate.

THE NO.1 INTERNATIONAL BESTSELLER

MARKUS ZUSAK

The Book Thief

'A novel of breath-taking scope, masterfully told'
Guardian

The Book Thief has spent over 500 weeks on the *New York Times*' bestseller list.

Review and Reflect

1. Who wrote *The Book Thief*?
2. Where is it set?
3. Name the main characters.
4. Do you think it is interesting that the author chose to write the story from the viewpoint of Death?
5. What is interesting about Death telling Liesel, 'I am haunted by humans'?
6. Do you think that the theme of death is an important one for religions? Explain why or why not.

Revision Questions

Enquiry

1. Name **three** songs in which you can identify religious themes.
2. How is the character of E.T. messiah-like?
3. Name a contemporary artist who uses religious themes.
4. Who narrates the story in *The Book Thief*?

Exploration

1. Think and write about the themes in the songs you listen to, the books you read or the films you watch.
2. Think and write about whether you relate to these themes.
3. Think and write about the influence that world views and beliefs, religious or non-religious, have on contemporary culture.

Reflection and Action

- In pairs, research a poem that explores one of the following religious themes:
  - The meaning of life
  - Death
  - God/Gods
  - Prayer
  - Morality
- Make a presentation of your findings to the class.

22 Living Your Beliefs

Learning Outcome 2.8

Present stories of individuals or of groups in the history of two major world religions that have had a positive impact on the lives of people because of their commitment to living out their beliefs.

Learning Intentions

By the end of this chapter I will:

- Know the story of two individuals and/or groups who are committed to their religion
- Understand how the individuals and/or groups have had a positive impact on the lives of others
- Realise how the faith of the individual and/or group is connected to their commitment to making a positive impact on the lives of others
- Reflect on how my own faith or personal beliefs can have a positive impact on others

Key Skills and Wellbeing

- Being creative
- Managing information and thinking
- Being literate

I have become aware of the positive influence of religious belief in my community and around the world. I realise that my beliefs, both religious and non-religious, can have a big impact on the lives of others. From my new understanding, I will strive to have a positive impact on the lives of others.

Keywords

devotion ▪ ecumenism ▪ reconciliation

Introduction

Faith is a powerful motivator. It can make people do all sorts of things. In most cases, faith encourages people to do good, helpful and kind acts for other people. Unfortunately that is not always the case. When people misinterpret sacred texts and teaching, or when evil people become religious leaders, sometimes the followers of that faith can do hurtful, wicked things instead.

This chapter does not dwell on evil things. Instead it looks at how people who have strong faith live out their beliefs in order to help others, and make a positive impact on the lives of people all around the world.

Icebreaker

1. Make a list of all the things you have done to help other people. Include as many as you can think of!
2. Once your list is complete, write down beside each one why you did it.
   - Did someone tell you to?
   - Did you do it because something inside told you it was the right thing to do?
   - Did you learn something in school or while at worship that made you think it was the right thing to do?
3. Discuss your good deeds and your motivations for doing good and helping others with the rest of the class.

"If we're on earth to help others, how do I go about becoming an 'other'?"

Over to You – Exploration

Carefully examine the cartoon above. Reflect on what you think it means and then discuss the following questions with a classmate.

1. What message do you think the cartoon is trying to get across?
2. If you were asked this question, what would your answer be?
3. Who are the 'others' in your life?

Brother Roger

Brother Roger Schütz was born on the 12 May 1915 in Provence, Switzerland. His father was a Lutheran pastor and his mother was a French Protestant. Brother Roger showed an early interest in living a life of faith and studied reformed theology at university. He was a leader of the Swiss Student Christian Movement. Brother Roger witnessed some of the horrors of the Second World War. He felt a calling to help those suffering, just like his grandmother, who had helped refugees during the First World War.

Brother Roger Schütz spent many decades of his life helping people at Taizé. This photo shows him at work in the 1970s.

The Founding of the Taizé Community

In 1940, Brother Roger left his home in Switzerland and travelled to his mother's country of birth – France. Taizé was a small village in Vichy France that was near the border with the Nazi-occupied region. Brother Roger felt this would be a good place to shelter refugees fleeing the war. He took out a loan and bought a house and outhouses that had been left empty for years. He asked his sister Genevieve to help him to take care of the war victims. Soon it became known as a place of safety, and friends of Brother Roger gave out his address in Taizé to people needing help.

Brother Roger and Genevieve's parents were worried about the danger their children faced. They asked a friend, a retired French official, to keep an eye on them and warn them of any danger. In 1942, he told Brother Roger that the Gestapo (Nazi secret police) had found out about their refuge. Brother Roger and Genevieve had to flee. Brother Roger went to Geneva and lived there with other religious brothers for two years, until he returned to Taizé in 1944.

Refuge for Victims of War

In 1945, Brother Roger was asked to take in children who had been orphaned by the war. Once again, he asked his sister to help him and together they offered a place of safety to people harmed by the effects of the Second World War.

Others heard of the great work Brother Roger was doing. On Easter Sunday 1949, seven people joined Brother Roger's community. They committed themselves to a life of **devotion**, helping others, in Taizé.

Brother Roger devoted his life to peace and **reconciliation**. He wanted to help those who were in need of safety. When the war was over, Brother Roger's commitment to his calling did not end. The community at Taizé continued to grow, and in the winter of 1952–53 Brother Roger wrote *The Rules of Taizé*.

What Does This Mean?

Devotion: When loyalty and dedication are shown. You can be devoted to another person in your life, a cause or a religion.

Reconciliation: Restoring relationships that have become hostile between people or groups. Persuading people or groups with opposing outlooks or beliefs to respect each other where previously they did not.

Taizé Today

Today, Taizé is a place of reconciliation, **ecumenism** and community. Brother Roger wanted Christians of all denominations to come together in peace and unity. Now, there are over 100 brothers working in Taizé, and several different orders of sisters help with welcoming and organising thousands of young people who visit every year. While visiting Taizé, young people are invited to discuss the Bible, develop their faith, spend time in silence and in work, and attend special prayer services and Mass.

In Taizé, everyone takes turns to help out cooking, feeding and cleaning.

Brother Roger was killed on 16 August 2005, aged 90. A woman, who was later diagnosed as being mentally ill, stabbed him during evening prayers. Taizé is now overseen by Brother Alois, whom Brother Roger had named as his successor a few years before his death.

Even though Brother Roger is gone, the spirit of peace and reconciliation he devoted his life's work to lives on in Taizé. This is through the thousands of people who go on pilgrimage there every year, and in the hearts of all the people he helped during the Second World War.

What Does This Mean?

Ecumenism: Bringing the different Christian churches closer together, to promote unity, co-operation and better understanding.

Over to You – Reflection and Action

In pairs, discuss and make a list of the ways Brother Roger's faith had a positive impact on the lives of others.

The Taizé ecumenical community pray together in the Church of Reconciliation.

Key Skill: Being Creative

- After you have read the story of Brother Roger's life above, divide his life into three stages.
- Divide the class into three groups, and assign each of the following roles to each member of the group: writer(s), director(s), actor(s), producer(s).
- Each group should take **one** stage in Brother Roger's life and create a short role play depicting that stage. Perform your role play for the rest of the class.

The Tzu Chi Foundation

Dharma Master Cheng Yen was born in 1937 in Qingshui, a small town in Taichung County, Taiwan. She founded the Tzu Chi Foundation in 1966 on the east coast of Taiwan. She became Buddhist when she was 21 years old after the unexpected death of her father. Cheng Yen began to question the meaning of life, death and suffering. When she was 25, she devoted herself to life as a Buddhist nun by shaving her head. In 1966 when she was 29, she founded Tzu Chi.

> Dharma Master Cheng Yen deeply believes that all people are capable of the same great compassion as the Buddha. True compassion, however, is not just having sympathy for another's suffering – it is to reach out to relieve that suffering with concrete actions.

Source: The Tzu Chi website

Inspired to Help Others

Cheng Yen and her disciples supported themselves by sewing baby shoes and other craftwork. The area in which they lived was very poor, and many families did not have enough money for food and medical care. Cheng Yen witnessed this firsthand when she was visiting a patient at a local medical clinic in 1966. She saw a pool of blood on the floor, which had come from a woman who lived in the mountains. The woman was having a complicated labour and her family had carried her down the mountain to seek medical help. But when they arrived, they did not have enough money to pay the medical fee and had to take her away. Cheng Yen was overcome with sorrow and immediately began to think of ways she could help these people.

Cheng Yen felt conflicted; Buddhism teaches love and compassion for all living creatures, but you must do good without seeking recognition. It would be impossible to ask people for charity to help others without them knowing that you were trying to help. She realised that a small but concentrated effort would make a huge difference and decided to set up the organisation anyway. Along with her disciples, she would do what she could for the poor. They would live out Buddha's teaching of compassion and love in a real, physical way.

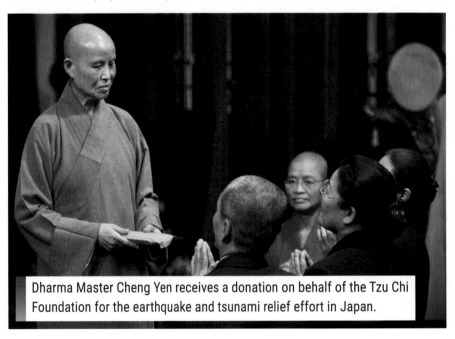

Dharma Master Cheng Yen receives a donation on behalf of the Tzu Chi Foundation for the earthquake and tsunami relief effort in Japan.

Tzu Chi Centres

Word spread quickly and many people wanted to give what they could to Tzu Chi or help in some way. Tzu Chi started to collect donations from villages further and further away. Today there are Tzu Chi centres in 47 countries, which provide aid to 69 nations. The Tzu Chi Foundation's 'Four Major Missions' consist of charity, medicine, education and humanity. They have also begun campaigns in bone marrow transplant, environmental protection, community volunteerism and international relief.

> In founding Tzu Chi, Dharma Master Cheng Yen wished to give ordinary citizens the chance to actualise their compassion, which will bring inner peace and happiness to the individual, and pave the way for world peace and harmony.

Source: The Tzu Chi website

The Tzu Chi Foundation helps many people, including those in this UNHCR refugee centre in Malaysia.

Over to You – Enquiry

1. Go to the website for the Tzu Chi Foundation. Discover what work the foundation is doing. Write down **one** thing it is doing to help others under each of the following four headings:
   - Mission of Charity
   - Mission of Medicine
   - Mission of Education
   - Mission of Humanity
2. Reflect on how the work this foundation is doing is guided by the teachings of Buddhism.

Revision Questions

Enquiry

1. Who was Brother Roger?
2. Where did he start his community?
3. Who helped him?
4. Name **two** things Brother Roger did.
5. What happens in Taizé today?
6. How many brothers live and work in Taizé now?
7. What happened to Brother Roger?
8. What is Cheng Yen's religion?
9. How did she show that she was committed to her faith?
10. What event did she witness?
11. What Buddhist values did Cheng Yen want to live by?
12. List the Tzu Chi Foundation's Four Major Missions.
13. Does the Tzu Chi Foundation work in any other areas? If so, name them.

Exploration

1. Why did Brother Roger want to help the victims of the Second World War?
2. In your opinion, what motivated Brother Roger to set up the community at Taizé?
3. Do you think a community like Taizé has a good impact on the world? Why or why not?
4. What religious values are evident in the life of the people at Taizé?
5. What effect did her experience in the local medical centre have on Cheng Yen?
6. How does Cheng Yen show her compassion and love?
7. Which of the Four Major Missions do you feel is the most important? Give a reason for your answer.

Reflection and Action

- Do you know anyone in your community who lives the positive message of their beliefs by helping others? It could be a family member who gives time or donates to charity. Or it could be someone who volunteers in the community or abroad.
- Or do you know of a person or organisation that has helped humanity and made a positive impact on the world through living their beliefs?
- Research the founding story of an organisation that helps others, or research the background story of a person who helps others. Find out their mission and the work that they do. Create a leaflet on this person or group. The back page of the leaflet should show how their beliefs have guided their actions.
- The person or group should have close ties with one of the five major world religions.

Dialogue for Peace 23

Learning Outcome 1.10

Discuss the importance of dialogue and interaction between major world religions and within major world religions in promoting peace and reconciliation in the world today.

Learning Intentions

By the end of this chapter I will:

- Know and be able to give an example of dialogue between major world religions
- Know and be able to give an example of dialogue within major world religions
- Understand the importance of dialogue between the major world religions for promoting peace in the world today
- Reflect on the importance of dialogue within religions for promoting peace and reconciliation

Key Skills and Wellbeing

- Working with others
- Being creative
- Communicating
- Being literate

I am aware of my thoughts and feelings. I feel listened to and valued. I appreciate how my actions impact on the wellbeing of myself and others, locally and globally.

Keywords

dialogue ▪ ecumenism ▪ interaction ▪ intercultural dialogue ▪ peace ▪ reconciliation

Introduction

This chapter is about **dialogue** and **interaction** between different religions and the various groups within religions. It explores how these are important for encouraging peace between people. As we have seen, there are many different religious viewpoints in the world. It is important that the religions and groups within them are able to work together, to share ideas and to help to create a more peaceful and understanding society. Whatever the differences of belief, we all share this world and it is vital that we do so in harmony.

What Does This Mean?

Dialogue: A conversation between two or more people.

Interaction: Communication or involvement with someone or something.

Icebreaker

1. In pairs, list your similarities and differences, including likes and dislikes.
2. Discuss why you have these differences.
3. Consider the following questions:
   (a) Is it good to be different?
   (b) Is it okay to have different likes and dislikes or different opinions?

What do you think helps people from diverse cultures and backgrounds get on well together?

The Importance of Communication

Throughout this course, we have explored the five major world religions: Hinduism, Judaism, Buddhism, Christianity and Islam.

These religions started in different times and places and have emerged over thousands of years. Some have close links to each other, such as Judaism and Christianity. Unfortunately, people have not always respected religious views that are different from their own. Often, religion is used as a way to divide people, to encourage mistrust between them and even as an excuse to fight, to hate and to kill. This is not what these religions are trying to achieve, and goes strongly against their main teachings and the visions of their founders. For example:

In Islam, this saying is attributed to the Prophet Muhammad: 'To you be your religion, to me be mine.'

Jesus taught his followers to 'love their neighbour as themselves' and to treat others are they would like to be treated. He did not say this applied only to other Christians.

In Judaism, the command to care for the 'stranger' is mentioned 36 times in the Torah, more than any other command. For example, the Book of Exodus says, 'Do not ill-treat a stranger or oppress him, for you were strangers in the land of Egypt.'

The spiritual leader of Tibetan Buddhism, the Dalai Lama, has said, 'Peace does not mean an absence of conflicts; differences will always be there. Peace means solving these differences through peaceful means; through dialogue, education, knowledge; and through humane ways.'

A famous verse from Hindu scripture says, 'This person is my relative and that person is a stranger, says the small-minded one; for the one who knows the truth, the whole world is a family.' The phrase 'The whole world is a family' from this verse is engraved in Sanskrit in the entrance hall of the parliament of India.

What Is Dialogue?

Dialogue is a conversation between two or more people. When thinking about communication between people from different religions or different religious subgroups, we need to define **intercultural dialogue**.

What Does This Mean?

 Intercultural dialogue: An open and respectful exchange between individuals and groups belonging to different ethnic, cultural and belief backgrounds that leads to a deeper understanding of the other's and one's own perspective.

Over to You – Enquiry

 Intercultural dialogue leads to a 'deeper understanding of the other's and one's own perspective'. In pairs, discuss why that is important.

Dialogue Between the Major World Religions

The Faith & Belief Forum is an example of efforts to get people of different religions and beliefs to communicate and develop good relationships. The organisation was founded in 1997 as the Three Faiths Forum to encourage friendship, goodwill and understanding between people of different faiths, especially between Muslims, Christians and Jews. Over the years, its work expanded to include people of all faiths and beliefs, both religious and non-religious. In 2018, it changed its name to the Faith & Belief Forum to better reflect this inclusive ethos.

The organisation runs programmes in schools, universities, workplaces and the wider community where people can engage with questions of belief and identity and meet people different from themselves. Overall, its aim is to build good relations between people of all faiths and beliefs, and to build a society where difference is celebrated.

The goal of the Faith and Belief Forum is to be:

> ' a supportive society where people of different faiths, beliefs and cultures have strong, productive and lasting relations. We believe the future belongs to people of all beliefs, that religious intolerance has no place in society and that diversity adds value. '

Source: The Faith and Belief Forum website

Over to You – Exploration

1. In groups, discuss the following statement: 'The work of an organisation like the Faith and Belief Forum is more important in the world today than ever before.'
2. Research the following organisations. Find out what they do to help the different religions to work together and to engage in dialogue in Ireland:
   - The Irish Council for Christians and Jews
   - The Dublin City Interfaith Forum
3. Think of ways that you could help people of different religions feel included and accepted.

Why Is Dialogue Important for Peace?

Peace is about living in safety and without fear of violence. It is when people can live together in harmony and tranquillity. This concept will be explored further in Chapter 24.

What Does This Mean?

Peace: Living without conflict or hostility. It is living in harmony with one another, with peace of mind, freedom and security.

Dialogue is important for peace. If people talk to each other, they have a better chance of understanding the other person's point of view, even if they do not agree with it. Dialogue is not the same as a debate. It is not about making a case that everyone has to vote on; nobody wins in dialogue in the way they do in a debate.

The important things to remember when involved in dialogue are to:

- Take time to listen to both sides.
- Ask questions.
- Respect those you are in dialogue with. To respect is to have regard for the feelings, rights and opinions of others.

This is a quote on peace from the Buddhist monk and peace activitist Thich Nhat Hanh:

> To work for peace is to uproot war from ourselves and from the hearts of men and women. To prepare for war... is to plant millions of seeds of violence, anger, frustration, and fear that will be passed on for generations to come.

Buddhist monk and peace activist Thich Nhat Hanh

Dialogue is important for peace because:

- It gives an opportunity for people to feel listened to.
- Through dialogue, people become better informed and they no longer rely on hearsay or assumptions.
- It allows questions and understanding.

Interaction

If you understand someone, even if you do not share the same opinions or have the same beliefs, you are less likely to dislike them, to spread lies about them or consider them bad. If you feel listened to, you are less likely to feel frustrated and angry. You are less likely to resort to violence or aggression to express your feelings.

Interaction further helps understanding between different groups. Interaction may happen in different ways, for example: sharing space or resources, holding events together and discussing ideas about something. This can be helpful in bringing different religions together.

World Religion Day

> The Dublin City Interfaith Forum organises events like World Religion Day. The 2018 event was in the Bahá'í World Centre in Dublin. The theme for this event was Unity and the aim was to: unite people – whatever their faith – by showing that there are common foundations to all religions, and that we can work together to help humanity live in harmony.

Source: Dublin City Interfaith Forum website

The Interfaith Walk of Peace, organised by the Dublin City Interfaith Forum: Do you think events like this help members of minority religions in Ireland to feel more included?

Did You Know?

? In 1986 in Assisi, Pope John Paul II held an international World Day of Prayer for Peace. This inspired a Catholic community in Rome called Sant'Egidio to organise a meeting every year since called The International Prayer for Peace. This takes place in cities across Europe. Representatives from all the major world religions are invited to discuss issues of peace and take part in discussion panels and prayer services to encourage peace throughout the world.

Review and Reflect

1. What is dialogue?
2. How does dialogue happen?
3. Is dialogue important for peace? Why?
4. Give an example of an organisation that encourages dialogue between members of different world religions.

Dialogue and Interaction in a Major Religion

Within each of the major world religions are different groups, sometimes referred to as branches, sects, denominations or traditions.

- In Islam, there are two main groups – Sunni and Shia. There are also Ahmadiyya, Ibadi and Sufi Muslims.

- In Christianity, there are three main branches – the Orthodox Church, the Roman Catholic Church and Protestant Churches. Among the Protestant churches, there are many different denominations such as Church of Ireland, Methodist, Quaker, Presbyterian, Baptist, Seventh-day Adventist and Salvation Army.

- In Judaism, the different groups include Orthodox, Conservative, Reformed and Progressive.

- Buddhism has three main groups – Theravada, Mahayana and Tibetan.

- In Hinduism, the religion is varied depending on the worship of the different Gods, traditions and rituals. The two most popular Gods are Vishnu and Shiva, and they fall into two groups called Vaishnavism and Shaivism.

Religious Divisions

There are many reasons for there being subgroups in these religions. In some cases, divisions occur because of location, language or culture. However, in many cases an event, a person or a disagreement led to a split, e.g. the Reformation in Christianity. This can lead to problems between the subgroups and has often been very **divisive**.

Most followers feel that their branch, group or sect is the correct way to be a Hindu, a Jew, a Buddhist, a Christian or a Muslim. Groups may find it hard to work together and to accept their differences. The best way to overcome the division is to communicate, to discuss, to understand and to find common ground: to realise that each is just a different way of following a religion.

What Does This Mean?

Divisive: Causing disagreement or hostility between people.

Discussion is very important for overcoming division.

Healing Racism Series

Muslim Mythbusters

Why would a flyer for a 'healing racism' talk use images like these?

Review and Reflect

1. What are the **two** main groups found within Islam?
2. What are the **three** main branches of Christianity?
3. Who are the most popular Gods in Hinduism?
4. What does 'divisive' mean?
5. Are there many ways of following the same religion? Explain your answer.

Orthodox   Roman Catholic

Protestant

Did You Know?

? Cassius Clay was born in 1942. After converting to Islam, he changed his name to Muhammad Ali. Muhammad Ali was three times heavyweight champion of the world and an Olympic gold medal winner. His is considered by many to be the greatest boxer of all time.

Ali was drafted to the US Army to fight in the Vietnam War. When he refused, he was prosecuted and convicted. Ali issued the following statement:

> It is in the light of my consciousness as a Muslim minister and my own personal convictions that I take my stand in rejecting the call to be inducted. ... I find I cannot be true to my beliefs in my religion by accepting such a call. I am dependent upon Allah as the final judge of those actions brought about by my own conscience.

The Supreme Court eventually overturned Ali's conviction in 1971, but his stand cost him dearly. He lost all his titles and his licence to fight. Muhammad Ali died in 2016 aged 74.

The History and Development of Christianity

A basic look at Christian history shows the moments when division took place. Here is a brief outline of the events.

- For around 300 years from the time of Jesus, Christianity grew and spread throughout the Roman world, especially around the area of the eastern Mediterranean. This was despite persecution by the Romans. The community was made up of small groups with male and female leaders, who taught and led these early Christians. They often met in secret and were forced to hide their religion from the authorities. Some were killed by the Romans.

- In the fourth century, the Roman Emperor Constantine became Christian and the religion spread and developed. More churches were built, and the community formalised the statements of faith or creeds. It became more organised in terms of leaders and roles.

This ancient Byzantine mosaic in the Hagia Sophia in Istanbul, Turkey, depicts the Emperor Constantine offering gifts to Jesus.

- In 1054, the first big divide in Christianity took place. Known as the Great Schism, it divided Christianity into East and West. The Eastern Orthodox Church used Greek as its language and was centred on the city of Constantinople (now Istanbul). The Orthodox Church was led by the Patriarch of Constantinople. The Western Church used Latin as its language and was centred on the city of Rome. The Roman Church was led by the Pope or Bishop of Rome.

- In the sixteenth century, some people wanted to change or 'reform' the Western Church, which they felt had become corrupt. They disagreed with the Church on issues like the number of sacraments, the leadership of the Pope, transubstantiation (the belief that the bread and wine in the Eucharist turn into the body and blood of Christ), the need for priests to stay unmarried and the importance of Church teaching and tradition. In 1517 in Wittenberg, Germany, a monk named Martin Luther posted 95 theses against the selling of **indulgences** and other corrupt practices in the Roman Catholic Church. This event is seen as the beginning of the Reformation. This eventually led to a complete split in the Western Church, as it divided into the Roman Catholic Church and the Protestant Churches.

What Does This Mean?

Indulgence: A partial or full remission of the punishment of sin granted by the Roman Catholic Church. In the Middle Ages, this was seen as a way to shorten the person's time in Purgatory. This was where it was believed a person's soul went after they died and before they were accepted into heaven.

Did You Know?

? Protestant is a general name for the Churches that are seen as 'reformed' and do not accept the leadership of the Pope. There are many different types of Protestant, including Anglicans, Methodists, Presbyterians, Quakers, Baptists and more.

Three Branches of Christianity

There are many ways of being a Christian. All Christians have things in common as well as things that make them different and diverse. It is good to have diversity. Finding common ground and ways to work together are not about trying to make everyone the same.

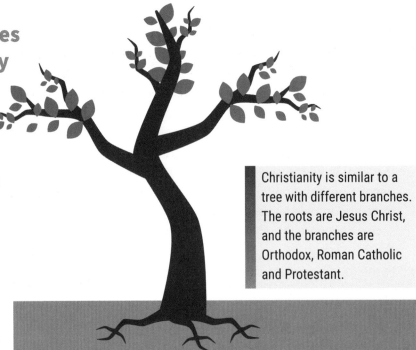

Christianity is similar to a tree with different branches. The roots are Jesus Christ, and the branches are Orthodox, Roman Catholic and Protestant.

Similarities	Differences
One God	Organisation: especially leadership roles
Followers of Jesus	Number and understanding of the sacraments
Bible is the main sacred text	Rituals and how they are carried out
The Golden Rule	Importance placed on Church teachings and traditions

Over to You – Exploration

Christians are all followers of Jesus Christ and all part of the one religion. It seems sad that, at times, Christians find it difficult to engage in dialogue with each other. In groups, discuss and answer the following:

1. Why do you think dialogue between different branches of Christianity has been difficult?
2. What problems can this cause?
3. How do you think it could be overcome?
4. If you were encouraging Christians from different branches to communicate better with each other, what points would you make?

The Irish Council of Churches

The Irish Council of Churches provides a platform for the different churches in Ireland to meet together and connect.

- Their vision is 'to be a benchmark for unity in Christ for Churches and Communities globally'.
- Their values include 'respecting and seeking to understand each other's beliefs; we are aware of our diversity while recognising the presence of Christ in each other'.

Source: The Irish Council of Churches website

The Global Christian Forum

The Global Christian Forum (GCF) is an organisation that promotes **ecumenism**. It aims to bring the different Christian Churches closer together. The GCF wants to help unity, co-operation and understanding between different Christian churches. The GCF is defined as follows:

> A gathering of global Christian churches and organisations bringing together all the major streams of world Christianity. The GCF is an open space where all Christians can meet to nurture unity by fostering mutual respect and understanding as well as by addressing together common challenges.

Source: Global Christian Forum website

The GCF brought together 230 leaders from all the main Christian traditions at a conference in 2007. The GCF is about:

> bringing into conversation with one another Christians and churches from very different traditions that have had very little contact or never even talked to each other. It is about building bridges where there are none, overcoming prejudices, creating and nurturing new relationships.

Source: Global Christian Forum website

On 24 April 2018, the Global Christian Forum gathered in Bogotá under the theme of 'Let mutual love continue'.

Photo © Albin Hillert/WCC

Over to You – Enquiry

1. Find out the names of **10** different churches and organisations involved in the GCF.
2. Which continents and countries do they come from?
3. Find out the locations of the **three** big global gatherings organised by GCF in 2007, 2011 and 2018.
4. What was the theme for each of these meetings?
5. How many participants were involved?
6. The Global Christian Forum has a weekly prayer cycle. Research the different prayers and discuss how relevant they are for the world today.
7. Do you think the Global Christian Forum is a good example of ecumenism (see definition on page 189)? Explain why or why not.
8. Do you think it is an important forum for promoting peace and reconciliation between Christians in the world today? Explain why or why not.

Challenges to Dialogue and Peace

What Is Islamophobia?

- **Islamophobia** is the dislike and fear of Muslims and prejudice against the Islamic faith.
- Islamophobia is a form of racism.
- Islamophobia can lead to **discrimination** against Muslims.
- Islamophobia **stereotypes** Muslims; it portrays all Muslims as being the same.
- Islamophobia can lead to the abuse of people who are Muslim, including mental and physical bullying or attacks.

Ireland and Islamophobia

Sadly, Islamophobia happens in Ireland. In 2016 the *Irish Times* reported a serious rise in Islamophobia in Ireland. The article by Sorcha Pollak reported that the director of the European Network Against Racism Ireland (Enar), Shane O'Curry, claimed that:

> Islamophobic language, and references to Muslims as terrorists, bomb makers and members of Islamic State, is becoming increasingly apparent in Irish society... the rhetoric used overseas towards Islam is being 'recycled in Ireland'. It's as if the language of Islamophobia is international but being spoken with an Irish accent.

Dr James Carr is a sociologist and lecturer in the University of Limerick who researches Islamophobia. He wrote the book, *Experiences of Islamophobia: Living with Racism in the Neoliberal Era*. In an interview with RTÉ, Dr Carr pointed out that in his research he had engaged with 343 Muslim men and women in Ireland. Over 36 per cent of them had experienced anti-Muslim hostility and discrimination.

Over to You – Exploration

1. In pairs, think of the different ways Muslim adults and children experience racism in Ireland. Share your ideas with the class.
2. Discuss how this might make Muslim people living in Ireland feel.
3. Discuss ways that this problem can be addressed.
4. Suggest ways your school or local community could take steps to actively combat this form of racism.

The Media and Islamophobia

Islamophobia is often associated with seeing Muslims as a political force in the world and as a source of terrorism. In Britain, the media have faced a lot of criticism for the way they report on the Muslim community. This reporting has contributed to a rise in anti-Muslim racism, especially following the 9/11 attacks in New York in 2001, attacks in Paris in 2015 and in London in 2017. Research published by the University of Cambridge in 2016 showed that: 'Mainstream media reporting about Muslim communities is contributing to an atmosphere of rising hostility towards Muslims in Britain.'

What the media fail to report is that the vast majority of Muslims are against terrorism. Many Muslims are victims of extremists, and most Muslims want to help work with others to combat terrorism. This is also a serious issue in the USA, a problem made worse by the anti-Muslim remarks made by President Trump.

Photo: Mark Henderson

Is this image of young Muslim girls one that you see in the media? Does it fit with the stereotype?

The image is of Diverse City FC from Sport Against Racism Ireland's (SARI) Hijabs and Hat-tricks programme. They were playing at the SARI/UNHCR Ireland World Refugee Day Fair Play Cup event.

Review and Reflect

1. Whom do you think the media is appealing to when it reports on the Muslim community in a biased and unfair way?
2. Are politicians involved in creating hostile attitudes towards Muslims?
3. Do you think the media plays a big role in how people view minority religions?
4. Do you think journalists are responsible for the way they report? Should they take into account the influence they have on other people?
5. Discuss the difference between a fact and an opinion. How is that relevant to the issue of Islamophobia?

Sectarianism

Sectarianism is hatred of some people because they belong to a different group (sect) of a religion.

- Sectarianism is caused by misinformation, fear and ignorance. It occurs when people do not respect, trust or want to understand each other.
- Sectarianism is a serious problem in society. When people are treated unfairly, not given the same opportunities and not allowed the same rights (to go to certain places, or to have certain jobs), this is called discrimination.
- Sectarianism leads to discrimination and is damaging to people, relationships and society. It has no place in a peaceful society, where people should be able to live in harmony and be free from fear or violence.

Northern Ireland has had problems with sectarianism. Only through a peace process, which involved a lot of dialogue and interaction, has this been addressed and is beginning to be overcome.

The British army patrolled the streets of Northern Ireland during the Troubles.

Why do you think someone has written graffiti about the Pope on the wall?

Corrymeela Community

For over 50 years, the Corrymeela Community has worked for peace and understanding in Northern Ireland. It was founded in 1965 by Ray Davey, a former Second World War chaplain, with some students from Queen's University in Belfast. Their original motivation was to create a place where people of goodwill could come together and be a community. The growing sectarianism in Northern Ireland at that time concerned people like Ray. His experiences during the war, particularly witnessing the bombing of Dresden, encouraged Ray to actively promote peace. Ray was:

> ... concerned at the tensions brewing between people of different political, religious and ideological differences in Northern Ireland. Corrymeela grew out of this concern. It began before the Troubles and continued after the Troubles, promoting tolerance between people of differing backgrounds and beliefs. Corrymeela offers space for an analysis of the underlying dynamics of conflict, fracture, scapegoating and violence that we see across so many spheres of our world today.

Source: Corrymeela Community website

Corrymeela and Reconciliation

Corrymeela promotes **reconciliation** through encouraging interaction, building positive relationships and healing social, political and religious divisions. Corrymeela has a residential centre on the north coast that hosts over 11,000 people every year. The community also has an outreach programme that involves going out to work with communities, schools, families, youth groups and others.

Corrymeela has an international reputation for peace-building and reconciliation. It now has 150 members, 50 associate members and friends all over the world.

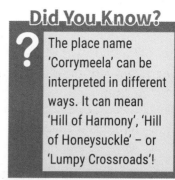

CORRYMEELA IS A COMMUNITY OF CHRISTIANS COMMITTED TO PEACE AND RECONCILIATION

CORRYMEELA CENTRE

A SAFE PLACE FOR ALL
FOR ENCOUNTER, MEETING AND DIALOGUE

WELCOME

The Dalai Lama visiting Corrymeela

People attend the Corrymeela Centre to learn about peace and reconciliation.

Review and Reflect

1. Define sectarianism. What causes sectarianism?
2. When was Corrymeela founded?
3. Why was it started?
4. Do you think Ray Davey's experiences as a chaplain in the Second World War would have influenced his interest in peace and reconciliation? Explain why or why not.
5. Do you think a community like Corrymeela can help to bring people together and to promote peace? Explain why or why not.

Expressing Beliefs

Revision Questions

Enquiry

1. What is a dialogue?
2. Give an example of dialogue between major world religions.
3. What is interaction?
4. Give an example of interaction between different branches of Christianity.
5. What is peace?
6. What is reconciliation?
7. Name an organisation that works to promote peace and reconciliation.

Exploration

1. Think about the importance of dialogue in promoting peace. Share your thoughts with the class.
2. Think about the need for reconciliation between members of different branches of the same religion. Share your thoughts with the class.
3. Think about the need for peace in the world and the responsibility of every person towards contributing to a peaceful society. Share your thoughts with the class.
4. Explore with your class ways that you can contribute to a more peaceful world.

Reflection and Action

- Find out about the Buddhist leader and pacifist Thich Nhat Hanh. Make a presentation about him for the class. Discuss the impact his teaching has on the world and the contribution he makes to promoting peace and understanding.
- Research the World Council of Churches (WCC). Find out when it was founded, what it does and the impact it has on the world in terms of promoting peace and reconciliation. Make a presentation for your class and discuss the contribution the WCC makes to promoting peace.
- Research more about Corrymeela. Make a presentation to the class about the work it does and discuss the contribution the Corrymeela Community makes to peace-building and reconciliation.
- As a class, create a mural, poster or exhibition promoting peace between the different world religions and different branches of the different world religions.

Organisations for Justice

Learning Outcome 1.11

Research religious or other organisations, working at a national or international level to promote justice, peace and reconciliation and consider how their work is an expression of their founding vision.

Learning Intentions

By the end of this chapter I will:

- Know what is meant by peace, justice and reconciliation
- Know the names of organisations that work on the issues of peace, justice and reconciliation
- Reflect on how the work of these organisations is an expression of their founding vision

Key Skills and Wellbeing

- Managing information and thinking
- Being creative
- Working with others
- Communicating

I am aware of my values and the influences on my decisions. I am aware of my ability to contribute to a more just and peaceful society.

Keywords

justice ▪ peace ▪ reconciliation

The atomic bomb exploding in Hiroshima, Japan and its aftermath. How do you reconcile people after events like these?

Introduction

In this chapter, we will research national and international organisations working for **justice**, **peace** and **reconciliation**. These are serious issues in today's world. History shows how much war has destroyed people's lives. Today, threats to peace and stability come in many forms: from disputes over land, the desire for resources and opposing political outlooks. The organisations working to promote justice, peace and reconciliation can be national (working within a country) or international (working between many countries). The work that they do is very important, and it is often a reflection of the beliefs and vision of a founder or of a group of people.

Icebreaker

 Brainstorm
1. What is justice?
2. What happens when people are not treated fairly?

 ## Action Verb Focus: Research

Research: To find information, sort, record and analyse it.

When we research something, we find out as much as possible about it. We can use books and the internet, and we can ask people questions. Research can include doing surveys or studying something by making observations and recording what has been discovered. When we research, we take notes and sift through all the information that is available to us before deciding what is most useful. Then, we can consider what we have learned to come to a fuller understanding of the topic and to come to a conclusion about it.

Justice

Justice is treating people equally, fairly and respectfully. Justice is also connected with human rights. The Universal Declaration of Human Rights states:

> recognition of the inherent dignity and of the equal and inalienable rights of all members of the human family is the foundation of freedom, justice and peace in the world.

Laws are important in making sure society is just and fair. They can make all people equal and ensure that people are treated well. Good laws force governments and individuals to treat people fairly and with respect. Laws reflect the societies that make them; therefore, an unjust society can have unjust laws.

> Why do you think Lady Justice is depicted blindfolded?

Peace

In Chapter 23 we looked at the concept of peace. Peace is living without conflict or hostility. It is living in safety and without fear of violence. It is when people can live together in harmony and tranquillity.

The United Nations charter is primarily about working for peace and harmony in the world. It states that:

> we, the peoples of the United Nations, determined to save succeeding generations from the scourge of war ... and for these ends to practise tolerance and live together in peace.

This sculpture was created by Swedish artist Carl Fredrik Reuterswärd. It is called *Non-Violence*. What other symbols of peace can you think of?

* Many would say peace is an absence of war, but it is more than that. It is living with peace of mind, freedom and security. It is living in harmony with one another and meeting the needs of people. It is giving people their dignity and rights. It is a society where all can flourish and develop and nobody is marginalised or threatened.

Reconciliation

Reconciliation is about bringing people together after an argument, a disagreement or a conflict. It involves asking people to build a positive relationship with each other even when they have opposing beliefs or viewpoints. Reconciliation restores damaged relationships and broken communities or societies. It is not easy to achieve and it needs time and a commitment from both sides. As we saw in Chapter 23, reconciliation needs dialogue and interaction from both sides in order to work.

Shaking hands is often seen as a symbol of reconciliation and peace. Why? Do you think it is a powerful symbol?

? The sacrament of reconciliation is one of the seven sacraments of the Roman Catholic Church. It involves a person seeking forgiveness and absolution from God for wrongdoing. The reconciliation is the repairing of the person's relationship with God through participation in the sacrament. It is also known as the sacrament of penance and confession. In it, the priest absolves the person, granting them 'pardon and peace'.

The following organisations work to promote justice, peace and reconciliation. Some of these organisations are national and some international. Some international organisations have national sections in Ireland or associated Irish groups. We will consider how their work is an expression of their founding vision.

Glencree: Peace and Reconciliation Centre

Background to Glencree

Glencree was founded in 1974 as a response to the increasing violence in Northern Ireland. It is a place for people to come together from both sides of the divide to share their stories and work together for a better future. People can start to reconcile and learn how the world can be peaceful, in contrast to violence, conflict and sectarianism. It demonstrates a way to transform society through dialogue, non-violence and reconciliation.

The values of Glencree are impartiality, respect, non-violence and inclusivity.

Vision and Beliefs

> Glencree believes in a shared world; where human rights are protected; where diversity and different identities are cherished; where all can live free from the fear of violence, abuse and with dignity and respect; and where differences and conflicts are transformed peacefully.

The mission of Glencree is:

> to help deepen reconciliation within and between communities on the island of Ireland and in selected contexts internationally.

Source: Glencree website

The Work of Glencree

Some of the work that Glencree has been involved with over the past 40 years includes:

- Working with victims and survivors of conflict alongside former combatants. This work helps people to see each other as fellow human beings, rather than as enemies.

- Working with and educating young people and getting young people together from different backgrounds, religions and communities. Glencree currently has a programme to train young peace-builders.

- Working with communities and politicians to help them to build a more peaceful future in Ireland.

- Working with refugees. Glencree engages in cultural diversity programmes. These help host communities and immigrants to find mutual understanding. They help people to integrate into their new communities and work to combat racism, including Islamophobia.

- Working with women on issues of gender violence and equality. Glencree helps women become more involved in leadership roles for peace and reconciliation.

International Work

Glencree has become a beacon to the wider world. It has been involved in community building, reconciliation and bridge-building between people from other countries and war zones. It gives them a place that is neutral and understanding, somewhere to share their stories and express their feelings to one another. Glencree's international work has seen them host workshops and other programmes with people involved in conflicts in places such as Israel, Palestine, Sri Lanka, Colombia, Liberia, Nepal, Afghanistan and Liberia.

Glencree is a neutral and secure place where important dialogue can take place. It has become a place with an international reputation for peace-building.

The Founding Vision of Glencree

Many of Glencree's founders were motivated by a Christian understanding of peace and love, and bringing about the Kingdom of God. The community is not affiliated to any church or religious organisation. It is inclusive of all people, whatever their background – religious or non-religious. The Glencree Community's work for peace and reconciliation today is still very much connected with the past and their vision for a shared world. It comes from the 'conviction that there must be a better way than violence and vandalism, intolerance and sectarianism' (Source: Glencree website).

Reconciliation and peace-building need people to be creative and imaginative. Most of all they need people to get involved.

Over to You – Exploration

1. When was Glencree founded?
2. What was the motivation for starting a peace and reconciliation centre in Glencree?
3. What type of work does it do?
4. What are the issues in the world today that Glencree addresses?
5. Do you think the work that the Glencree community does is difficult? Explain your answer.
6. Do you think the work it does is important or relevant in today's world? Explain your answer.
7. Research more about Glencree. Find out about the impact Glencree has had on communities and individuals.

The St Vincent de Paul: A Just Society

Background to the Society

The Society of St Vincent de Paul is a charity that aims to 'fight poverty in all its forms through the practical assistance to people in need'. The society was founded by Frédéric Ozanam in 1833 in Paris. Frédéric was only 20 when he and some student friends started the organisation to help the poor. Frédéric once said:

Society of St. Vincent de Paul

> You must not be content with tiding the poor over the poverty crisis. You must study their condition and the injustices which brought about such poverty, with the aim of long-term improvement.

Frédéric and his friends named their organisation after a seventeenth-century French priest, Vincent de Paul. He was famous for his charitable work and compassion and was made a saint in 1737.

Vision and Beliefs

The Society of St Vincent de Paul has branches in 140 countries. Its 1.5 million volunteers and 700,000 members help 30 million people. It is a truly international organisation.

The society is based on Christian values. The mission statement of the Irish branch, founded in 1844, says it 'seeks to respond to the call of every Christian to bring the love of Christ to those in need'.

The vision of the Irish society is:

> To make Ireland a fairer place; where caring for each other and our children, older people and people with disabilities is valued and supported; where individuals, families and communities can participate fully in work and society; and where an adequately resourced state, a strong economy, employment and business support the type of society that we wish to live in.

Source: St Vincent de Paul website

What motivates people to give to charity?

Working for a Just and Inclusive Society

The main aim of the society is to provide support and friendship to people, to help people become self-sufficient and to work for social justice. The society's work includes:

- Providing services to people, such as shops, resource centres, social housing projects, daycare centres and hostels
- Working with policymakers to lobby on issues such as more affordable education
- Helping low-income families to manage bills

Over to You – Enquiry

1. Discuss the link between the work of the Society of St Vincent de Paul and the concept of justice.
2. Reflect on the founding vision of Frédéric Ozanam and the work that the society does today.

The Red Cross/Red Crescent

Background to the Red Cross

The origins of the International Committee of the Red Cross (ICRC) go back to 1863 when a group met in Switzerland to organise a neutral independent organisation to care for wounded soldiers. Henry Dunant, a devout Christian, was one of the five members of the first committee. Henry had witnessed a bloody battle and written a book about it. The book, *Souvenir de Solférino*, called for better care for wounded soldiers.

Since 1863, the Committee of the Red Cross has evolved into an organisation with the primary goal of helping victims of war and conflict.

The work of the ICRC involves creating rules regarding war, on issues such as:

- The use of weapons
- The treatment of prisoners
- The protection of civilians
- The protection of medical officers in conflict situations

The ICRC also:

- Visits prisoners of war
- Helps reunite families following conflict
- Provides food, water and medical aid in conflict situations
- Searches for missing persons

It promotes respect for international humanitarian law, especially the Geneva Conventions.

IFRC

 # International Federation of Red Cross and Red Crescent Societies

The International Federation of Red Cross and Red Crescent Societies (IFRC) was founded in 1919 in Paris. Following the First World War, many thought that a federation of Red Cross Societies would be a good idea.

> The first objective was to improve the health of people in countries that had suffered greatly during the four years of war. Its goals were to strengthen and unite, for health activities, already-existing Red Cross Societies and to promote the creation of new societies.

The vision of the IFRC is:

> To inspire, encourage, facilitate and promote at all times all forms of humanitarian activities by National Societies, with a view to preventing and alleviating human suffering, and thereby contributing to the maintenance and promotion of human dignity and peace in the world.

Source: International Federation of the Red Cross and Red Crescent website

The work of the IFRC includes disaster response, disaster preparedness and healthcare in the community. It is a strong advocate for humanitarian values and has worked tirelessly with refugees and other victims of both human and natural disasters.

The Irish Red Cross is a member of the IFRC, which includes 190 national Red Cross and Red Crescent societies worldwide.

The Syrian Arab Red Crescent helps displaced people in the civil war in Syria. How important is this work in Syria? What difference do these volunteers make?

Over to You – Enquiry

 Research more on **one** of the following:

- The work of the Irish Red Cross
- The Geneva Conventions
- Henry Dunant and the beginnings of the Red Cross Society
- The work of the ICRC or IFRC at the present time

Pax Christi: An International Organisation for Peace

Background to Pax Christi

Pax Christi is a Catholic organisation that was set up in 1945. It was formed to encourage reconciliation between countries and people following the Second World War.

Pax Christi is an international movement, with over 100 independent member organisations in over 50 countries and five continents.

Vision and Beliefs

Pax Christi is:

> working toward reconciliation, peace and justice, and building bridges with civil society in the secular world, as well as with people working for justice and peace in other Churches and Faiths.

Source: Pax Christi website

It is a faith-based movement with a commitment to prayer, study and action for peace:

> It strives for dialogue and co-operation with non-governmental organisations and movements working in related fields – whether they are Christian, Muslim, Jewish, Buddhist, or non-religious groups.

Source: Pax Christi website

The Work of Pax Christi

The work of Pax Christi includes the following:

- Dialogue and discussion on peace
- Organising anti-war demonstrations
- Highlighting the illegal arms trade
- Consulting with the United Nations, the Council of Europe, UNICEF and UNESCO
- Providing opportunities for interfaith dialogue and co-operation
- Sending messages of hope to people in conflict situations
- Education and youth work

What Does This Mean?

Pax Christi: Latin for 'Peace of Christ'.

What symbols for peace do you recognise?

Pax Christi Ireland

Pax Christi started working in Ireland in 1958. Its work here has involved campaigning on issues around nuclear disarmament, child soldiers, landmines, the sale of small arms and light weapons, and promoting peace and reconciliation in Northern Ireland.

Pax Christi's founding vision is that peace is possible. The basis for its work was the desire for reconciliation after the Second World War. It was inspired by faith and based on the Gospel of Jesus Christ. Since its foundation the organisation has evolved:

> from a desire for reconciliation between nations, the pathway has led to all aspects of life: the economics of the arms trade, the theology of inter-religious dialogue, the ethics of globalisation, and the practice of nonviolence.

Source: Pax Christi website

The work it carries out today is still true to that founding vision as the organisation continues to work for peace, respect for human rights, justice and reconciliation.

Do you think protests against war, nuclear weapons or other issues can make any difference? Do they give an alternative viewpoint?

Review and Reflect

1. Why was the organisation Pax Christi originally founded?
2. How has its vision and work developed?
3. How many countries have member organisations?
4. What issues has the Irish member organisation worked on?
5. Do you think the values of Christianity have been an inspiration for the work of Pax Christi? Explain why or why not.
6. Do you think that Christians should involve themselves in movements like Pax Christi? Explain why or why not.

ICAN

The International Campaign to Abolish Nuclear Weapons (ICAN) was founded in 2007. It is a coalition of non-governmental organisations working to abolish nuclear weapons, to promote a more peaceful world and to highlight the humanitarian impact of nuclear explosions. In 2017, ICAN was awarded the Nobel Peace Prize.

Setsuko Thurlow and Beatrice Fihn from ICAN, receiving the Nobel Peace Prize Medal and Diploma in Oslo on 10 December 2017

Did You Know?

The Women's International League for Peace and Freedom (WILPF) was founded in 1915 during the First World War in the Netherlands. It has branches in 33 countries. The WILPF brings women together for peace and aims to create a peaceful world with justice and equality for all.

Over to You – Enquiry

1. Find out how many countries have nuclear weapons.
2. Research the Treaty on the Prohibition of Nuclear Weapons that was adopted by the United Nations in 2017. How many countries have signed the treaty so far?
3. What is the Irish government's position on nuclear weapons?
4. Which is the only country to have used a nuclear weapon in a war?
5. Find out more about the humanitarian impact of nuclear weapons.

Over to You – Reflection and Action

1. Discuss how much of a threat nuclear weapons are to world peace.
2. Write an essay addressed to the leaders of countries with nuclear weapons asking them to abolish them.

   Or

   Design a poster campaigning for nuclear weapons to be abolished.
3. Research more on the work of the Women's International League for Peace and Freedom.

Revision Questions

Enquiry

1. Define the following terms:
    - Peace
    - Justice
    - Reconciliation
2. Name **one** international organisation working for a more peaceful world.
3. Name **one** national organisation that helps to reconcile people.
4. Connect an organisation's work with its founding vision and give an example.
5. Do you think work for peace, justice and reconciliation is important? Give reasons for your answer.

Exploration

1. Research **one** of the following organisations and find out what work it does for justice, peace or reconciliation.
    - The Peace People, Northern Ireland – building a just and peaceful society
    - Christian Aid – international organisation for a just world
    - Amnesty International – working for justice and human rights
2. How much is the work it does connected with its founding vision?

Reflection and Action

- Think about what makes a peaceful society.
- Consider what the obstacles to reconciliation are.
- Reflect on the work of organisations in the world today that promote a more just society.
- Reflect on the efforts made by some people and groups to work for peace.
- Start a poster campaign in your school to encourage your school community to act in a peaceful manner.

25 Life's Big Questions

Learning Outcome 2.2

Consider responses from one major world religion and from a non-religious world view to some big questions about the meaning of life, such as, Why are we here? How should we live? What happens when we die?

Learning Intentions

By the end of this chapter I will:
- Be able to list what the big questions about the meaning of life are
- Understand the concept of the 'meaning of life'
- Have explored where people find meaning in life
- Have learned about a religious and non-religious understanding of life's big questions

Key Skills and Wellbeing

- Being creative
- Staying well
- Working with others
- Managing information and thinking

I am aware of my thoughts and feelings and I can make sense of them. I feel listened to and valued.

Keywords

materialistic ▪ philosophy ▪ purpose

This sculpture is by the French artist Auguste Rodin. It is called *The Thinker*. What is it all about?

Introduction

People from different cultures and traditions around the world have wondered about life's big questions. For example: Why we are here? What is life all about? They think about the meaning of life, death and the existence of God. This chapter focuses on how these questions find expression and considers how different world views – including religious ones – answer them.

 Action Verb Focus: Consider

Consider: To think carefully about something.

Sometimes, you consider things when you have a decision to make and you are reflecting on various possibilities or choices. When you consider something, you might find it useful to discuss it and to think about different opinions or ideas around it. To consider can involve reflecting upon the significance of something.

For example, you might consider how important your family is to you when deciding whether to move away from home for work. You might be asked to consider someone's feelings when you have upset them. Here, we are considering different responses that people have to the big questions about life.

Icebreaker

 In pairs, write **three** questions for each other:

1. The first question should be something that is easy to answer.
2. The second question should be difficult, but one that has an answer.
3. The third question should be something the other person simply could not know (in fact, nobody could).
4. Discuss the questions in life that we may never fully know or understand and share your ideas with the class.

Finding Meaning in Life

People want their lives to have meaning. Some people find meaning through their relationships with other people, some through doing the things they love, and others from believing in something and seeing themselves as part of a bigger plan for the world.

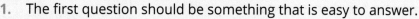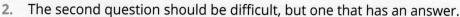
What Does This Mean?

Philosophy: The 'love of wisdom'. Philosophy has different branches – it includes asking questions about the world and reality, about morals or what is good, and about knowledge (how we know what we know).

Many people look to religion for answers to the questions they have in life. Others look to **philosophy**, and some think it is for each person to find their own meaning to life.

The world view of individuals is shaped by many factors:

- How they are brought up
- What their religious understanding and background is
- How they live
- What they experience in life

Difficult Questions

Some of the questions that many people think about do not have easy answers.
These might include:

- Why do I exist?
- Does my life have a bigger purpose or meaning?
- What happens to me when I die?
- Is there a God or Gods?
- How do I live a good life?

Some people block their search for meaning because:

- They are too busy to seek answers to the questions.
- They are not having their basic needs met.
- They live in a **materialistic** society that replaces meaning with objects.
- They experience too many problems in the world, leading to apathy and indifference.

What Does This Mean?

Materialistic: Concerned with material things. A materialistic person is someone who is focused on possessions and money.

Searching for Meaning

From ancient times to the present day, people have wondered about the world and their place in it. People have asked questions like: Why are we here? What happens when we die? How should we live? These questions have been expressed through art, story and ritual. In ancient times, people placed goods in the graves of those who had died, showing their belief in an afterlife of some kind. Ancient stories and myths explored questions about the origins of the world, and the ancient philosophers considered the question of how we know what is good, true or beautiful.

Over to You – Exploration

1. In groups, think about the phrase 'the meaning of life'.
   - What do you think it means? What does it make you think of?
   - Where can people try to find an answer to the question: 'What is the meaning of life?'
   - Do you think there is a meaning to life? Explain why or why not.
2. Discuss your ideas in the group and then share them with the rest of the class.

Shared Religious Themes

Religions try to explain and to give answers to the difficult questions listed below. The answers may not always satisfy everyone in that religion, but they give guidance to those people seeking solutions.

- Each religion sees human existence as part of a bigger plan, that people have a purpose and meaning.
- They believe that there is a reason for human existence, that individuals matter and that their lives have meaning.
- They believe that there is a good and bad way to live.
- They believe that people have free will in choosing how they live their lives.
- They believe that there is a spiritual existence, as well as a physical one. They believe in some form of afterlife – something that exists beyond the physical world.

Man's Search for Meaning

People are always searching for meaning. Viktor Frankl's book *Man's Search for Meaning* describes his time in a concentration camp and how, even when suffering, people need to feel a sense of meaning. He wrote: 'Those who have a "why" to live, can bear almost any "how".'

We will briefly explore what each of the five major world religions and humanism teach about finding meaning in life and answering the big questions.

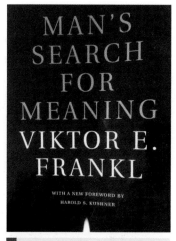

Man's Search for Meaning by Viktor Frankl

Hinduism

In the Hindu understanding of the world, all living things are part of a universal soul called Brahman. Every soul (**atman**) is going through a process of reincarnation called *samsara*, with continuous life cycles until the soul finally reaches *moksha* or union back with Brahman. *Karma*, the law of cause and effect, impacts each life cycle and brings the person or soul either closer to or further away from Brahman. If a person does bad deeds, they will create bad *karma* and in their next life, they will be further away from achieving *moksha*. However, doing good deeds creates good *karma* and brings that person closer to achieving *moksha*.

When Hindus die, their bodies are cremated to release the soul for reincarnation.

Dharma

Dharma, or sacred duty, informs people how to live for each stage of their life. For young people, their duty is to study and respect their parents, while a parent's duty is to look after their family and provide for them.

Moksha means 'liberation'. It is freedom from desires and attachment to worldly possessions, freedom from the sorrows and suffering of this life. *Moksha* breaks the cycle of *samsara*, the soul's passing from one body to another.

In this way, Hindus have an understanding of how to live a good life and their place in the world, the bigger purpose of life and the answer to the question of the afterlife.

Judaism

In Judaism, God is the source of the whole world. God has reached out to the people through revelations and prophets and wants to have a relationship with the people. In Judaism, that relationship is through the covenant, or agreement, between the people and God. The Torah, which is the 'law' or 'instruction', is the side of the agreement the people should live by, and it shows every person how to live a good life.

Afterlife

There are varying traditions and understandings in the Jewish sacred texts about an afterlife. Some talk about a place and others about a spiritual resurrection. In the Tanakh, *sheol* is the place where the dead go. In other Jewish writings, there is mention of a world to come for those who are spiritually resurrected. There are also references to *Gan Eden* (the Garden of Eden) as a place where the righteous will go.

The different branches of Judaism have different understandings about an afterlife. Many say the important thing is to live by the covenant, follow the Torah, carry out good deeds (*mitzvot*) for their own sake, and leave the issue of reward and punishment to God. Within a Jewish understanding, there is a bigger purpose to the world: each person is important as part of God's creation and there is a way to live a good life.

In the Talmud, an important Jewish text, it states: 'Whoever saves a life, saves the entire world'. This shows how connected all life is and that each life matters. All of this gives followers of Judaism a sense of purpose and meaning, and a way to think about the big questions in life.

A girl celebrates her *bat mitzvah*.

Buddhism

In Buddhism, the purpose of each person's life is to reach a state of enlightenment called *nirvana*. As in Hinduism, all people go through many life cycles by being reincarnated. In Buddhism, this will happen until they reach *nirvana*. *Nirvana* is to be awakened, to have freedom from suffering and desire, to know and understand the world, and to have found meaning in life. Buddhists have a clear guide to follow in trying to achieve this state of enlightenment through the Noble Eightfold Path.

The Four Noble Truths also help Buddhists to understand the world and suffering. The Eightfold Path represents the eight steps to follow in order to reach your enlightenment. The steps include:

1. Right view
2. Right intention
3. Right speech
4. Right action
5. Right livelihood
6. Right effort
7. Right mindfulness
8. Right concentration

In this way, Buddhism gives people a way to seek understanding and answers to the big questions in life, and it tells each Buddhist how to live a good life.

A Buddhist monk meditating

Islam

Islam understands the whole world as belonging to Allah. Life is a gift from Allah and Allah cares for each person as a unique part of this creation. Through the Prophet Muhammad, Allah has shown how each person can live a good life. Muslims follow the Five Pillars of Islam to give meaning and purpose to their lives. The Five Pillars are:

- *Shahadah*
- *Salat*
- *Zakat*
- *Sawm*
- *Hajj*

Islam teaches that there is an afterlife or existence after death and that this depends on a person's behaviour in this life. When someone dies, Muslims believe that their deeds in this life will be judged, that the good and bad are held into account.

For Muslims, Allah is merciful and compassionate, and submitting to Allah's will is the way to achieve peace. To submit to the will of Allah is a choice, and all are given free will and choice over their lives. There is a bigger picture to life in Islam. When someone dies, there is a popular phrase from the Quran that is often said: 'Indeed we belong to Allah and indeed to Him we will return'.

People taking part in the *Hajj*, the annual Islamic pilgrimage to Mecca

Christianity

In Christianity, all people are considered to be made in the 'image and likeness' of God.

- Everyone is a unique creation, with purpose and meaning.
- There is a clear understanding in Christianity that God is the source of all life.
- God wants to have a close relationship with people.
- God does not control a person's actions and each person has free will.
- People choose the way they live, and move either closer to God or further away from God depending on how they live their lives.

God's most important revelation to people was through the person of Jesus. Through Jesus' life and teaching, people have an understanding that there is a good way to live and that there is life after death. The teachings of the Bible outline the idea of resurrection and everlasting life: that all can be saved and that God is forgiving.

There are consequences to people's behaviour, and they will be judged according to how they have lived their life. Christians are to work towards bringing about God's kingdom on earth. They should live their lives to reflect that goal, seeing all people and the earth as belonging to God and worthy of respect and love.

Prayer can be a way of reflecting on life, responding to mystery and thinking about what is important.

Humanism

In humanism, meaning is something that individuals must create for themselves. The famous French philosopher and humanist Jean-Paul Sartre said, 'man first of all exists, encounters himself, surges up in the world – and defines himself afterward'.

For many humanists, the world has no other meaning than the meaning individuals make for themselves. There is no higher plan. People are born in a particular time and place, and it is up to them, through their choices and decisions, to make their own meaning.

Personal Responsibility

In humanism, personal responsibility is emphasised. People are responsible for making something of their existence. Humanists believe that people have a responsibility to help other people and to advance humanity. Everything is achieved by human reason and understanding.

The purpose of life is to live the best life possible, to seek happiness and help others to do the same. For humanists, there is no evidence of an afterlife. People live on in the memory of others, in what they have achieved that helps future generations, or through the genes that they may have passed on to their children or grandchildren.

Each generation searches for a sense of meaning and purpose.

Review and Reflect

1. Where do each of the five major world religions and humanism see the purpose or meaning of life coming from?
2. What does each say about the question of an afterlife?
3. What do they say about how to live a good life?

Finding Meaning through Ritual

A ceremony or ritual, whether religious or non-religious, can add meaning to an important event in a person's life. The different words, gestures and symbols show the importance a person's belief has when it comes to marking the special times in life. Here are some examples:

Birth

- In Islam, the first thing a baby should hear is the **adhan**, or call to prayer.
- In Christianity, a baby is baptised, welcoming it into the community as part of God's family.
- In humanism, a naming ceremony is a way to welcome a new life into the family and community.
- In Hinduism, a baby's first haircut represents the removal of bad *karma* from a previous life.

Marriage

- At a Jewish wedding, the couple stand under a canopy. This symbolises the idea that God provides.
- At a Hindu wedding, the couple walks around the sacred flame, **arti**, taking steps to represent love, life, happiness, children, wealth, God and strength.
- At a humanist wedding, the couple are showing their love for each other publicly and making a commitment to each other in front of friends and family.

Death

- In Hinduism, the body is cremated. This allows the soul to be released for reincarnation. The flame is lit by the closest relative and prayers are said.
- In Islam, a person is buried facing Mecca and the site of the Kaaba. Prayers are said for Allah to be merciful.
- In Buddhism, death marks the transition to a new existence. It is an opportunity for all to be reminded of the teaching of the Buddha about the impermanence of this life.
- In Christianity, a person's life is celebrated at a funeral. When the body is buried or cremated, prayers are said. Though people are sad, the belief in resurrection and a person returning to God can be a source of comfort for some people.

The sacred fire is used in Hindu rituals and acts of worship. The most frequent is the *arti* ceremony.

Over to You – Exploration

1. In pairs, find out more about rituals for birth, marriage and death in **one** of the traditions.
2. Create a presentation about it for your class.
3. Explore ways in which this ritual gives meaning to a special event and reflects the person's belief about life and the meaning of life.

Finding Purpose

Many people look to things other than their beliefs to give themselves a sense of **purpose** and meaning.

Family

For many people, family gives them a strong sense of identity, a feeling of belonging and, most importantly, love. Love is one of our most basic needs. If our needs are not met, we cannot realise our true potential. A family can be a source of meaning for many people, giving a feeling of value and importance, that our lives matter.

Friends

For some people, friends give a strong sense of identity and connectedness. Friends are there for each other in happy and sad times. They are important for helping a person feel accepted and valued. Like family, friends can help a person to realise their potential. Friends can help us to feel that our lives matter.

Work, Hobbies, Sport

Work and achievement in their career or in an activity that they enjoy, such as a sport, music or art, give some people a sense of purpose and meaning. For example, a scientist discovering new ways of doing things, a researcher looking for cures to help people or an artist creating beautiful work all lead fulfilling and meaningful lives.

The Natural World

For some people, an appreciation of nature helps them to find meaning. Seeing themselves as a part of the natural world, exploring, appreciating and understanding nature, can help some people in their search for meaning. Finding ways to connect with nature, care for it and have a commitment or goal in looking after it can give people a sense of purpose.

Understanding nature can help some people in their search for meaning.

Helping Others

For some people, charity work, giving to others, helping people or working for social change give their lives a sense of meaning and purpose. Many individuals volunteer to provide care for others, to build homes for people, to distribute much-needed supplies in wars, famines or other disasters, to fundraise for good causes or to campaign for human rights. These people are trying to make the world a better place. This is often linked with giving people a sense of purpose, happiness and fulfilment.

The charity Médecins Sans Frontières helping refugees in Greece

Key Skills: Being Creative

Design a T-shirt with images, symbols or words that illustrate the things in life that give you a sense of meaning or purpose. Each person's design can be cut out and displayed around the room.

Revision Questions

Enquiry

1. What does the phrase the 'meaning of life' refer to?
2. What questions might a person ask in their search for meaning?
3. Where do people look for meaning in life?
4. What is the humanist approach to finding meaning in life?
5. How does **one** of the major world religions help a person to find answers to the search for meaning and purpose?

Exploration

1. Think about and make a list of the people and things in life that might give a person a sense of purpose or meaning.
2. Compare the humanist response to how people find meaning with a religious response.

Reflection and Action

- Research how searching for meaning in life and asking the big questions has been given expression in works of art or music.
- Reflect on the search for meaning as a part of the human experience.
- Research a philosopher's views on finding meaning in life.

26 Understanding the Divine or Transcendent

Which image is God?

Introduction

When we study the different world religions, we find a variety of beliefs about God or Gods. But what exactly do people mean when they talk about a God or a higher being? This is something we need to try to grasp so that we can better understand the major world religions and what their followers believe. We can do this by researching how religions talk about God or Gods and what their important writings say. The way followers carry out different rituals and acts of **worship** can help us in our attempt to interpret this further.

Sometimes when talking about God, people use the term 'the **Divine**'. The Divine is something that is of or relates to God. When we talk about a divinity, we are really talking about a God. There are many ways of understanding the Divine, and different religions understand it in different ways. Another way of talking about God is to say God is transcendent. The **Transcendent** refers to a spiritual being or force that is able to exist outside of the limits of the material universe, often referred to as God.

Icebreaker

Brainstorm

In pairs, discuss the questions below about what people mean when they talk about a 'God'. Bullet point your ideas. Share them with the class.

1. What is God?
2. Who is God?
3. Where do people get their image of God from?

Understanding God

When we study how the different religions understand the Divine or the Transcendent, we are limited in the language we can use. The major world religions are either monotheistic, believing in one God, or polytheistic, believing in many Gods.

Through their **sacred texts** and how they worship or carry out rituals, each religion reveals how it understands the Divine. This understanding is only a part of how people understand God. Whether or not a person believes in God, they have an idea as to what people mean when they use the word 'God'. This is not necessarily the idea shared by others.

In this chapter, we look at how the major world religions understand the Divine and see how that expresses itself in symbols, rituals and words.

Alpha and *omega* are the first and last letters of the Greek alphabet. In Christianity, it is said that God is the *alpha* and the *omega*, the beginning and the end. In religious understanding, God is beyond time and there is no time when God did not exist. God does not rely on anything or anyone else for God's existence.

The Monotheistic Religions

Judaism, Christianity and Islam are monotheistic religions. While we know this means that their followers believe in one God, we need to further develop our understanding by exploring the following points:

- Who is God?
- What is God like?
- The characteristics of God
- The relationship with God
- The impact on followers of this understanding

The sources for the followers of Judaism, Christianity and Islam for understanding God are:

- Judaism: the Tanakh
- Christianity: the Bible
- Islam: the Quran

These are the sacred texts or writings of these religions. They are considered to be important and sacred or holy. Some people in these religions believe that they are the direct word of God, while others believe that they are divinely inspired, written by people but with God's inspiration. Some people see them as having important truths and lessons to help believers live good lives and to have a better understanding of and relationship with God.

Sacred writings are often used in religious worship. They may also be used when seeking advice on a moral issue, or when reflecting on the nature of God and the meaning of life.

How important are sacred writings in religion?

Listed below are the features of God common to all three of the monotheistic religions. God is:

- Pure spirit – with no body and neither male nor female
- Ethical – God cares if people do right or wrong
- Creator – God gives life and is the source for the whole world
- Personal – in the sense of being able to have a relationship with people and caring about humankind
- Revealed – both general revelation in God's creation and in particular revelation through individuals and events
- Omnipotent – all-powerful
- Omniscient – all-knowing

Over to You – Enquiry

1. What does each of these quotes below say about God?

> Where shall I go from your spirit, or where shall I flee from your presence?
> **Psalm 139**

> ... when Allah created you and whatever you make ...
> **Quran 37: 96**

> I will walk among you and be your God, and you will be my people.
> **Leviticus 26: 12**

> I will comfort you there like a mother comforting her child.
> **Isaiah 66: 13**

> God cares for you, so turn all your worries over to him.
> **1 Peter 5: 7**

> Allah has power over all things and that Allah encompasses all things in His knowledge.
> **Quran 65: 12**

> Great is our Lord and mighty in power, his understanding has not limit.
> **Psalm 147: 5**

> ... teaching them to observe all things I have commanded you. And remember, I am with you always, even to the end of the age.
> **Matthew 28: 20**

> ... and learn to live right. See that justice is done. Defend widows and orphans and help those in need.
> **Isaiah 1: 17**

> To God belongs whatever is in the heavens and whatever is on earth. He will repay those who do evil according to their deeds, and recompense those who do good with the best.
> **Quran 53: 31**

2. What are the similarities between a Jewish, Christian and Muslim understanding of God?

God in Islam, Judaism and Christianity

Islam

In Islam, God is called Allah. Allah has 99 attributes, which include being the creator, the merciful, the provider, the all-knowing, the impartial judge, the loving one and the forgiving one. Allah's will is revealed through the Quran and the example of the Prophet Muhammad. Muhammad, the last and greatest prophet, has revealed Allah's will to the people, and they must worship and respect Allah through following the Five Pillars of Islam. Islam does not allow images of Allah or Muhammad. Allah is too amazing for humans to be able to imagine or draw, and creating images can lead to false idols – worshipping something other than God.

Judaism

In Judaism, God has made a covenant, or agreement, with the people. God is a lawgiver, and the people are the people of God. God is particularly concerned with how people treat each other. Jews understand God as being concerned with right and wrong behaviour. This can be referred to as 'ethical monotheism'. God is a liberator; God rescued the people from slavery in Egypt and intervened in history to save the people.

These pictures show Moses parting the Red Sea (below) and Moses receiving the Ten Commandments (above). What do these events teach about how God is understood in Judaism?

Christianity

In Christianity, God has been revealed through the prophets and events in history. God's most important and ultimate revelation was through the person of Jesus. Jesus is God incarnate, in other words, he is God in the flesh. God wants a personal, close relationship with people and understands human experience and suffering. God is shown through the teachings of Jesus to care for the poor, oppressed and marginalised. God's power is demonstrated when Jesus performs miracles. God is three in one. God can be encountered through the Holy Spirit.

> This picture shows Christ healing a blind man. What does this painting teach us about the Christian understanding of God?

Over to You – Exploration

Create a Venn diagram making a comparison of the understanding of God in Islam, Judaism and Christianity.

Hinduism: Gods and Goddesses

In Hinduism, there are many Gods and Goddesses. They are all part or faces of the divine soul known as Brahman, which runs through all life and provides life to everything that lives. Each person has a soul that is part of Brahman. *Atman* is the word used for a person's soul. The God Brahman is unknowable and beyond human understanding so people worship the many different Gods instead.

The three main Gods in Hinduism, known as the *Trimurti*, are called Brahma, Shiva and Vishnu. Their roles are to create, preserve and destroy. There are female wives, or consorts, for each of these main Gods.

Brahma

 Chapter 1

Brahma is the creator. He is shown as having four faces, representing the four Vedas, which are the sacred writings of Hinduism. Brahma is full of all the knowledge of the world that he creates. He has four arms pointing in each direction: he is everywhere. He holds in his hands a book representing his intelligence, a string of beads representing time, and a water pot representing the idea that all life came from the ocean. His fourth hand is in a giving position, showing that he bestows life to all.

Brahma is seen with a book in his hands, which represents the knowledge needed to create.

Saraswati

Saraswati is the Goddess of knowledge and the wife of Brahma. She holds a string of beads and a musical instrument, and she is always shown with a swan or goose. Saraswati represents beauty and knowledge, including artistic or creative knowledge and the ability to use that knowledge for good. She is popular with people seeking knowledge and is worshipped by teachers, scientists and students.

Do you think having female images of God could help some people relate more to a Transcendent being?

Vishnu

The God Vishnu is a very popular Hindu God. Vishnu is the preserver God. He sustains life and the world, especially when it is in danger. Vishnu has taken many different forms in Hindu stories; nine times in the past he has descended to earth in the form of a different God to help sustain life. The nine incarnations so far have included:

- Rama, a popular God and hero of the Hindu writings the *Ramayana*
- Lord Krishna, the blue-skinned God, who features in Hindu writings, including the *Mahabharata* and the *Bhagavata Purana*
- Buddha, the spiritual founder and teacher of Buddhism

Which form is Vishnu shown as in this picture?

Each time Vishnu descends, the form he takes is known as an **avatar** of Vishnu. *Avatar* means 'one who descends'. According to Hindu tradition, Vishnu will return to earth one more time in the future. This last time, he will take the form of a man called Kalki on a white horse.

Lakshmi

Lakshmi is the wife of Vishnu. She is the Goddess of fortune and a very popular Goddess in Hinduism. She is worshipped during the festival of light called **Diwali**. 'Lakshmi' means 'goal'. The fortune she brings is both material and spiritual. Lakshmi is shown holding a lotus flower, which in Hinduism is a symbol for purity and goodness. Her other hand is shown in a giving position and during the festival of Diwali, people place coins in her hand.

Did You Know?

? The ancient epic poem *The Ramayana* has over 24,000 verses, while another ancient Hindu poem, *The Mahabharata*, is over 100,000 verses long!

Lakshmi, wife of Vishnu

Shiva

Shiva, the third God of the *Trimurti*, is the destroyer God. He is shown holding a trident and with his snake, Vasuki. The snake represents power. Shiva has a third eye, which represents his all-seeing wisdom and insight. Shiva's destruction of the universe is essential for its recreation and Hindus see his role as a very positive one. Shiva is often referred to as the 'Lord of Dance'. It is his dance of death that brings about the destruction of the universe.

Why is Shiva often called the 'Lord of Dance'?

Parvati

Parvati is the Goddess of love, devotion and family and Shiva's wife. She is the perfect wife and mother. Parvati can also take other forms and is seen by some as the feminine force in the universe. Her other forms include Durga and Kali. Parvati and Shiva are the parents of a favourite Hindu God, Ganesh. Ganesh is the Hindu God with an elephant's head. He is a very friendly and warm God. Ganesh is said to remove obstacles. He brings success and therefore many worship him when they are starting a new venture or going on a journey.

Parvati, wife of Shiva

The Transcendent in Worship and Festival

In Hinduism, people see the Gods and Goddesses as personal. They relate to them, they ask for their help and they try to make them happy. Offerings of food, flowers, milk and incense are made to the Gods. Hindus look to the various Gods for help with different things going on in their lives. They see the Gods as intervening in this world and as being a force for good and a source of energy and strength. The Gods will help when they should, but they are superior to humans in their knowledge and wisdom. They know what is best for people.

The Ganesh Chaturthi Festival

During the Ganesh Chaturthi Festival celebrating the God Ganesh, people put clay statues of Ganesh in their homes. In public places, giant statues of the God are displayed. People carry out acts of worship in their homes. There are lots of celebrations. People buy new clothes to wear and exchange gifts. They eat special foods. When the festival is over, the statues of Ganesh are brought to the sea to be immersed in the water and dissolve. Hindus have a final ceremony to say farewell to Ganesh. They feel like they are saying goodbye, as he has been a friendly, helpful and lucky presence in their homes.

How all the different Gods and Goddesses are shown and how they are worshipped give us an indication of how Hindus understand the Transcendent.

How do Hindus understand the Gods and their relationship with people?

Review and Reflect

1. What is the name for the universal soul that, according to Hinduism, lives in all life?
2. Name the three Hindu Gods of the *Trimurti* and explain their role in the world.
3. How is Brahma shown in Hindu tradition? What does each of the things he holds represent?
4. Name the wife of Brahma.
5. What do Hindus believe about Vishnu?
6. What does Lakshmi's name mean? What festival honours her?
7. What is the weapon carried by Shiva?
8. Describe the God Ganesh.

Understanding the Transcendent in Worship and Ritual

Judaism	- *Shema*: 'Hear O Israel the Lord our God is one' - Praying to God - Wearing symbols to show respect to God - Following the Torah, including eating only *kosher* food - Carrying out rituals, e.g. marriage under a canopy - Touching the *mezuzah* on the way in and out of their homes
Christianity	- Creed: 'I believe in God the Father almighty, maker of heaven and earth' - Listening to the word of God, with special reverence for the Gospels - Carrying out the sacraments - Praying to and worshipping God - Wearing symbols and blessing oneself - Carrying out rituals, e.g. offering a sign of peace
Islam	- *Shahadah*: 'There is no God but Allah' - Praying five times a day - Submitting to the will of God - Praying towards the Kaaba or house of God in Mecca - Following the Five Pillars of Islam - Reading and respecting the Quran
Hinduism	- Having statues and shrines to the Gods - Making offerings to the Gods - Carrying out a **puja** (act of worship), including *arti* or worship of the sacred flame - Rituals, e.g. the Sacred Thread ceremony - Believing in *karma* - Using symbols to decorate homes and temples

Did You Know?

? In Hinduism, the Sacred Thread ceremony is a rite of passage. It marks the stage when a person is old enough to study the sacred writings.

Why do Muslims not have any images of God?

Over to You – Reflection and Action

- Choose **one** of the above religions and in a group create a poster.
- Use words and images to show how the rituals, worship and beliefs create an understanding of God or the Gods for that particular religion.

Buddhism: No Gods

The belief in a God or Gods is not a part of Buddhism. The Buddha taught about suffering, the release from suffering and the path to spiritual enlightenment known as *nirvana*. The Buddha did not teach about God. Some Buddhists do believe in a God, while others are agnostic and do not know whether or not a God exists. Others still are atheists and do not believe in God at all.

Buddha reaching enlightenment

For many Buddhists, whether or not there is a God does not matter. It is a question that people may never fully answer or truly understand and therefore is not of value to them. Buddhism teaches the Four Noble Truths about human existence and how to overcome suffering. Life is suffering caused by attachment to things, the desire to have and control things. This suffering can be overcome through following the Noble Eightfold Path. These were the basic teachings of the Buddha.

When suffering is ended, a person has reached *nirvana*, which brings complete freedom from attachment, suffering and the desire to control everything. In some ways, this is a Transcendent state of being. It is a spiritual state beyond the normal, physical, human experience.

Revision Questions

Enquiry

1. What is the difference between monotheism and polytheism?
2. List **three** common features of God found in Islam, Judaism and Christianity.
3. Choose **one** of the monotheistic religions – Judaism, Christianity or Islam – and briefly give the understanding of God found in that religion.
4. How do Hindus understand the role of Gods in the world?
5. What sources do the religions have that give them their understanding of their God or Gods?

Exploration

1. Compare the understanding of God found in **two** of the major world religions.
2. Why do you think people have different understandings of God?
3. How do people demonstrate their understanding of God in their lives?

Reflection and Action

Research images of God or Gods and how they reflect the understanding of God found in that religion.

27 Sources of Values

Learning Outcome 3.1

Examine different sources of values and ways in which the values of a person relate to their everyday life choices, their relationships, and their responsibilities to others.

Learning Intentions

By the end of this chapter I will:
- Know what sources of values are
- Know where people source their values
- Understand the impact values have on life choices, relationships and responsibilities to others
- Realise what my own values are and how they impact on my life

Key Skills and Wellbeing

- Managing myself
- Staying well
- Working with others

I have identified the values that help to shape my actions, thoughts and words. I now realise what the source of my values are. I understand that values of others vary widely and that the sources of these values have a big effect on how we all live our lives and interact with each other.

Keywords

integrity ▪ Universal Declaration of Human Rights ▪ values

Introduction

Everyone has **values**, ways that they decide what is significant to them. Some of these values are deeply rooted since childhood, while others come much later. There is always time to uncover new values no matter what age or stage of life you are at. Values can also change over time. People who live by their values are said to have **integrity**.

The source or origin of these values can vary greatly. Humans can be influenced by many different things. The diagram below shows some of the sources of values for people today.

🔗 Chapter 19

What Does This Mean?

Integrity: The quality of being honest and having strong moral principles. Someone who stands by their values and stands up for what they believe to be right has integrity.

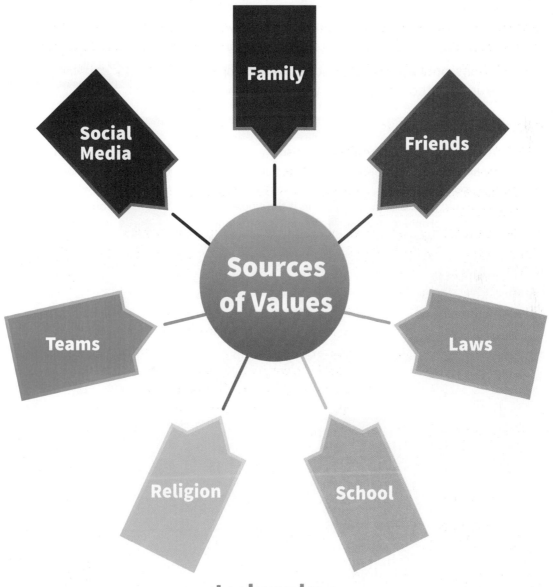

Icebreaker

 Identifying My Values
1. Take a few moments to reflect on your personal values. As a class, write up the values you share on the whiteboard.
2. Create a class values poster with all the values the people in your class think are important. Display it in the classroom.

Family

Family is the original and most influential source of thoughts, actions and words. It is the strongest source of values for many people. From the moment of birth, children live and learn the beliefs and values of family members. Children love to repeat what they hear at home, and how a child acts outside the home gives a good indication of the values held at home. A child who is brought up in a home that values equality will look at everyone as equal, whereas a child whose family looks down on or makes fun of someone who is 'different' will often do the same outside the home.

Religion

Religious teachings can be a strong and sacred source of values for many people all over the world. In 2015, there were 7.2 billion people living on the planet, 6 billion of whom subscribe to religious belief. This is one of the main reasons why religious education is vital for everyone – it helps us to understand the people around us.

The wording of the Golden Rule varies between the five major world religions, but the values of kindness and compassion it promotes are clear no matter which way they are written.

Christianity
In everything, do to others as you would have them do to you; for this is the law and the prophets.

Judaism
What is hateful to you, do not do to your neighbour. This is the whole Torah; all the rest is commentary.

Buddhism
Treat not others in a way that you yourself would find hurtful.

Hinduism
This is the sum of duty: do not do to others what would cause pain if done to you.

Islam
Not one of you truly believes until you wish for others what you wish for yourself.

Social Media

This is the age of social media. If an event isn't posted online, to many it might seem as if it didn't even happen. This has become an unhealthy obsession for many people today. A lot of people cannot even eat their breakfast without posting it online, and entire concerts are watched through the screen of a phone. Individuals have made millions by telling other people what to wear and how to behave, as online 'influencers'.

However, social media can also be positive. Because of social media, people are exposed to more information and news than they would have been. It is much easier to stay in contact with others, and to keep up to date on the important events in the lives of our friends

Social media is useful for keeping in touch with the news or with friends far away.

and family. By being exposed to so many opinions and thoughts, people are now presented with many more alternative values to add to their own.

Over to You – Exploration

Decide on a list of **five or six** values that the class agree are important.

- Write each value in the middle of a sheet of paper and spread them out around the room.
- Now divide the class into the same number of values you have chosen.
- Each group has one minute at each value. They should write down one way the value impacts on a person's life choices, relationships and/or responsibility to others.
- Once each group has worked on each value, discuss the answers given for each value as a class.

Universal Declaration of Human Rights

The **Universal Declaration of Human Rights** (UDHR) is a list of all the basic values that every human should have. It was adopted by the United Nations in 1948 and contains 30 Articles. It has been translated into over 500 languages. The first article on the declaration is: 'All human beings are born free and equal in dignity and in rights'. This article means that every person deserves dignity and everyone is granted these rights equally. The important values highlighted in this article are dignity, respect and equality.

Chapter 18

What Does This Mean?

Universal Declaration of Human Rights: A very important document which was drawn up so everyone would know what they have a right to.

The Universal Declaration of Human Rights

- **Article 1** Right to equality: You are born free and equal in rights to every other human being. You have the ability to think and to tell right from wrong. You should treat others with friendship.

- **Article 2** Freedom from discrimination: You have all these human rights no matter what your race, skin colour, sex, language, religion, opinions, family background, social or economic status, birth or nationality.

- **Article 3** Right to life, liberty and personal security: You have the right to live, to be free and to feel safe.

- **Article 4** Freedom from slavery: Nobody has the right to treat you as a slave, and you should not make anyone your slave.

- **Article 5** Freedom from torture and degrading treatment: Nobody has the right to torture, harm or humiliate you.

- **Article 6** Right to recognition as a person before the law: You have a right to be accepted everywhere as a person according to law.

- **Article 7** Right to equality before the law: You have a right to be protected and treated equally by the law without discrimination of any kind.

- **Article 8** Right to remedy by capable judges: If your legal rights are violated, you have the right to fair and capable judges to uphold your rights.

- **Article 9** Freedom from arbitrary arrest and exile: Nobody has the right to arrest you, put you in prison or to force you out of your country without good reasons.

- **Article 10** Right to fair public hearing: If you are accused of a crime, you have the right to a fair and public hearing.

- **Article 11** Right to be considered innocent until proven guilty: (1) You should be considered innocent until it can be proved in a fair trial that you are guilty. (2) You cannot be punished for doing something that was not considered a crime at the time you did it.

- **Article 12** Freedom from interference with privacy, family, home and correspondence: You have the right to be protected if someone tries to harm your good name or enter your house, open your mail or bother you or your family without good reason.

- **Article 13** Right to free movement: (1) You have the right to come and go as you wish within your country. (2) You have the right to leave your country to go to another one, and you should be able to return to your country if you want.

- **Article 14** Right to protection in another country: (1) If someone threatens to hurt you, you have the right to go to another country and ask for protection as a refugee. (2) You lose this right if you have committed a serious crime.

- **Article 15** Right to a nationality and the freedom to change it: (1) You have the right to belong to a country and have a nationality. (2) No one can take away your nationality without a good reason. You have a right to change your nationality if you wish.

- **Article 16** Right to marriage and family: (1) When you are legally old enough, you have the right to marry and have a family without any limitations based on your race, country or religion. Both partners have the same rights when they are married and also when they are separated. (2) Nobody should force you to marry.

- **Article 17** Right to own property: (1) You have the right to own things. (2) Nobody has the right to take these things from you without a good reason.

- **Article 18** Freedom of thought, conscience and religion: You have the right to your own thoughts and to believe in any religion. You are free to practise your religion or beliefs and also to change them.

- **Article 19** Freedom of opinion and information: You have the right to hold and express your own opinions. You should be able to share your opinions with others, including people from other countries, through any ways.

- **Article 20** Right to peaceful assembly and association: (1) You have the right to meet peacefully with other people. (2) No one can force you to belong to a group.

- **Article 21** Right to participate in government and elections: (1) You have the right to participate in your government, either by holding an office or by electing someone to represent you. (2) You and everyone has the right to serve your country. (3) Governments should be elected regularly by fair and secret voting.

- **Article 22** Right to social security: The society you live in should provide you with social security and the rights necessary for your dignity and development.

- **Article 23** Right to desirable work and to join trade unions: (1) You have the right to work, to choose your work and to work in good conditions. (2) People who do the same work should get the same pay. (3) You should be able to earn a salary that allows you to live and support your family. (4) All people who work have the right to join together in unions to defend their interests.

- **Article 24** Right to rest and leisure: You have the right to rest and free time. Your workday should not be too long, and you should be able to take regular paid holidays.

- **Article 25** Right to adequate living standard: (1) You have the right to the things you and your family need to have a healthy and comfortable life, including food, clothing, housing, medical care and other social services. You have a right to help if you are out of work or unable to work. (2) Mothers and children should receive special care and help.

- **Article 26** Right to education: (1) You have the right to go to school. Primary schooling should be free and required. You should be able to learn a profession or continue your studies as far as you can. (2) At school, you should be able to develop all your talents and learn to respect others, whatever their race, religion or nationality. (3) Your parents should have a say in the kind of education you receive.

- **Article 27** Right to participate in the cultural life of community: (1) You have the right to participate in the traditions and learning of your community, to enjoy the arts and to benefit from scientific progress. (2) If you are an artist, writer or scientist, your work should be protected and you should be able to benefit from it.

Michelle Bachelet, the United Nations High Commissioner for Human Rights

- **Article 28** Right to a social order: You have a right to the kind of world where you and all people can enjoy these rights and freedoms.

- **Article 29** Responsibilities to the community: (1) Your personality can only fully develop within your community, and you have responsibilities to that community. (2) The law should guarantee human rights. It should allow everyone to respect others and to be respected. (3) These rights and freedoms should support the purposes and principles of the United Nations.

- **Article 30** Freedom from interference in these human rights: No person, group or government anywhere in the world should do anything to destroy these rights.

Over to You – Enquiry

1. Read through the Universal Declaration of Human Rights again.
2. Select the top **five** human rights that you think are most important.
3. Why did you select these five?
4. What values are shown in the five values you have chosen? Share your thoughts with the class.

Revision Questions

Enquiry

1. What is a value?
2. What is integrity?
3. List **five** sources of values.
4. Where do children get their values?
5. What values are shown in the Golden Rule?

Exploration

1. Select **one** value you find important and outline how this value impacts on your daily life choices.
2. Select **one** value your school holds important and outline how this value impacts on the relationships within your school community.
3. Select **one** value the country of Ireland holds important and outline how this value impacts on the responsibilities Ireland has towards its citizens.

Reflection and Action

1. Research any **two** other sources of values from the diagram on page 247 or of your choice.
2. Write a report outlining how the values gained from this source could affect someone's life choices, relationships and responsibility to others.

Understanding Compassion

28

Why do you think these people are handing out hot drinks on a cold night?

Introduction

The four concepts of **compassion**, **justice**, **peace** and **reconciliation** are vital to people's happiness. By showing compassion, seeking justice, striving for peace and accepting reconciliation, we can become better people and help to make the world around us a better place. The five major world religions all hold these four concepts as essential to living a good life. Before we dive into the understanding of these concepts in two of the major world religions, we need to understand what these concepts mean.

Icebreaker

 Carousel

Divide the class into four groups.

- Write each of the four concepts of compassion justice, peace and reconciliation onto large sheets of paper.
- Each group should spend a few minutes at each sheet discussing the concept.
- After some discussion, the group writes down what they feel the concept means and how one could put that concept into action.

Compassion

Have you ever witnessed a homeless person struggling to stay warm? An injured animal, frightened and alone? A lost child, crying, looking for his mother? If these experiences tugged at your heartstrings and caused sadness, then you are feeling sympathy. If you have an urge to do something that might ease their pain or suffering, you have compassion. Compassion is a beautiful thing. It is what makes people search for ways to help those in need. Charity would not survive without compassion.

How could you show compassion in this situation?

Key Skill: Communicating

- Think about times in your life when you have shown compassion to another person, and times when you have received compassion from someone.
- In pairs, discuss these times and these experiences. Listen carefully to your partner's stories and reflect on the compassion shown.
- Discuss how you could bring more compassion into your life.

Justice

We all crave equality: to be treated the same as everyone else. When the world is equal, the world will be just. But life is not always just, and injustice can make us angry, upset and frustrated. We can experience injustice on a small scale, such as your sibling getting a treat when you do not, or on a large scale, such as a woman being paid less than a man for doing the same job. Injustice is all around us. It is how we deal with injustice and seek to make the world a just place that matters.

Scales are often used as a symbol for justice. Why do you think this is?

Over to You – Enquiry

1. Read the following scenario and discuss it.

   Sarah gets to work on time every day. She leaves five minutes earlier than she needs to just in case there is heavy traffic on the way. Her only coworker, Kevin, is always late, usually by 15 minutes. He blames everything else: traffic, weather, car trouble, the dog escaping ... the list goes on. One day, after Kevin arrived particularly late, Sarah's boss calls both of them into his office. He is really annoyed and says that due to the amount of time lost because of Kevin's late arrivals each morning, they are several hours behind. Both Sarah and Kevin will need to come in on Saturday to make up the lost time, unpaid! Both Sarah and Kevin are angry.

2. Why is Sarah angry?
3. Why is Kevin angry?
4. Who has been treated unfairly?
5. What would be the fair thing to do?
6. Is there anything Kevin can do to make it fair for Sarah?

Injustice Around the World

Unfairness is a frustrating thing to deal with. But on a worldwide scale, injustice has serious consequences, especially for vulnerable members of society.

- Worldwide, one in six children between the ages of 5 and 14 are engaged in child labour.
- Around the world, over 115 million children are not in education.
- Nearly 1 billion people in the world cannot sign their own name.
- One in seven people on the planet is malnourished.
- In July 2018, there were 3,867 children in emergency accommodation in Ireland.
- Some 8.6 per cent of the world's population owns 85.6 per cent of the world's wealth.

Do these facts sound fair to you? Does it sound like justice?

Peace

Peace is time that is free from disturbance; a time when there is no war or conflict. It is a time when people can live in freedom and security and their rights and dignity are respected. There are many types of peace: peace from war, inner peace, peace that comes from calmness.

In 1998, the Good Friday Agreement was signed. The aim of this agreement was to bring an end to the Troubles in Northern Ireland. The sectarian violence in Northern Ireland had claimed many lives and caused years of suffering. While the Agreement itself did not end violence immediately, it did mark the beginning of the path to peace.

The signing of the Good Friday Agreement was facilitated by Taoiseach Bertie Ahern, UK Prime Minister Tony Blair, US President Bill Clinton and negotiator George Mitchell.

Over to You – Exploration

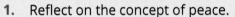

1. Reflect on the concept of peace.
2. Using your creativity, draw an image of what peace means to you. Under your image, write down **three** ways you can influence the peace in your life and the peace in the world around you.

Reconciliation

Reconciliation is when two people or groups come together and restore their good relationship. For a relationship to break down, one or both sides could have been at fault. Sometimes, it can be difficult to say 'I'm sorry'. To genuinely forgive someone can be even harder.

True reconciliation requires one, or both, sides to realise their wrongdoing, to want to make amends, and not want to do harm again. The other side needs to realise that the apology is genuine and agree to leave the episode in the past. It can be hard to trust that the other person will not hurt you again, but if you hold onto suspicion and anger, there can be no true reconciliation.

Buddhism: Concepts in Action

Love and compassion are necessities, not luxuries. Without them, humanity cannot survive.

The 14th Dalai Lama

Buddhists all over the world practise justice, compassion, peace and reconciliation in their daily lives.

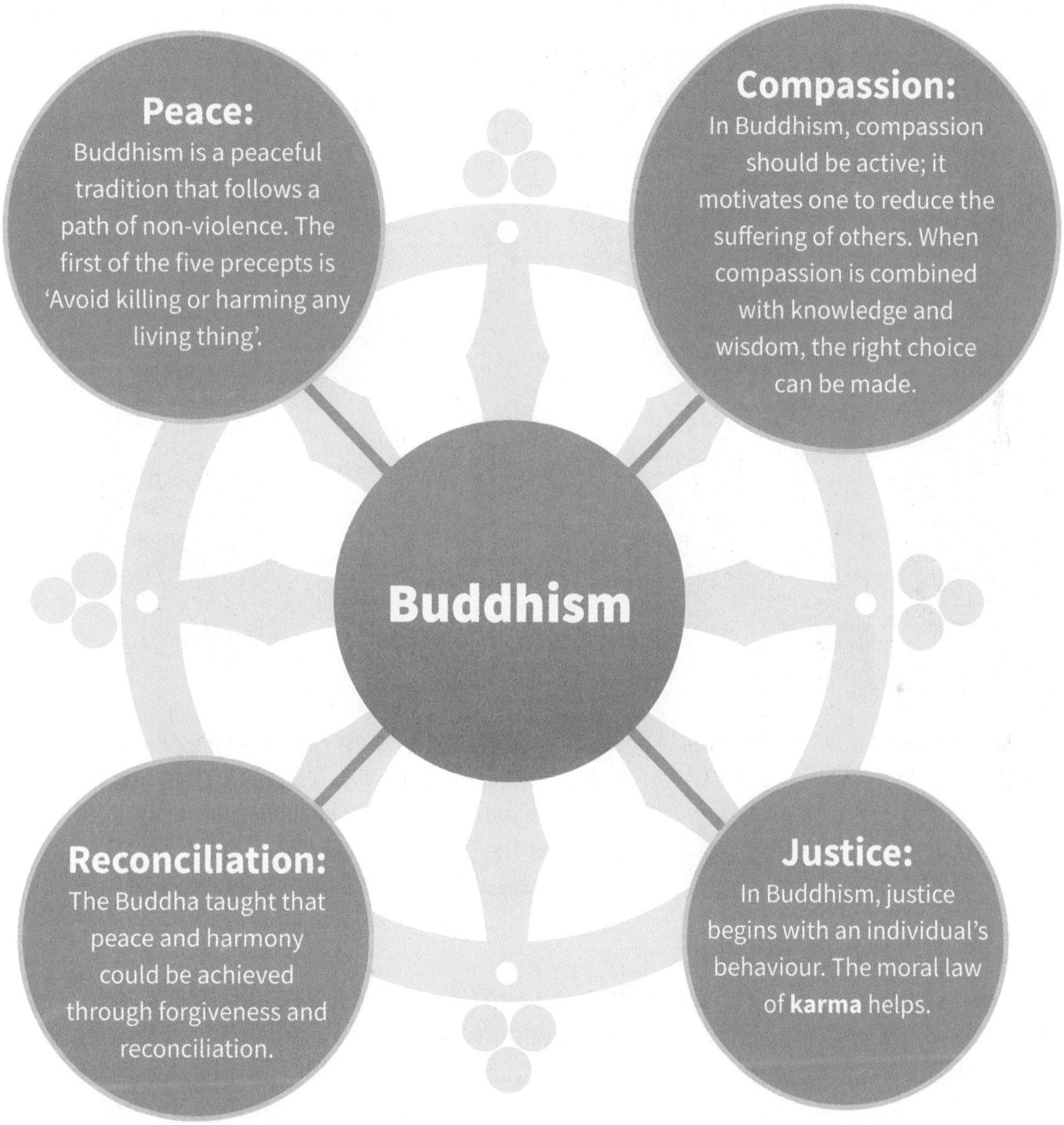

Peace:
Buddhism is a peaceful tradition that follows a path of non-violence. The first of the five precepts is 'Avoid killing or harming any living thing'.

Compassion:
In Buddhism, compassion should be active; it motivates one to reduce the suffering of others. When compassion is combined with knowledge and wisdom, the right choice can be made.

Buddhism

Reconciliation:
The Buddha taught that peace and harmony could be achieved through forgiveness and reconciliation.

Justice:
In Buddhism, justice begins with an individual's behaviour. The moral law of **karma** helps.

Did You Know?

? The tagline for the Buddhist Peace Fellowship is 'Cultivating Compassionate Action'. The Buddhist Peace Fellowship works for peace from diverse Buddhist perspectives. It advocates non-violent, peaceful social activism.

Buddhism and Compassion

The Buddhist understanding of compassion can be seen clearly in the fact that many Buddhists are vegetarian. Buddhists believe they are lessening the suffering of other living creatures by refusing to eat meat. This choice also shows their commitment to non-violence and their refusal to kill other living creatures.

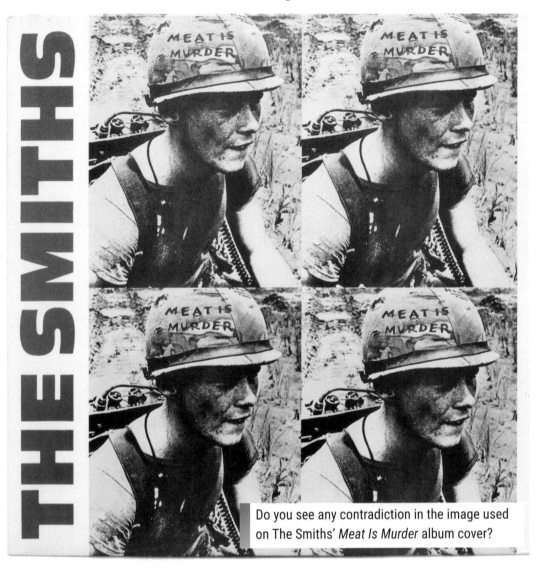

Do you see any contradiction in the image used on The Smiths' *Meat Is Murder* album cover?

The Noble Eightfold Path

Nirvana is a state of perfect happiness, truth and peace. It is the release from selfishness, craving and suffering. The end of suffering can be achieved by following the Noble Eightfold Path, which not only brings inner peace to Buddhists, but also makes the world a more peaceful place. In a physical sense, Buddhists have a firm commitment to non-violence and conflict resolution through peaceful methods.

Buddhists' strong belief in karma helps them to make good moral choices. However, *karma* is not the universe serving out justice for wrongdoing. It is the belief that good action will be rewarded with something positive in the future. This encourages Buddhists to be a force for good in the world and to work for justice.

Reconciliation involves a return to friendliness. It is different from forgiveness in that reconciliation requires trust. Each path in the Noble Eightfold Path contains the word 'right': you must live in right compardsion, right speech, right effort and so on. In order to achieve the right relationship with the Noble Eightfold Path, followers should seek to reconcile their relationship with themselves, other people and the world around them.

Islam: Concepts in Action

" Believers in doing good to each other and in being merciful and compassionate to each other are like one body. "

The Holy Prophet Muhammad

Muslims all over the world practise justice, compassion, peace and reconciliation in their daily lives.

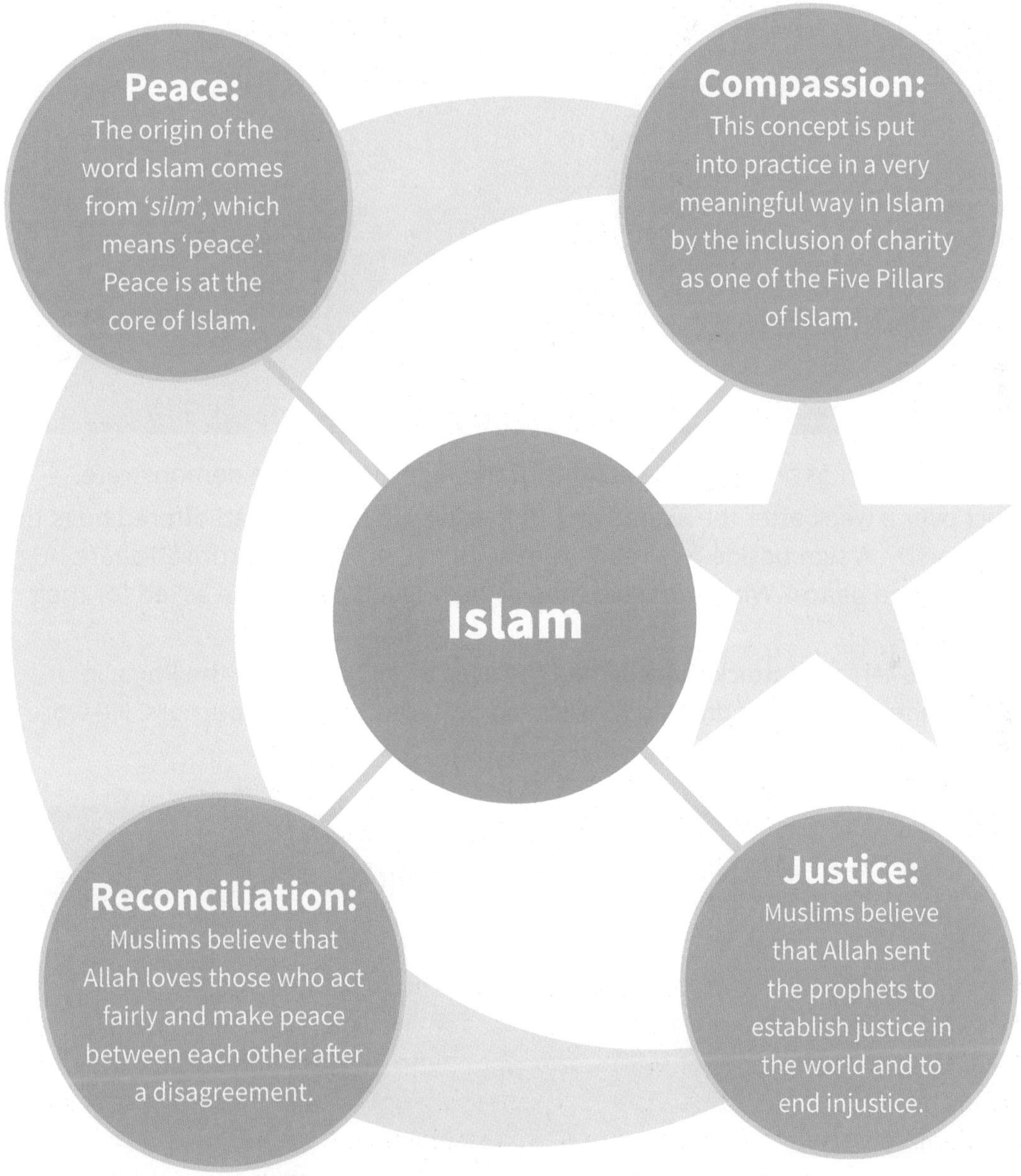

Peace:
The origin of the word Islam comes from 'silm', which means 'peace'. Peace is at the core of Islam.

Compassion:
This concept is put into practice in a very meaningful way in Islam by the inclusion of charity as one of the Five Pillars of Islam.

Islam

Reconciliation:
Muslims believe that Allah loves those who act fairly and make peace between each other after a disagreement.

Justice:
Muslims believe that Allah sent the prophets to establish justice in the world and to end injustice.

Did You Know?

? The Yemeni journalist Tawakkol Karman is an advocate for women's rights and seeks justice and peace in the world. She founded the movement Women Journalists Without Chains. She has led dozens of peaceful protests and was awarded the Nobel Peace Prize in 2011.

A Peaceful Religion

In August 2017, a 22-year-old man drove a van into a crowd of pedestrians on Las Ramblas, in Barcelona, Spain. Thirteen people were killed that day, and 130 injured, one of whom died 10 days later. The man killed another person in order to steal his vehicle to make his getaway. Four days after the attack, he was shot and killed by Spanish police. Before he died, he shouted 'Allahu Akbar', which means 'Allah is the greatest' in Arabic. This man claimed to be carrying out the will of Allah, but anyone who understands Islam knows that this is not the case.

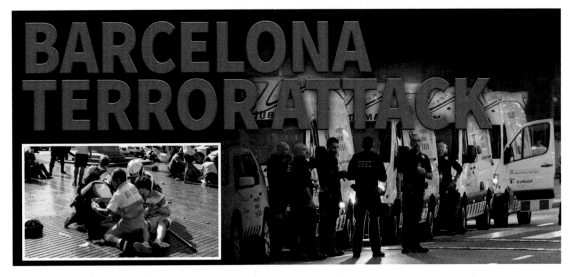

Islam is a religion of peace, as the actions of the following people demonstrate.

- Just over a week after the events on Las Ramblas, a Muslim man offered hugs to passersby. A sign beside him read: 'I am Muslim, I am not a terrorist. I share hugs of love and peace.' Witnesses said that, as he hugged people, he asked for their forgiveness.
- After the terrorist attack that claimed the lives of 130 people in the Paris, in November 2015, a blindfolded Muslim man offered hugs to mourners. He wore a sign saying, 'Do you trust me?'

Hugging can be a physical sign of reconciliation. Why do you think this is?

Over to You – Exploration

 How did the actions of these people show compassion, justice, peace and reconciliation?

Revision Questions

Enquiry

1. What does compassion mean?
2. How could someone show compassion to another person?
3. What does justice mean?
4. What impact does injustice have on vulnerable people?
5. What does peace mean?
6. What benefit is peace to the world?
7. What does reconciliation mean?
8. How can reconciliation help two people who have had an argument?

Exploration

1. Which of the **four** concepts – compassion, justice, peace and reconciliation – do you think is the most important? Explain your answer.
2. How can you put these **four** concepts into action?

Reflection and Action

- Research the concepts of compassion, justice, peace and reconciliation in any of the other **three** world religions: Judaism, Christianity or Hinduism.
- Outline how these concepts are put into action by members of the world religion you have chosen.
- Put your findings together in a PowerPoint presentation or on a poster and present them to your class.

29 Stewardship and Wellbeing

There is only one world for us to live on. How well do we take care of it?

Introduction

Over the past decades, we have seen how much damage has been done to the natural world. There are many people working to take care of the earth and to address the problems it faces. All the major world religions see the earth as something valuable and important and teach the **relevance** of looking after it. Although these religions are ancient in origins, they show an understanding of the importance of taking care of the environment and how a bad environment can affect the **wellbeing** of people.

Icebreaker

Watch a short video or YouTube clip on the topic of climate / climate change / the environment / the world we live in, for example the trailer for *An Inconvenient Sequel: Truth to Power* or part of the final episode of *Blue Planet II*.

- List the environmental problems the world faces today.
- Discuss the relevance of these issues for all of us.

What Does This Mean?

Relevance: How something relates to or is useful with regard to what is happening. When we think about environmental issues, understanding how people view the world and their place in it is relevant.

Wellbeing: Feeling healthy, comfortable and happy.

Wellbeing

Our environment can influence our wellbeing. If we live in a bad environment, where the earth is not looked after, this can affect our welfare, health, comfort, security and safety.

🔗 Chapter 16

Wellbeing and the Planet

The problems that occur when we do not look after the earth are enormous. Not caring about the planet has damaged the ozone layer, and led to climate change and global warming. Industrial development over the last 200 years has led to deforestation, water and air pollution, and the extinction of many animal species.

- Climate change can lead to the destruction of people's homes and of animal habitats.
- Global warming causes extreme weather events. These can lead to flooding, droughts and poor harvests, which can result in famines.

All of this seriously affects the wellbeing of millions of people and many animal species. The Sustainable Development Goals (SDGs) of the United Nations Development Plan prioritise protecting the planet, by tackling climate change, protecting life below water and on land, and by creating sustainable communities and cities.

What are the reasons for animals becoming endangered?

Care for the Earth

The term '**interconnected**' refers to the fact that all living creatures and all communities are connected in some way. Everything is in a complex relationship. We all share the same planet, the air, the sea and the land. All of this connects us. How we grow food, how we travel, how we get our energy, the many ways we use the earth and its resources, all have an effect on other people and communities.

Many organisations and individuals – religious and non-religious – campaign on the issues of the environment, climate change, food production, sustainable living, the survival of species and the future of the planet. This shows genuine concern about the wellbeing of the planet and of people.

What Does This Mean?

Interconnected: The complex relationship between all living things on the earth.

Who is responsible for the natural world and the environment?

The Earth in Religions

We have studied the major world religions and humanism. We have looked at how they affect moral decision-making, and how individuals' belief systems influence their values and thinking. The future of the planet is a hugely important issue. So, it is worth investigating what the major religions say about caring for the earth. It is something everybody – whatever their beliefs – should be informed on.

Judaism and the Earth

In Judaism, the earth and everything that is in it belongs to and is a gift from God. Psalm 24 of the Jewish writings says that 'the earth is the Lord's and everything in it'.

The world is for people to live in and each person has a responsibility to take care of it. The idea of separating the natural world from people would have made no sense to those who wrote the Jewish sacred writings.

People rely on the natural world for food, health and wellbeing. People are stewards, or managers, of the environment, with a duty to protect it. This idea is known as **stewardship**.

What Does This Mean?

Stewardship: To take care of something, to look after it and to manage it. To be a steward of something is to be put in charge of looking after it, for it to be entrusted to your care and for you to protect and preserve it.

In the creation story, a repeated phrase that follows each day of creation is 'and God saw that it was good'. The whole creation that humans had the job of looking after was 'good'. It is clear that God cared for the whole of the world: the sky, seas, mountains, plants, animals and finally humans.

Repairing the World

Tikkun Olam is a Jewish concept meaning 'repairing the world'. It is interpreted in many different ways and includes taking action to combat injustice and to help create a fairer society. It can also refer to taking care of the environment and creating a sustainable society.

> How does this poster show concern for the earth in Judaism?

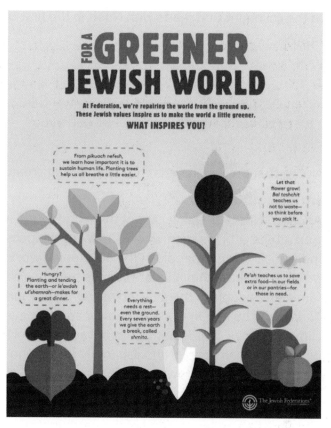

The Law and the Land

In Jewish tradition, as shown in the Book of Leviticus, which is part of the Torah, taking care of the land is important. The law instructs about having a Sabbath year. Every seven years the land should be left fallow, so, 'the land is to have a year of rest'.

The Torah refers to fair distribution of food and land, as well as not allowing unnecessary suffering to animals. This is seen in Exodus where it says, 'during the seventh year let the land lie unploughed and unused. Then the poor among your people may get food from it, and the wild animals may eat what is left.'

The command to rest on the seventh day, the Sabbath, is not just about humans having time to rest and worship God, it is so 'your ox and your donkey may rest'. These traditions show an order to creation that needs to be carefully maintained. Every creature, the land and people are interconnected and interdependent.

Promoting the wellbeing of all creatures is a way of respecting the whole of creation.

Living Our Values

In the covenant God made with Noah in the first book of the Jewish Torah, Genesis, it says:

> I establish my covenant with you, and with your descendants after you, and with every living creature that is with you, the birds, the livestock, and every beast of the earth with you.

Notice that the covenant is with 'every living creature', not just with humans.

God as Liberator

Another aspect of taking care of the world found in the Jewish texts is the idea of God as liberator, as seen when God frees the people from slavery in Egypt. Many individuals think of people in the developing world as needing to be freed from poverty and hardship. Climate change and the related problems of drought and famine hit people in the developing world far more than those in wealthy countries. Those who believe in God as liberator see it as everyone's duty to tackle the issue of climate change. This is not just as a way to respect the natural world, but also as a way of respecting all people, and especially those who need to be liberated. In the Jewish tradition, all of this shows respect, ultimately, to God.

Christianity and the Earth

The Christian understanding of the earth is similar to the Jewish one. Most Christians understand that the processes involved in creating the earth include it continually evolving and changing. They believe that the earth and everything in it belongs to God. The phrase 'the earth is the Lord's and everything in it' from Psalm 24 is quoted in the New Testament in 1 Corinthians 10. The earth is a gift from God and something that human beings have a duty to look after on behalf of and for God.

The earth is not for people to exploit but for people to respect and to do everything possible to sustain. The world includes every living creature from the depths of the oceans to the highest mountains. The central understanding in Christianity is that God loves the world. God loves people so much that God gave Jesus as a sacrifice for the sins of the whole world, so that people could have everlasting life and freedom. The New Testament writing on this includes the phrase that God so 'loved the world'. Notice that it says God loved the world and not just that God loved humans.

A New Beginning for the World

In Christianity, the death of Jesus marks a new beginning for the world, a new creation. This creation is to be a good world, a Kingdom of God, one in which people love one another and love God. To love God includes loving the world that God has given to people. This shows how important it is in Christianity to be stewards of the earth, to take care of every living thing and to not be disrespectful of this gift. There is a Christian hymn, 'Look at the World', by John Rutter, which includes the following lyrics:

> Give us thankful hearts that we may see,
>
> All the gifts we share and every blessing,
>
> All things come of thee,
>
> Every good gift, all we need and cherish,
>
> Comes from the Lord in token of his love,
>
> We are his hands, stewards of all his bounty.

In Christianity, as in Judaism, taking care of the oppressed and the poor is very important. God is liberator and Jesus further emphasised this in his teachings. He constantly reached out to the marginalised and forgotten.

For Christians, it is very important to acknowledge that climate change and environmental problems have the biggest impact on people in the poorest parts of the world. For Christians, the issues of wellbeing and care for the earth are very relevant.

> **Why should Christians show concern for the earth?**

Islam and the Earth

In Islam, as in Judaism and Christianity, the earth and everything that is in it belongs to and is a gift from Allah (God). The Quran chapter 13.3 says:

> … and it is He who spread the earth and placed thereon firmly set mountains and rivers; and from all of the fruits He made therein two mates; He draws the night as a veil over the day. Indeed in that are signs for a people who give thought.

Islam teaches that there is a oneness or wholeness to the world and each part is necessary for harmony and balance. There is a *hadith*, or tradition of the Prophet Muhammad, that 'the earth is green and beautiful, and Allah has appointed you stewards over it'. It is important to respect the earth and everything in it as this shows respect for God.

People should also show compassion and empathy for all living things. In Islam, taking care of the earth and the environment is very important since it helps all living creatures, and is essential for the wellbeing of all people.

> **Is the wellbeing of people connected to our care for the earth?**

Buddhism and the Earth

Buddhism teaches that humans and nature must coexist, that life should be respected and that all life is interconnected. Buddhism emphasises awareness of all living things and encourages pure action as well as pure thought. Living in harmony with the world and showing respect for all life are fundamental principles in Buddhism. The first of the five precepts or rules of Buddhism is to avoid taking life. This shows the understanding that all life on earth should be respected and not harmed. Because of this rule, many Buddhists are vegetarian.

The Dalai Lama said:

> It is not difficult to forgive destruction in the past which resulted from ignorance. Today, however, we have access to more information, and it is essential that we re-examine ethically what we have inherited, what we are responsible for, and what we will pass on to coming generations.

Panels of solar batteries on the roof of a Tibetan Buddhist monastery

Hinduism and the Earth

Hinduism sees all life as part of the divine soul: Brahman. The world and each life on it go through cycles. The earth must be protected and sustained for each cycle to occur.

Ahimsa, or gentleness, is an important value in Hinduism. This is one of the reasons the cow is a sacred animal in Hinduism, as the cow is said to have a gentle nature. Through respect for the cow, Hinduism shows importance of animals as part of the universal soul. Many Hindus are vegetarian. Each soul goes through many incarnations, so the soul of a person may return in animal form. Many of the Hindu Gods take on animal as well as human form, again showing the interconnectedness of all forms of life.

The small arctic tern flies all the way from the Arctic to the Antarctic. The future of planet earth is linked to the future of all living creatures.

Humanism and the Earth

Humanism emphasises the responsibility of each person to live a good and moral life with respect for the welfare of others. Through reason and science, humanists believe individuals are capable of solving problems and helping everyone to live a happy life. As this is the only world people have, humanists believe people have a duty to take care of it for future generations. According to humanists, the welfare of people is dependent on the wellbeing and continued existence of the natural world. Therefore it is clearly in everyone's interest to take care of the environment.

Did You Know?

? Humanists for a Better World is a UK web-based interest group for people to share information and take action on many issues, including climate change and the environment. They list ten things you can do about climate change for anyone who 'cares about the future of humanity (or even just the future of their children or grandchildren or neighbourhood)'. These include:

- Political lobbying
- Eating less meat
- Planting a tree
- Using green energy
- Travelling less
- Supporting a wildlife or environmental charity
- Consuming and wasting less

Over to You – Exploration

1. In groups, design a poster for **one** of the above religions or humanism showing how the earth and caring for the earth is important for people who share that belief.
2. Put an image representing the earth at the centre of the poster.
3. Using words, pictures or symbols make a visual representation of care for the earth according to this particular belief.

Care for the Earth in Action

The Alliance of Religions and Conservation (ARC) was set up in 1995. Its origins go back to 1986 when the President of the World Wildlife Fund (WWF) invited leaders of each of the five major world religions to Assisi in Italy. They met to talk about how they could encourage people to become more aware of and more active in caring for the planet. As billions of people are part of the major world religions, what could they do to address this serious issue? How could they work together to help with environmental issues? How could they help to save the planet?

Photo: ARC/Katia Marsh

The ARC was a participant in this UN Faith in the Future Meeting, which took place in Bristol, UK. The meeting launched new Faith Commitments and discussed how to support the new United Nations Sustainable Development Goals.

How can individuals help to take care of the earth?

The Alliance of Religions and Conservation

At that first meeting, Father Serrini, a Franciscan priest, said:

> Each religion will celebrate the dignity of nature and the duty of every person to live harmoniously within the natural world. We are convinced of the inestimable value of our respective traditions and of what they can offer to re-establish ecological harmony; but, at the same time, we are humble enough to desire to learn from each other. The very richness of our diversity lends strength to our shared concern and responsibility for our Planet Earth.

At the original meeting, the five major religions issued a declaration on nature. Now there are 12 religions involved, each with its own statement and many with long-term plans to protect the living planet.

What Does This Mean?

Sustainable: Able to be maintained or continued over a long period of time. In relation to development or obtaining energy, sustainable refers to things that do not damage the environment and do not use up limited natural resources.

ARC has helped to develop many projects from 'faith in food' – which works to produce food in more **sustainable** and fairer ways – to forest and wildlife projects. It works with conservation groups, governments, the United Nations, communities and individuals. ARC 'helps the major religions of the world to develop their own environmental programmes, based on their own core teachings, beliefs and practices'. It works with 12 religions, helping them to link with key environmental organisations. Its vision is 'of people, through their beliefs, treading more gently upon the earth'.

To tread the earth gently is to consider how you use the natural environment. How does our lifestyle impact the earth?

Over to You – Exploration

1. Research **one** of the following organisations, or another organisation that you have heard of, which is concerned about the environment:
    - Eco Congregations is a project of the Irish Church in Society Forum that encourages churches of all denominations to be more eco-friendly in everything they do.
    - One Earth Sangha is a a Buddhist response to climate change, with a mission 'to bring the essential wisdom and practices from the Buddhist tradition to collective engagement on critical ecological crises'.
2. Make a presentation for your class on this organisation and include the answers to these questions:
    - What do they do?
    - Who do they work with?
    - Why do they do the work?
    - How do they want to help with the wellbeing of the planet and all people?
    - What recent work or news have they been involved in?

Pope Francis and Climate Change

Read these quotes from the Papal Encyclical 'Laudato Si: On Care for Our Common Home', Pope Francis's letter on ecology, published in 2015:

- Climate change is a global problem with serious implications, environmental, social, economic, political, and for the distribution of goods; it represents one of the principal challenges facing humanity in our day.

- Greater investment needs to be made in research aimed at understanding more fully the functioning of ecosystems and adequately analysing the different variables associated with any significant modification of the environment. Because all creatures are connected, each must be cherished with love and respect, for all of us as living creatures are dependent on one another.

- It is not enough, however, to think of different species merely as potential 'resources' to be exploited, while overlooking the fact that they have value in themselves. Each year sees the disappearance of thousands of plant and animal species which we will never know, which our children will never see, because they have been lost for ever. The great majority become extinct for reasons related to human activity.

- The deterioration of the environment and of society affects the most vulnerable people on the planet … the depletion of fishing reserves especially hurts small fishing communities without the means to replace those resources; water pollution particularly affects the poor who cannot buy bottled water; and rises in the sea level mainly affect impoverished coastal populations who have nowhere else to go. The impact of present imbalances is also seen in the premature death of many of the poor, in conflicts sparked by the shortage of resources, and in any number of other problems which are insufficiently represented on the global agenda.

- We have to realise that a true ecological approach always becomes a social approach; it must integrate questions of justice in debates on the environment, so as to hear both the cry of the earth and the cry of the poor.

Floods in Thailand destroy many homes.

Over to You – Enquiry

Using the information in these quotes, answer the following questions:

1. Does the Pope think that climate change is an important issue in the world today?
2. Does the Pope value the importance of scientific research?
3. How does the Pope view other species?
4. What example does the Pope give to show that environmental problems are having a greater impact on the lives of the most vulnerable people on the planet?
5. Do you think that religious leaders have a role in tackling the issue of climate change? Explain why or why not.

Over to You – Enquiry

The following questions are for you to discuss and to ask as an ongoing research project in class. You can do a survey, pool answers and add your own thoughts; research online and in libraries; contact your Green Schools group, or other environmental organisations; and keep up to date with news on environmental issues.

- Why does taking care of the earth matter?
- How does taking care of the earth help our wellbeing?
- What steps can we take to help the environment?
- What moral questions must we all face when it comes to the environment?
- What are your reflections on what you have learned?

Over to You – Reflection and Action

Write a letter to a world leader asking him or her to work towards combating climate change. Explain the problems that the natural world is facing and outline steps that could be taken to help the environment.

The world's leading climate scientists have warned there is only a dozen years for global warming to be kept to a maximum of 1.5°C, beyond which even half a degree will significantly worsen the risks of drought, floods, extreme heat and poverty for hundreds of millions of people.

The authors of the landmark report by the UN Intergovernmental Panel on Climate Change (IPCC) released on Monday say urgent and unprecedented changes are needed to reach the target, which they say is affordable and feasible although it lies at the most ambitious end of the Paris Agreement pledge to keep temperatures between 1.5°C and 2°C.

The half-degree difference could also prevent corals from being completely eradicated and ease pressure on the Arctic, according to the 1.5°C study, which was launched after approval at a final plenary of all 195 countries in Incheon in South Korea that saw delegates hugging one another, with some in tears.

Source: *The Guardian*, 8 October 2018

Revision Questions

Enquiry

1. What is the understanding of the earth found in **two** of the major world religions?
2. How relevant are the teachings of the religions on the earth and how people need to take care of it in today's world?
3. How is the wellbeing of the earth connected with the wellbeing of people?
4. What does humanism say about people's role in taking care of the earth?

Exploration

1. How important is it to take care of the earth?
2. Create a list of environmental problems occurring in the world today.
3. Discuss the importance of individual actions in combating climate change.
4. Discuss who is most responsible for taking care of the earth.

Reflection and Action

- Raise awareness of the problems the planet is facing by creating an information board or newsletter, organising an art competition or holding a fundraiser for a wildlife charity.
- In this project, include tips on things that people can do to be more environmentally friendly.

30 Debating a Moral Issue 3

Learning Outcome 3.6

Debate a moral issue that arises in their lives and consider what influences two different viewpoints on the issue.

Learning Intentions

By the end of this chapter I will:

- Have learned about a moral issue
- Have heard two different points of view on the issue
- Have learned about what influences different points of view on this issue
- Have participated in a debate

Key Skills and Wellbeing

- Communicating
- Managing myself
- Staying well

I feel listened to and respected.
I show care and respect for others.

Keywords

euthanasia ■ hospice ■ palliative care

Introduction

Earlier in this course, we explored what it means to be moral, moral codes and influences on morality. In Chapter 8, a moral decision-making process was outlined. We learned that moral issues are ones that have the potential to affect people for good or bad, and that influences can affect a person's character, development or behaviour. Chapter 9 looked at how to debate moral issues and Chapter 20 presented another topic for debate. The following points are important to remember:

- Moral issues involve choices.
- People have different opinions on moral issues.
- Different viewpoints are influenced by many issues.

 Chapters 8, 9, 20

In this chapter, we will debate another moral issue. Remember to debate is to set out a viewpoint or argument on a subject on which people have different views, supporting one's stance with evidence.

Icebreaker

 Discuss whether the following statements are true or false.

1. For something to be moral, it must involve a choice.
2. What one person thinks is right another can think is wrong.
3. A person's moral choice affects no one but themselves.
4. A person's own morality is more important than what the state says is legal.
5. In the end there is only one right answer when making a moral decision.
6. A person should carefully consider the consequences when making a moral decision.
7. Group moral decisions should be made on the basis of the opinion of the majority of people.

Here is a moral dilemma for you to think about.

The Runaway Train Dilemma

There is a runaway train heading down a track. If it continues on the track, it will hit five people on the track and kill them. There is a lever which you can pull, which will divert the train and change its course to a side track. The problem is there is a worker on the side track. If you pull the lever, the worker will be killed. What should you do?

Euthanasia

What Is Euthanasia?

The word '**euthanasia**' comes from two Greek words that roughly translated mean a 'good death'. To carry out euthanasia is to end a person's life when they want to die. Euthanasia is a deliberate act that aims to relieve suffering and to bring about death. There are some important distinctions that need to be made.

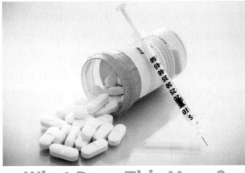

What Does This Mean?

Euthanasia: To end a person's life when he or she wants to die.

- Active euthanasia involves doing something to bring about death. It can include giving an overdose of sedatives or an injection to bring about death.

- Passive euthanasia means withdrawing treatments that will sustain life.

- 'Voluntary euthanasia' means the person has requested or asked to be euthanised.

- Non-voluntary euthanasia means the person is unable to request euthanasia and someone else makes the decision for them.

- 'Involuntary euthanasia' means the person is euthanised against their wishes. They are capable of making a decision but have not asked to be euthanised.

Assisted suicide is another related term. This is when a person helps someone else to take their own life. An example of this would be buying tablets on the internet and giving them to someone, knowing that they intend to use them to take an overdose. Both euthanasia and assisted suicide are illegal in Ireland. They are considered to be very serious crimes and can be punished by life imprisonment.

Countries that have legalised euthanasia are the Netherlands, Belgium, Luxembourg, Colombia and Canada. Switzerland and some states in the United States allow assisted suicide.

Ending a Life

This following important information on end-of-life rights in Ireland is adapted from the HSE website:

- All adults, as long as they are considered mentally able to make decisions, have the right to refuse medical treatment even if the treatment is needed to save their life.

- Individuals who know they may not be able to make decisions in the future are able to arrange in advance what procedures and treatments they want or do not want carried out.

- Some people choose not to allow resuscitation following cardiac arrest or respiratory arrest. This is called a DNAR order, which means 'do not attempt resuscitation'. This order needs to be put on a person's medical records. People who make this order usually have serious illnesses, where there is a real risk of cardiac or respiratory arrest. Individuals can change their minds about the DNAR order.

- When individuals are coming close to death, there is an option to give them palliative sedation. This makes them unconscious and unaware of pain. It is not intended to end a person's life but can risk shortening it.

- Life-sustaining treatments like feeding through a tube and use of dialysis and ventilators can be withdrawn by a doctor's recommendation. This is done only when the treatment is prolonging dying and there is no prospect of a person recovering.

Debate: For and Against Euthanasia

For Euthanasia

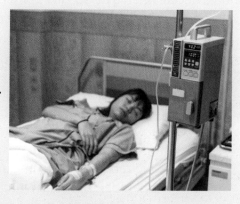

- A doctor could ease a patient's last moments if the person wants to die.
- Dying can cause a lot of suffering, pain and distress. Euthanasia can help to reduce this.
- Doctors have too much power over patients. Some people see palliative sedation and DNAR as a type of euthanasia. This needs to be controlled more, with proper laws introduced allowing for voluntary euthanasia.
- Patients should have more control over how and when they die. Many very ill people feel they have lost any control. Euthanasia gives people some say over their own lives. This is especially important in these difficult circumstances.
- Watching someone die is extremely difficult for individuals' relatives and friends. If a person wants to die, allowing them a quick and painless death will relieve their own and their loved ones' suffering.
- Keeping terminally ill people alive is expensive, and uses the time and skills of doctors, nurses and other health professionals. When a person wants to die, it is a misuse of resources in an already stretched health system.
- Euthanasia is about compassion and love. Ending a person's life in this way is not comparable to killing as it has a completely different motivation.

Against Euthanasia

- A doctor's role is to help sustain and preserve life, not to take it away.
- When people become seriously ill, or when they have been in a life-changing accident, they are not thinking rationally. They may go on to lead very full and happy lives, but if they were euthanised this could never happen.
- Doctors can make mistakes. People may be told they are not going to get better when they could make a recovery or have a very long remission. The decision to euthanise someone is irreversible.
- The state should never allow someone to take a person's life.
- Euthanasia leads people to think that some individuals' lives are less valuable than others. Old and sick people are vulnerable and could start to view themselves as a burden to their families. They might request euthanasia even when they do not want it.
- Euthanasia is unnecessary. There are alternatives, such as palliative care, which helps individuals to die naturally and with dignity and respect. In the right circumstances and with the right care, a person does not have to suffer intolerably.
- People asking for euthanasia are not thinking clearly. They may be upset and afraid. The best way to help them is to relieve their suffering not to end their life. Compassion and love are not expressed through killing someone.

These are just some of the arguments for and against euthanasia. You can probably think of many more. Many religious people view euthanasia as wrong as they believe only God should decide when a person lives or dies. Many humanists think that euthanasia should be legalised as it allows people to make decisions about their own lives.

Over to You – Enquiry

- Have a debate.
- You can do a walking debate or formal debate.
- It is a good idea to research this topic further ahead of doing a formal debate.
- If you are working in teams, divide the arguments between you, and try to avoid repeating the same arguments.
- Remember that life-limiting illnesses and end-of-life care are sensitive topics. Be mindful of the experiences of other people in your class when discussing this.

To Think About ...

In pairs, discuss the following questions and give feedback to the class.

1. Who should make the decision for someone to be euthanised if they cannot decide for themselves, for example, if they are in a coma?
2. Would allowing voluntary euthanasia inevitably lead to non-voluntary or involuntary euthanasia?
3. Why might individuals end up being euthanised against their wishes?
4. Should people be forced to go abroad to get the treatment that they want?
5. If euthanasia were introduced, should it only be for people who have terminal illnesses or are in extreme physical pain? What about people who just want to die?

Palliative Care

The Irish Cancer Society describes its **palliative care** as care which:

> ... aims to improve the quality of life of patients and their families when their cancer can no longer be cured. As well as providing relief from pain, nausea and other symptoms, palliative care offers support and comfort to patients. It involves caring for their physical, emotional and spiritual needs in the best way.

Irish Cancer Society

Palliative care is also given to patients with other life-limiting illnesses. Many terminally ill people are cared for in a **hospice**. The Irish Hospice Foundation has lots of information on what palliative care is.

The Irish Hospice Foundation

What Does This Mean?

Palliative care: Care for terminally ill patients and their families.

Hospice: A hospital that takes care of people who are dying. In a hospice, people's medical, physical, emotional and spiritual needs are taken care of.

Over to You – Reflection and Action

Some people see palliative care as a good alternative to euthanasia. What do you think?

Revision Questions

Enquiry

1. What is the difference between voluntary, non-voluntary and involuntary euthanasia?
2. What rights do people have over their medical treatment in Ireland?
3. Which countries allow euthanasia?
4. What is palliative care?

Exploration

1. Why would a person seek euthanasia?
2. What factors would influence a person's view on the issue of euthanasia?
3. Would allowing euthanasia change the outlook of people in Ireland in relation to illness, old age and dying?
4. How could the Golden Rule 'treat others as you want to be treated' be used to argue for or against the introduction of euthanasia?

Reflection and Action

- Research the work of the Irish Hospice Foundation. Find out how it helps people with life-limiting illnesses and their families.
- Choose **one** major world religion or humanism and investigate its teachings on the issue of euthanasia.

31 Religious Themes in Culture 3

Learning Outcome 1.5

Explore the presence of religious themes in contemporary culture through an examination of art, music, literature or film.

Learning Intentions

By the end of this chapter I will:

- Explore the use of religious themes in contemporary culture by examining art, music, literature and film
- Analyse religious themes in art, music, literature and film
- Evaluate the use of religious themes in different works of art, music, literature and film

Key Skills and Wellbeing

- Working with others
- Managing information and thinking
- Being creative
- Communicating

I am aware of the influences around me. I am connected with others and the wider world and respect the diversity of cultures, beliefs and opinions of others.

Keywords

analyse ▪ evaluate ▪ impact

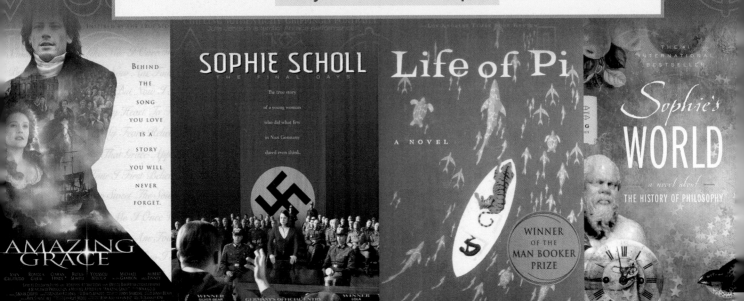

Introduction

In Chapters 10 and 21, we explored and compared religious themes in contemporary culture. In this chapter, we will again explore religious themes expressed through art. This time, we will **analyse** and **evaluate** the use of religious themes in different art forms.

Icebreaker

1. What are religious themes?
2. Make a list of films, songs, and works of art, poetry or stories with religious themes.

Action Verb Focus: Analyse and Evaluate

Analyse: To study or examine something in detail

When we analyse something, we break it down in order to bring out the essential elements or structure; to identify parts and relationships, and to interpret information to reach conclusions.

Evaluate: To collect and examine evidence and to make judgments and appraisals

When we evaluate something, we describe how evidence supports or does not support a judgement; we identify the limitations of evidence in conclusions; and we make judgments about ideas, solutions or methods.

Art

When you study the world religions,

🔗 Chapters 10, 21

you find certain themes and ideas emerge. Reconciliation is an idea found throughout world religions. This can be identified as a religious theme. Reconciliation is about bringing people together after an argument, a disagreement or a conflict. Forgiveness is often a part of reconciliation.

Reconciliation can also be between a person and God; it can be about repairing this relationship after something has damaged it. In the Roman Catholic Church, the sacrament of reconciliation is where individuals seek forgiveness from God for wrongdoing. They aim to reconcile their relationship with God. Reconciliation, whether between individuals or groups, is about healing a broken relationship. This has been a theme for some of the following works of art.

What religious themes are evident in this picture?

Hands Across the Divide

The sculpture *Hands Across the Divide* by Maurice Hannon was unveiled in Derry in 1992, 20 years after Bloody Sunday. It is a bronze sculpture with two men reaching out their hands towards each other. It is a symbol of hope and reconciliation. The sculpture has become a popular landmark and is mentioned in guidebooks. The two hands are reaching out but not touching. Many have interpreted this as a sign that healing is still needed between the two communities in Northern Ireland. It has been suggested that, in the future, when all past hurts are healed and the communities are fully reconciled, the two hands could be placed in a way that allows them to touch.

🔗 Chapter 24

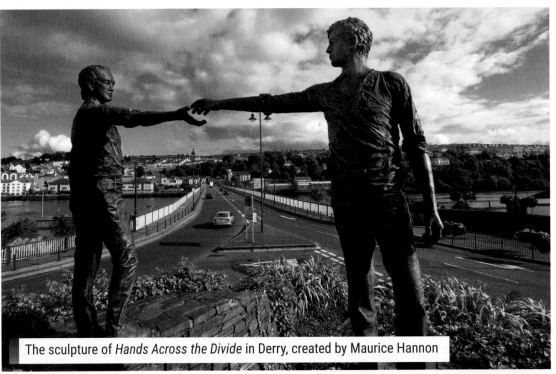

The sculpture of *Hands Across the Divide* in Derry, created by Maurice Hannon

The Prodigal Son

The Prodigal Son is a sculpture by Margaret Adams Parker. It was dedicated in 2005 in the Duke Divinity School in North Carolina, USA. It is a bronze sculpture depicting the story of the Prodigal Son as told in the Bible in Luke 15. It shows the father holding the younger 'prodigal' son while reaching out to his older son. The father is shown as full of compassion and understanding. The sculpture is the artist's way of representing a Christian understanding of God's forgiveness. At the same time it highlights the father's role in reconciling the two brothers.

Photo: Dwayne E. Huebner

The Prodigal Son is a sculpture by Margaret Adams Parker (www.margaretadamsparker.com).

Reconciliation

Another statue with the theme of reconciliation is by Josefina de Vasconcellos. This sculpture is found in Coventry Cathedral, in the UK. It shows a man and woman embracing and was originally created in 1977 and called *Reunion*. It was later renamed *Reconciliation*. The dedication underneath the statue reads:

> In 1995, 50 years after the end of the Second World War, this sculpture by Josefina de Vasconcellos has been given by Richard Branson as a token of reconciliation. An identical sculpture has been placed on behalf of the people of Coventry in the Peace Garden, Hiroshima, Japan. Both sculptures remind us that, in the face of destructive forces, human dignity and love will triumph over disaster and bring nations together in respect and peace.

Why do you think an identical casting of this sculpture was placed in the Japanese city of Hiroshima?

Over to You – Exploration

1. Research the background story of **one** of the three sculptures discussed above and how it came to be created.
2. Do you think the artist's own background and ideas influenced its creation?

Review and Reflect

1. Discuss how well the theme of reconciliation is expressed through these **three** sculptures.
2. Which of the **three** sculptures do you think best depicts the theme of reconciliation?
3. What aspects of this sculpture do you think convey its theme most?

Music

The song 'Hallelujah' was written by Leonard Cohen and has been covered by many artists, including the singer Jeff Buckley, and (for the film *Shrek*) by Rufus Wainwright. It was performed by Alexander Stewart in Canada at a tribute for the victims of the 2018 shooting in Danforth. This song is full of religious references and themes.

The repetition of the word 'hallelujah', which is an expression of praise or thanks to God, is instantly recognisable as a religious theme. The lyrics also refer to characters from the Jewish Tanakh. King David from the Tanakh is mentioned in the first verse, and the character of Samson in another. The relationships referred to are ones that are characterised as failing or causing the downfall of someone. The 'hallelujah', although an exclamation of praise to God, is sung with a sadness that does not seem to celebrate or be joyful. Is it all that is left when nothing else can be said?

The Canadian singer and songwriter Leonard Cohen wrote 'Hallelujah'.

- Is a comparison being made between the failed relationships of the biblical characters with a failed relationship of the singer?
- Can we all identify with a broken relationship, which leaves anger, hurt and feelings of rejection?
- Is it like losing faith?
- Has the singer given up on God? Is the 'hallelujah' ironic?

 Chapters 10, 21

No matter what happens, the singer keeps on repeating 'hallelujah' and at the end sings: 'And even though it all went wrong, I'll stand before the Lord of Song, With nothing on my tongue but hallelujah'.

This song is open to interpretation. People will have different viewpoints about what it means. However, the use of religious themes and references is clear. Themes of love, pain, jealousy, God, reconciliation and hope can be identified.

Over to You – Exploration

1. Before reading about this song, were you familiar with 'Hallelujah'?
2. Listen to different versions of the song 'Hallelujah'.
3. What feeling does the song convey?
4. Which version do you prefer?
5. Write down any words with religious meaning.
6. Do you think the song uses religious themes well? Explain why or why not.
7. Name any other songs you know that use religious themes.

Literature

Two books that delve into the theme of the search for meaning are *The Life of Pi* by Yann Martel and *Sophie's World* by Jostein Gaarder. These books explore this theme in very different ways.

The Life of Pi

Chapters 10, 21

The Life of Pi is a about a boy who is shipwrecked in the Pacific Ocean and spends 227 days surviving on a lifeboat with a Bengal tiger named Richard Parker. The story centres on the character of Pi Patel, a 16-year-old who had previously lived with his family in Pondicherry Zoo in India. While in India, Pi searches for meaning to life through his exploration of religion. He practises Christianity, Islam and Hinduism at the same time. He also studies zoology. But when he is shipwrecked, Pi's family are drowned and life becomes a matter of survival; he is faced with finding meaning in suffering.

The use of story to make meaning is a theme in this book. It starts with a writer in India meeting a man who tells him to find Pi Patel. Pi will tell him a story that will make him 'believe in God'.

When Pi is rescued, two officials, who are writing a report on the sinking of the ship, interview him. They find Pi's story of his time at sea with the tiger unbelievable, so Pi tells them another story that satisfies them. The reader now has two stories of Pi's time at sea, and it is up to the reader to decide which story to believe.

This book covers religious themes of God, suffering, love, faith, miracles, the nature of humans and animals, hope, morality, belief and meaning.

As the character Pi says:

> Love is hard to believe, ask any lover. Life is hard to believe, ask any scientist. God is hard to believe, ask any believer. What is your problem with hard to believe?

A still from *The Life of Pi* shows Pi on the boat with the tiger Richard Parker.

Sophie's World

Sophie's World is a book by Jostein Gaarder. The story centres on a 14-year-old girl called Sophie. She is introduced to a philosophy course through a letter arriving at her home. However, she finds herself in the middle of a mystery that requires philosophical thinking to work out.

The book is about the human search for meaning and understanding. It introduces the reader to many of the most famous philosophers in history, including Socrates, Descartes and Kierkegaard.

The author of *Sophie's World*, Jostein Gaarder, said in an interview with the *Irish Times* in 2005:

> My experience from travelling all over the world is that human beings are human beings are human beings. I was in a classroom in Tokyo and I asked the young students there, 'What are the most profound human questions?', and they gave me exactly the same questions I would have got from students in Norway.

A still from *Sophie's World*

Review and Reflect

1. Which religious themes do the books *Sophie's World* and *The Life of Pi* share?
2. In the quote from *The Life of Pi*, what point is the character Pi Patel making?
3. When interviewed in 2005, what did Jostein Gaarder say that he noticed about human beings?

Key Skill: Being Creative

Draw a picture of Pi Patel on the boat in the Pacific Ocean with the tiger Richard Parker.

Over to You – Enquiry

1. Read the first chapter of either *Sophie's World* or *The Life of Pi* and discuss the setting.
2. Do you think it is a good setting for discussing the meaning of life in a story?
3. Do you think the main characters are a good choice for setting out on a journey to explore meaning of life questions?
4. What is your first impression of the story?
5. Would you like to read more? Explain why or why not.

Film

Amazing Grace and *Sophie Scholl* are two films that deal with the **impact** religious belief and faith can have on individuals' moral decisions and the outcome of their lives, the lives of others and their legacy. Both of these films are based on true stories. The central characters had strong religious convictions that led to them act in a way that was radical for their time and had long-lasting consequences.

What Does This Mean?

Impact: To have a strong effect on something or someone.

Amazing Grace

Chapters 10, 21

Amazing Grace is based on the story of the campaign to end slavery in Britain during the eighteenth and nineteenth centuries. The main character is William Wilberforce, who was deeply religious. He believed that, to truly live out his Christian life, he must do all in his power to improve the lives of others. So, he spent most of his political life campaigning to abolish slavery. The film features his friendship with the prime minister, William Pitt, and his old preacher, John Newton, who wrote the famous hymn the film is named after, 'Amazing Grace', and his marriage to Barbara Spooner. The theme of religious belief and its impact on social action, morality and sacrifice is strong. The film starred Ioan Gruffudd, Romola Garai, Albert Finney and Benedict Cumberbatch.

The experience of seeing a slave ship first hand and of hearing the story of a former slave had an impact on the character of William Wilberforce.

How Do the Themes Emerge?

- William Wilberforce is seen at the beginning of the film stopping someone from beating a horse.
- He is shown to be deciding whether he wants to become a minister of the church or go into politics.
- He is haunted by the fact that he has not succeeded in abolishing slavery. It affects his sleep and health. He is shown to have a very strong conscience.
- He talks to John Newton about matters of faith and about his mission to end slavery.
- The name of the film is also its opening song – 'Amazing Grace'. This was written by John Newton and reflects his experiences, conversion and belief in the love of God.

Sophie Scholl

Sophie Scholl is a German film based on the interrogation and trial of Sophie Scholl and her brother, Hans Scholl, in Nazi Germany. They were accused of being members of the White Rose – a group of students at the University of Munich, who opposed the Nazis and distributed anti-Nazi literature.

The film deals with Sophie's interrogation by the police inspector Robert Mohr. These scenes are an opportunity to deal with issues of morality and how a person views right and wrong.

The police inspector uses the law as his source for what is considered good or bad. His opinion on morality is that if you break the law, you suffer the consequences. He looks to no higher authority and does not see much value in personal conscience.

Sophie thinks about morals, conscience and God. She will do what is right even when the state thinks it is wrong, and even when it endangers her life. She lives by her conscience and her own moral compass. She has a strong personal faith.

The film also shows the influence of Sophie's parents on her life, and on her moral development and belief. This is revealed when she prays in her cell and when she asks the priest to bless her.

A still shows Sophie and Hans Scholl from the film *Sophie Scholl*.

How Do the Themes Emerge?

- Sophie Scholl is seen as very selfless. She wants to protect others and is willing to sacrifice herself to protect her friends.
- Sophie discusses morality with the police inspector.
- Sophie's father, Robert Scholl, says 'There is a higher justice'.
- She prays in the cell.
- Sophie's mother tells her, 'Don't forget, Sophie. Jesus.'
- Sophie asks the priest to bless her and he tells her, 'No one loves more than one who dies for friends.'

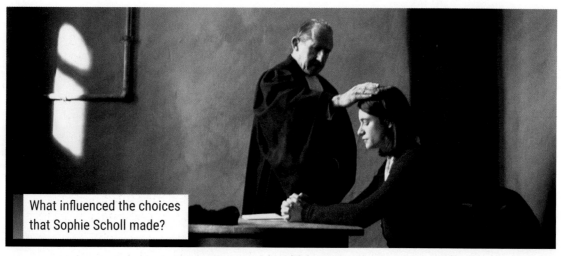

What influenced the choices that Sophie Scholl made?

Review and Reflect

1. What themes are dealt with in both *Amazing Grace* and *Sophie Scholl*?
2. Do you think that the themes are easy to identify?
3. Is the fact that they are based on real events important?
4. How important was the faith of both William Wilberforce and Sophie Scholl in their lives and choices?
5. Does the theme of the impact of religious belief occur in other films or books that you know?

Revision Questions

Enquiry

1. How do you identify religious themes in art?
2. How do you identify religious themes in music?
3. How do you identify religious themes in literature?
4. How do you identify religious themes in film?
5. What are the main religious themes found in contemporary culture?
6. Name a work of art, a book, a film and a piece of music and identify **one** religious theme for each.
7. Compare **one** religious theme in **two** pieces of art, music, literature or film.

Exploration

1. Think about how often religious themes emerge in contemporary culture.
2. Keep a list of times when you notice religious themes in contemporary culture. Share the list with others in your class.
3. Create a list wall in your classroom.
4. Design posters for religious-themed films, books, music and art.

Reflection and Action

- Watch the film *Sophie Scholl* or *Amazing Grace*. Research more about the story that the film is based on and evaluate how well the film tells the story.
- Read the book *Sophie's World* or *The Life of Pi* and write a review.

32 Archaeology, Art and Architecture

Learning Outcome 2.1

Research artistic, architectural or archaeological evidence that shows ways in which people have searched for meaning and purpose in life.

Learning Intentions

By the end of this chapter I will:

- Know how archaeology, art and architecture show the human search for meaning and purpose
- Be able to give examples of how the search for meaning and purpose is seen in archaeology, art and architecture
- Be able to identify shared themes in the human search for meaning as expressed in art and architecture

Key Skills and Wellbeing

- Managing information and thinking
- Being creative
- Being numerate

I feel connected to the wider world and I respect the different world cultures and expressions of meaning.

Keywords

archaeology ▪ Book of the Dead ▪ catacombs

Cave drawings from ancient times reflect the ultimate questions of life, purpose and meaning for the people who made them.

Introduction

Throughout history, people have asked questions about life and what it means. Individuals have considered the world, their place in it and the idea of God or a higher being. In every era, these big questions have been considered and expressed artistically in different ways.

For ancient history, we rely on the evidence of archaeologists to piece together the ideas of our ancestors. The art and architecture of the ancient world can show us how people thought about life, God, their purpose and death.

Whether we are studying ancient, medieval or modern times, there is physical evidence of how people have expressed their search for meaning and purpose in life. We are going to explore some of that evidence and look for common themes and ideas.

Icebreaker

1. What are the physical things people leave behind that show what they believed?
2. If a person in the future were studying the archaeological remains of today, what things would show what people believe now?
3. What things in art or architecture might give a clue as to how we search for meaning?

1. The Stadio Olimpico in Rome, **2.** the Sagrada Familia in Barcelona, **3.** the Blue Mosque in Istanbul and **4.** Glasnevin Cemetery in Dublin: can buildings be an indication of what people think is important in life?

The Search for Meaning and Purpose

Before we begin to identify the ways in which people have expressed their search for meaning and purpose through art and architecture, let us recap what questions that search poses. Some of these have been explored in Chapter 25, Life's Big Questions. We can list them here as:

- Is there a purpose to life?
- Do individuals matter?
- Is there an afterlife?
- Does God exist? And if so, what is the world's relationship to God? What is God's role and what is God like?
- What is the relationship between humans and the natural world?

🔗 Chapter 25

Throughout history, people have searched for meaning and purpose in life, and expressed these questions in art and architecture. We can identify some shared ideas or expressions, even though they are found in different parts of the world, at different times and in different cultures. Some of these ideas include:

- The idea of God or the Gods in the heavens. This is often shown in art and architecture.
- The use of tombs or graves and the artistic ways in which these are structured and decorated. This is often a way of representing the beliefs of the people who built them.
- The statues of the Gods or God and how these are a way of showing the importance of the divine.
- The important place that survival plays in every culture and how that is linked to meaning and purpose.
- The drawing of animals in symbolic ways.

People have often imagined God or Gods in the heavens.

People have always found ways to make sense of death. Ancient megalithic tombs, graveyards and memorials show how people try to find meaning in death, as well as in life.

Archaeology

The word '**archaeology**' means 'ancient study'. The work of an archaeologist is to study the past by looking at the remains below or above ground and even sometimes under water. Archaeologists look for clues when deciding to dig in a particular area. They may find remains above ground pointing to the possibility of more below, they may have seen an old map or have heard a story that suggests an area would be good to dig, or they may see patterns in the soil indicating an area of interest. The dig is carried out carefully and all is recorded and dated. The artefacts and other evidence archaeologists find are useful for finding out more about our ancient ancestors.

Archaeologists helped to discover the Egyptian pyramids, the cave paintings of France and Spain and the ancient sites of Newgrange and Stonehenge. It was through archaeology that we discovered more about the Aztecs, the Mayans and the Incas in Central America.

What Does This Mean?

Archaeology: The study of history by excavating old sites and analysing the artefacts found. It is often used for studying ancient times, as it relies on finding objects or material evidence to help us to find out about the past.

Wall paintings of animals in the Lascaux cave in France

The Great Sphinx of Giza with the Great Pyramid of Kufu in the background in Giza, Egypt

Archeological Discoveries

Sometimes, archaeologists notice patterns in stonework that may have had a meaning for the people who created them. Or they might notice how a body is placed in a grave or the way a structure is built. Much of the understanding of what these things mean is a matter of interpretation. We may never fully understand what the people who created them believed or thought.

Let us examine some of these ancient sites. We will see if they reveal any clues to the search for meaning and purpose, and if they point to the beliefs of the people who built them.

Machu Picchu is an ancient Incan city of temples, terraces and water channels built on a mountain top in Peru.

Newgrange

Newgrange in Co. Meath is the most famous Neolithic (New Stone Age) site in Ireland. The Boyne Valley area has a number of passage graves, of which Newgrange is the largest and most impressive. The grave has a central chamber, with three chambers leading out from it. It contains a passageway from the entrance to the inner chamber. The passage slopes upwards. When you are in the centre chamber, you can look out to the entrance, where there is a roof-box above the door. This roof-box is the most impressive feature. During the winter solstice, light enters through the roof-box and illuminates the central chamber.

Newgrange, a prehistoric monument built during the Neolithic period, is located in Co. Meath. It is a UNESCO World Heritage Site.

Light shines into the burial chamber in Newgrange during the winter solstice.

Features at Newgrange

Another feature of Newgrange are the spiral, artistic designs found inside and outside the tomb, especially the ones on the very large stones at the entrance.

The discovery of Newgrange and how the roof-box worked has led people to wonder about its purpose and meaning for the ancient people who built it. Newgrange clearly functioned as a grave, but could it also have been a sort of calendar for these people?

- Why did they bury their dead this way?
- Was a grave this impressive for a special person or people?
- What do the designs mean?
- Were the stone basins where the ashes of the dead were placed significant?
- Why did they cremate the dead first and then ceremonially place them here?

Spirals engraved into the entrance stones at Newgrange

Many people think that the people who built Newgrange saw it as a sacred place. They believe that the spiral designs on the stones were important symbols; perhaps they worshipped the sun as a type of God. After all, survival was dependent on the growth of crops, which require warmth and light from the sun. The fact that the chamber lights up at the turning point of the year, when the sun appears to have lost its power, but then regenerates and regains it, may reinforce this idea.

Over to You – Enquiry

1. Design a poster about Newgrange and include drawings, history and statistics.
2. Write a story about the people who built Newgrange.

Ancient Egypt

The temples and pyramids of ancient Egypt (3000 BCE–30 CE) reveal a lot about the beliefs and ideas of the ancient Egyptians. As the ancient Egyptians tried to make sense of the world and their place in it, they were concerned with the order of things and the need for survival. These people depended on the River Nile to flood in order for the crops to grow. The Ancient Egyptians believed that their many Gods were responsible for the Nile flooding, crops growing and the people surviving. The Gods were worshipped and glorified in the building projects they carried out.

The Book of the Dead

The ancient Egyptians believed in a soul that lived on after death, but it needed the body. Therefore the body had to be preserved. When a wealthy person died, the body was mummified, placed in a tomb and surrounded by statues and spells to protect it. The body might be partly wrapped in papyrus, which contained the **Book of the Dead**. Or the book could be rolled up and placed in a hollow statue next to the body. The Book of the Dead is a collection of spells, passwords and useful information for the spirit to move through the netherworld or underworld; this is where the person went immediately after death.

A papyrus of The Book of the Dead

The Underworld

When the soul moves through the netherworld, the heart is weighed to decide the person's fate. If the heart is too heavy, it is eaten by the devourer monster and ceases to exist. If the heart is the correct weight, the person is welcomed by the God of the Underworld, Osiris. Once here, the person may join the Gods and travel by day with the Sun God, Ra, re-entering the mummified body at night and worshipping Osiris. Or, in what was seen as a better fate, the individual enters a place known as the 'field of reeds', where a kind of Egyptian paradise exists and nobody goes hungry. This place is filled with waterways on which you can sail and fields of crops.

Did You Know?

? People who were worried about the heart-weighing ceremony had a spell inscribed on a heart amulet, to prevent their heart from 'betraying' them.

A human-faced, heart scarab of the type that was placed on the deceased's heart

Over to You – Enquiry

1. What is the Book of the Dead and what did it contain?
2. Why did ancient Egyptians believe they needed the Book of the Dead?
3. How was a person finally judged in death, according to the ancient Egyptians?
4. Who was the God of the Underworld?

Key Skill: Managing Information and Thinking

1. Find out about the great Sphinx of Giza and what purpose it served in ancient Egypt.
2. Write down **10** facts from what you find out.

Stonehenge

Dating from the Bronze Age (3000 BCE–1200 BCE), Stonehenge is one of the most famous stone circles in the world. Its elaborate design is hugely impressive, considering the time in which it was built.

The people who built Stonehenge are referred to as the Beaker people, named after the pottery discovered there on archaeological digs. These people, like those who built Newgrange, worshipped the sun. There appears to be careful planning around the stones' alignment, which allows the sun to shine through the stone arches. The stones also follow the light of the moon. Some think it was built to observe the movement of the sun and the moon.

The people may have seen this place as sacred, and there is evidence they buried their dead here. Was it a special place for connecting the two worlds: the world of the dead and the world of the living? Did these people, living thousands of years ago, have a sense of the sacred and a belief in some form of afterlife or further purpose?

A huge amount of time and effort was put into the construction of this magnificent stone circle, despite the lack of tools and machinery. This circle was built over many lifetimes. It was important for these people to complete it or to keep adding to it. It is thought that they carried out rituals and ceremonial gatherings here. They were making meaning of the world as they knew it and of life and its ending.

Stonehenge is made from two types of stone: sarsens and bluestones. The bluestones include many from the Preseli Hills in Wales, which is nearly 250 km away.

Did You Know?

 According to John Martineau in a book called *Megalith*, the builders of Stonehenge may have used Pythagoras's theorem 2,000 years before Pythagoras was born!

Key Skill: Communicating

1. Discuss the purpose of a stone circle.
2. Discuss possible uses that Stonehenge could have served for the people that used it.
3. Discuss the importance of archaeology for finding out more about the human search for meaning and purpose.

Art

Art is how humans use their creativity and imagination to express themselves. Humans have created art since ancient times. In September 2018, archaeologists discovered a drawing in South Africa that they believe dates back 73,000 years.

Art can take many forms, including paintings and sculpture. Most art is made to be beautiful or to express an emotion that is hard to put into words. Through art, people have conveyed ideas or thoughts, which other people can interpret and understand.

🔗 Chapters 10, 21

Catacomb Paintings

The **catacombs** are a series of tombs found under the ground in Rome, Italy. They were built and used from the second to fifth centuries by Christians, Jews and sometimes pagans. They were outside the walls of the city of Rome and away from view, so that Christians could bury their dead and use Christian symbols without fear. The Christians used art to decorate these tombs, some of which survives today. It is an artistic expression of their beliefs and a symbolic way of showing what gave their life meaning.

What Does This Mean?

Catacombs: Underground tunnels used as burial sites in the ancient world.

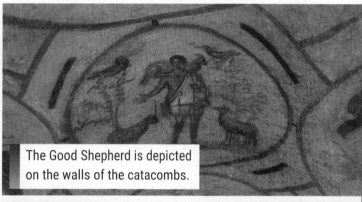

The Good Shepherd is depicted on the walls of the catacombs.

The catacombs of Rome

The Samaritan woman at the well is drawn on the walls of this tomb.

Over to You – Enquiry

1. In groups, discuss the images from the catacombs.
2. What story is behind each image?
3. How important was art for the early Christians in expressing their beliefs and giving sense or purpose to their lives?
4. Do these images still have any meaning or relevance for Christians today?

Statues

Hindus often use images and statues to represent their Gods. They believe in many Gods and they show devotion through acts of worship, which include giving offerings to the Gods. Hindus believe life is about trying to reach *moksha*, which is the ultimate goal and purpose of life. To do so, they must live the perfect life as a Hindu. The statues of the Gods are an artistic image of their important beliefs, and they bring a sense of meaning to the lives of Hindus.

Murudeshwar Statue

This statue of Shiva at the Murudeshwar Temple in India stands 37.5 metres high. It is the second biggest statue of Lord Shiva in the world. The tallest is found in Nepal and is an impressive 44 metres. The site of the Murudeshwar statue is particularly spectacular as the temple is surrounded by the Arabian Sea, creating an amazing view of the statue and coastline. Hindus aim to create good *karma* and wish to carry out their *dharma*, or sacred duty. This statue and others like it are reminders to people of what is important and meaningful in life.

The statue of Shiva at the Murudeshwar Temple in India

Over to You – Enquiry

 Find out more about the tallest statue of Shiva in Nepal.

1. When was it built?
2. Where exactly is it?
3. How tall is it?
4. How does it give people a sense of purpose?

Architecture

Architecture is the way buildings are designed and constructed. It can be an artistic way of expressing something. Many of the most famous buildings in the world are considered to be architectural works of art. These structures are built in a certain style to make a statement or point.

The architects of medieval gothic buildings used techniques such as pointed arches, rose windows and thin pillars to create high, bright interiors. They built tall Christian cathedrals and churches that gave a sense of power and otherworldliness as they pointed heavenwards.

Temple of Jerusalem

Architecturally, the Jewish First and Second Temples in Jerusalem were magnificent structures showing how important God was to the people. The Temples gave a sense of meaning to the people who built and used them. The Temple was a sign of devotion to the one God. Important rituals took place there.

The Romans destroyed the Second Temple in 70 CE, leaving only one wall – the Western or Wailing wall – standing. This wall still stands today, and is one of the most symbolic pieces of architecture in Judaism. It is called the Wailing Wall because people were so upset at the destruction of the Temple that they went there to 'wail' its loss.

For Jewish people, three things had become the focal points of their belief: the Promised Land, the Torah and the Temple. The Temple was an architectural expression of their sense of meaning and purpose in life. This life centred on the covenant with God and was structured around following Jewish law.

People praying at the Western Wailing Wall of the Temple in Jerusalem

The Kaaba

The Kaaba in Mecca is the most holy place in the world for Muslims and the symbol of their belief in one God. When Muslims pray in the direction of the Kaaba, they are submitting to the will of God. Islam is peace through submitting to the will of Allah; this gives Muslims meaning and purpose in their lives.

The Kaaba's structure is an important reminder of that meaning. It is a simple, stone building that is covered in a black cloth. Muslims believe it was first built by Ibrahim and his son Ishmael to worship God. Later, it was used for worshipping false idols, until the Prophet Muhammad restored it to its proper use and purpose.

Musilims pray in the direction of the Kaaba five times a day. They use a compass called a *qibla* to show its direction. Mosques also have a wall that shows this direction.

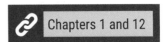
Chapters 1 and 12

The Kaaba in Mecca is a site of pilgrimage.

Key Skill: Being Numerate

1,2,3...

1. Notice the similarities between the meaning and purpose of the Kaaba and the Temple in Jerusalem.
2. Create a Venn diagram showing the similarities and differences between the two buildings.

Over to You – Exploration

There are many other examples of things found in art and architecture and discovered by the study of archaeology that you can explore to find out more about people's search for meaning and purpose. The following are suggestions for you to consider:

- The temples of the Inca or Aztec people
- The tunnels found beneath the ancient Mayan temple
- The Terracotta Army built on the orders of Qin Shi Huang in his pursuit of immortality, which includes 8,000 soldiers, 130 chariots and 520 horses
- The use of totem poles by Native American tribes
- Carvings, pendant necklaces and figurines of the Maori people
- The caves found in Altamira, Spain, or Lascaux, France
- Chinese or Japanese pagodas

Revision Questions

Enquiry

1. What does the search for meaning involve?
2. Explain archaeology.
3. Name **three** pieces of art or architecture that are examples of the search for meaning and purpose.
4. In which country will you find the following?
   - Newgrange
   - Stonehenge
   - The Pyramids
   - The catacombs
   - The Murudeshwar Temple
   - The Kaaba
   - The Wailing Wall
5. Mention themes that are shared among the different forms of art and architecture in the search for meaning and purpose.

Exploration

1. Think about how people have searched for meaning and purpose from ancient times to today.
2. Do you think it is important to use archaeology to help us understand the beliefs and ideas of people in ancient times? Explain why or why not.

Reflection and Action

- Choose **one** of the pieces of art, architecture or archaeology that we explored, or another one you are interested in. Make a presentation for your class about it.
- You can use any medium you wish to make your presentation, including a poem, story, drawing, oral presentation, short film or PowerPoint.

Glossary

adhan: the Muslim call to prayer

arti: the sacred flame ceremony, a very popular ritual in Hinduism

atman: the word for an individual's soul in Hinduism

ahimsa: the Hindu principle of nonviolence

analyse: to study or examine something in detail, to break it down in order to bring out the essential elements or structure; identify parts and relationships, and to interpret information to reach conclusions

anti-Semitism: disliking Jewish people and showing hostility towards them

archaeology: the study of history by excavating old sites and analysing the artefacts found. It is often used for studying ancient times, as it relies on finding objects or material evidence to help us to find out about the past.

asceticism: showing devotion to something through experiencing hardship

avatar: one who descends

Aum: the main symbol for Hinduism. It represents the Divine and is the sound that began the universe and the sound of deepest meditation.

BCE: Before the Common Era

belief: to hold a strong opinion or viewpoint on something

believers: people who have a religious faith and believe in the truth of something

bias: to have an unbalanced opinion. People tend to prefer some things or people over others.

Bible: the Christian holy book or sacred text

biography: an account of a person's life written by someone else. It is similar to an autobiography, which is a person's own account of his or her life.

Bodh Gaya: the place where the Buddha first reached enlightenment

Book of the Dead: a collection of spells, passwords and useful information for a spirit to move through the netherworld or underworld; this is where the person went immediately after death

Brahma: the Hindu God of creation; one of the three Gods that make up the *Trimurti*

Brahman: the universal soul or God in Hinduism. Brahman is the source of all life; part of Brahman exists in all living things.

catacombs: underground tunnels used as burial sites in the ancient world

CE: the Common Era

celebration: an occasion to be joyful and happy about something

census: an official count or survey of a population

choice: an act of making a decision when faced with two or more possibilities

chronology: arrangement of dates or events in order of their occurrence

community: a group of people with something in common

compassion: a strong feeling of sympathy and concern for the suffering of other people. A person with compassion will show care, kindness and a willingness to help other people.

concern: to be worried about or have an interest in someone or something

contemporary culture: art, music, literature and film created today

covenant: an agreement. In Judaism, the covenant is an agreement or promise between God and the people. It was first made by Abraham.

culture: the way of life, especially the customs and beliefs, of a group of people

decision-making process: a step-by-step process that provides a person with a framework for making a moral decision

devotion: when loyalty and dedication are shown. You can be devoted to another person in your life, a cause or a religion.

dharma: the Hindu word for sacred duty

dharmachakra: one of the most important symbols in Buddhism. It represents the teachings of the Buddha. Also known as the *dharma* wheel.

dialogue: a conversation between two or more people

dignity: the sense of self-worth and respect each person should have

discrimination: the unfair treatment of people, especially because of their race, religion, gender or sexuality. When a person is discriminated against, they are treated differently from the way other people are treated.

diversity: the variety within groups of people regarding cultures, religions, race, age, gender and so on

Divine: something that is of or relates to God

divisive: causing disagreement or hostility between people

Diwali: Hindu festival of lights; it celebrates the victory of good over evil

early followers: people who early on became a part of a religion. They were the first followers of a particular founder or belief system.

ecumenism: bringing the different Christian churches closer together, to promote unity, co-operation and better understanding

empathy: being able to image and understand how other people might feel

engage: to participate or become involved in something, allowing it to occupy your interest or attention

enlightenment: In Buddhism, enlightenment is when a person realises the truth about life. To be freed from the birth-death-rebirth cycle, a person must achieve enlightenment.

ethos: the set of values associated with a group of people or a particular type of activity

Eucharist: the sacrament in which Christians remember the Last Supper, when Jesus gave his disciples bread and wine and commanded them to 'do this in memory of me'.

euthanasia: to end a person's life when he or she wants to die

evaluate: to collect and examine evidence and to make judgments and appraisals. To describe how evidence supports or does not support a judgement; to identify the limitations of evidence in conclusions; to make judgments about ideas, solutions or methods.

evidence: the body of facts or information about something or someone. It helps us to build up a picture or understanding about a situation or person. It gives us the information we need.

expansion: when something develops or gets bigger

explore: to systematically look into something closely for the purpose of discovery; to scrutinise or probe

fact: a thing that is known or proved to be true

faith: to have trust or confidence in someone or something. A strongly held belief that may be based on a spiritual or religious conviction.

faith community: a group of people who share a faith

Five Pillars of Islam: guide to living as a Muslim. They are the foundation for any Muslim in living out their faith.

Five Precepts: the five rules of Buddhism

foundational: forming the base from which everything else develops

founder: a person or a group of people who have started something. In religion, there is a founder, or founders, who began a particular belief system or way of life. The founder of Christianity was Jesus of Nazareth; the founder of Islam was the Prophet Muhammad.

Four Noble Truths: the teachings of the Buddha, which explain the cause of human suffering and how to overcome it

freedom: the power or right to act, speak or think as one wants

Golden Rule: a code for how to behave found in the major world religions. It is rooted in the belief that everyone should treat other people the way that they would like to be treated by others.

Gospels: meaning 'good news'. The Gospels contain stories about the life of Jesus. The Bible contains four Gospels: these are Mark, Matthew, Luke and John.

Hadith: the words and deeds of the Prophet Muhammad; it is an important part of Islamic tradition

halal: meat that is prepared so it complies with Islamic teachings

Hajj: the fifth of the Five Pillars of Islam, requiring Muslims to go on the pilgrimage to Mecca

Hanukkah: the Jewish festival of lights, which commemorates how the Temple was restored and rededicated to God

heritage: the traditions, language and buildings that were created in the past and still have historical importance

Hijrah: when Muhammad was forced to flee Mecca in 622 CE and went to the town of Medina. This event is the start of the Islamic calendar.

hospice: a hospital that takes care of people who are dying. In a hospice, people's medical, physical, emotional and spiritual needs are taken care of.

Humanism: a system of thought that attaches prime importance to human rather than divine or supernatural matters

hunger: The short-term, physical discomfort caused by a chronic food shortage. When severe, it is a life-threatening lack of food.

impact: to have a strong effect on something or someone

indulgence: a partial or full remission of the punishment of sin granted by the Roman Catholic Church. In the Middle Ages, this was seen as a way to shorten the person's time in Purgatory. This was where it was believed a person's soul went after they died and before they were accepted into heaven.

influence: the capacity to have an effect on the character, development or behaviour of someone or something

initiation: the act of admitting someone into a new group or society

integrity: the quality of being honest and having strong moral principles. Someone who stands by their values and stands up for what they believe to be right has integrity.

interaction: communication or involvement with someone or something

interconnected: the complex relationship between all living things on the earth

intercultural dialogue: an open and respectful exchange between individuals and groups belonging to different ethnic, cultural and belief backgrounds that leads to a deeper understanding of the other's and one's own perspective

Islam: one of the five major world religions. 'Islam' means 'peace through submission to Allah'.

Islamophobia: the dislike and fear of Muslims and prejudice against the Islamic faith

justice: treating people fairly or equally

karma: the Hindu law of cause and effect. It means that from good comes good, while from bad comes bad. Hindus believe this will affect a person's next life.

kashrut: the food laws in Judaism

Ketuvim: Jewish writings that include the proverbs and psalms; one part of the Tanakh

key people: people who are considered important in relation to something

kosher: food that is allowed to be eaten in Judaism. *Kosher* food satisfies the food laws.

law: the rules agreed upon by people and governments that regulate the behaviour of people living in society

locality: An area or a neighbourhood, or the place where something is found or happens

Lord Krishna: one of the forms that the Hindu God Vishnu took when he descended to earth

Love Command: the teaching of Jesus to 'love God' and to 'love your neighbour as yourself'

magisterium: the Teaching Authority of the Roman Catholic Church. It is made up of the Pope and the bishops in union with him.

materialistic: concerned with material things. A materialistic person is someone who is focused on possessions and money.

mature: when someone or something is fully developed or fully grown

Messiah: from the Hebrew, meaning anointed or chosen one. Christians believe that Jesus is the Messiah.

mezuzah: found on the doorpost of Jewish homes. It contains the words of the *Shema*, 'Hear, O Israel, the Lord is one'.

Mishnah: a Jewish sacred writing, a commentary on the law

mitzvah: a good deed or unit of the Jewish law

mitzvot: Plural of *mitzvah*

moksha: the ultimate goal in Hinduism; when a person no longer needs to be reincarnated and is reunited with Brahman

monotheism: the belief in one God

monotheistic: a word used to describe a system of belief in one God

moral: whether something is considered right or wrong; deciding if an action or idea is good or bad

moral issue: an issue that has the potential to affect ourselves and others, for good or bad

morality: concerned with the principles of right and wrong behaviour

MUAC: mid-upper arm circumference. Aid agencies often use a MUAC band to determine if a child is malnourished. The bands measure the upper arm.

myth: a story full of symbols that expresses truths or beliefs about life at a particular time

narrative: a description of events that actually happened or that are invented

Nevi'im: the Prophets; one part of the Tanakh, the Jewish sacred writings

New Testament: the second part of the Bible. It includes the Gospels, Acts of the Apostles, Letters and Revelation. It is very important for Christians, as it tells the story of the life and death of Jesus Christ.

Nirvana: the state of enlightenment that Buddhists are trying to reach

Noble Eightfold Path: the eight steps outlined by the Buddha for his followers to help them to reach enlightenment

non-religious: unrelated or unconnected to religion or religious belief

Old and New Testaments: the two sections of the Christian Bible

Old Testament: the first part of the Bible, which contains the Jewish sacred writings of the Tanakh

opinion: a view or judgement formed about something, that is not necessarily based on fact or knowledge

origins: where or how something began

Pali Canon: the sacred writing of Buddhism

palliative care: care for terminally ill patients and their families

patron saint: a heavenly advocate of a country, place, activity, craft, person or family

patriarch: male leader of a tribe or group of people. In Judaism, the patriarchs are the founding fathers of the religion.

Pax Christi: Latin for 'Peace of Christ'

peace: living without conflict or hostility. It is living in harmony with one another, with peace of mind, freedom and security.

penitence: when asking for God's forgiveness, e.g. if a person hurts someone they love

petition: when asking for something, e.g. help to cope with stress before an exam

Pharaoh: a king or emperor in Egypt

philosophy: the 'love of wisdom'. Philosophy has different branches – it includes asking questions about the world and reality, about morals or what is good, and about knowledge (how we know what we know).

pilgrimage: a journey to a place of importance to a religion. The journey may be difficult and is undertaken to show devotion.

place of worship: a place set aside by a faith community for worship. This may be somewhere that people go to pray and carry out rituals or ceremonies. Most places of worship are a focal point for the community that uses them. They can be used for many different functions.

point of view: a way of considering something or an opinion

polytheism: the belief in many Gods

praise: When praising or glorifying God, e.g. when realising how beautiful a sunset is

prayer: a two-way conversation between humans and the sacred or holy

primary sources: sources from the time being studied, e.g. artefacts, manuscripts, diaries, official documents or ruins

Prince Rama: one of the forms that the Hindu God Vishnu took when he descended to earth. Rama is the hero of an epic saga the *Ramayana*

Prince Siddhartha Gautama: the founder of Buddhism

prophet: a messenger of God, someone who brings the message of God to the people in Judaism, Christianity or Islam

puja: an act of worship carried out by Hindus

Puranas: Hindu holy writings; they tell stories about the creation of the world and the legends of the Gods, and they explain how to perform religious rituals

purpose: a reason for something to be done or to exist

qibla: a compass that shows the direction of Mecca for prayer five times a day

Quran: the sacred writing of Islam

racism: prejudice and discrimination against people from a different race

Ramadan: the holy month of prayer and fasting in Islam

reconciliation: restoring relationships that have become hostile between people or groups. Persuading people or groups with opposing outlooks or beliefs to respect each other where previously they did not.

redeem: to compensate or to make amends for something bad. It is doing something good in exchange, to make up for wrongdoing.

reincarnation: the belief that when a person dies, his or her soul is reborn into a new life in this world

relevance: something that is relevant relates to what is going on now and is appropriate or connected to what you are considering, discussing or studying. It is pertinent to society at this time.

religious ritual: a ceremony performed according to a prescribed order, consisting of a series of actions that have religious and symbolic values attached to them

religious theme: a theme that involves a religious idea or concept

respect: to have proper regard for the feelings and rights of other people. When we respect a thing or idea, we consider it important and take care of it.

resurrected: to be raised from the dead

revelation: when God (or Gods) make something known to people

rishis: unknown wise men, the founders of Hinduism

ritual: the traditions, habits and actions that are repeated in a family, community or society

sacrament: a ritual in the Christian Church involves the use of symbols that represent the loving presence of God

sacred space: a place considered holy or sacred by a religious community. It is a place seen as special and significant to members of the religion that it is associated with.

sacred texts: the important writings of a religious community

sadaqah: refers to charity in Islam. This type of charity is voluntary.

saint: a good and holy person who is worthy of special honour

salat: the second of the Five Pillars of Islam, requiring Muslims to pray five times a day in the direction of Mecca

samsara: in Hinduism, the soul (*atman*) goes through a process of reincarnation called *samsara*, with continuous life cycles

sawm: the fourth of the Five Pillars of Islam, obliging Muslims to fast during the month of Ramadan

scholar: a person with great knowledge and who is a specialist in a particular branch of study

seal of the prophets: the final prophet, the last prophet of God (Allah) – there is no need for further prophets, as the final message has come from the seal-'closing' prophet

secondary sources: sources created about an event after it has happened, e.g. books, documentaries, reconstructions, drawings or diagrams produced later

sectarianism: hatred of some people because they belong to a different group (sect) of a religion

segregated: when some people are forced to live separately from others

Shahadah: the first of the five pillars of Islam; the statement of faith, 'There is no God but Allah and Muhammad is his prophet'

Shema: the Jewish statement of faith, 'Hear O Israel the Lord our God, the Lord is one'

Shiva: the Hindu God of destruction; one of the three Gods that make up the *Trimurti*

significance: to have importance in relation to something

situation: the particular circumstance or place that someone or something is in

society: people living together in an organised community, sharing laws and customs

source: anything that gives us information about something or someone. It is where the information comes from about the thing we are studying or trying to find out about.

sources of morality: the things that influence a person's moral decisions or ideas of right and wrong. They include family, friends, the media, law and religion.

stereotype: an oversimplified idea or image about a person or thing

stewardship: to take care of something, to look after it and to manage it. To be a steward of something is to be put in charge of looking after it, for it to be entrusted in your care and for you to protect and preserve it.

story: a description of events that actually happened or that are invented

subject: the person or thing that is being discussed or described

Sunnah: practices, customs and traditions of the Prophet Muhammad. These are seen as the perfect example for Muslims to follow.

sustainable: able to be maintained or continued over a long period of time. In relation to development or obtaining energy, sustainable refers to things that do not damage the environment and do not use up limited natural resources.

Talmud: Jewish sacred writing, commentary on the Jewish law or Torah

Tanakh: the sacred writings of Judaism, made up of the Torah, Nevi'im and Ketuvim

thanksgiving: when giving thanks to God, e.g. when someone has arrived safely after a journey

Ten Commandments: the centrepiece of the Jewish law or Torah. Also known as the Decalogue. These are 10 important laws that govern a person's relationship with God and other people.

theme: an idea that recurs in a film, a work of art, a piece of music or literature

timeline: a visual representation of a time period on which important events are marked

tolerance: being kind and understanding; showing respect for other people and their beliefs; not intentionally hurting someone or treating them badly

Torah: the Jewish law or instruction

tradition: a custom or practice that is repeated over a long time. It may be within a small group of people or a large community. It is significant and holds meaning for the people carrying it out.

Transcendent: something beyond the normal, physical, human experience

Trimurti: the three main Gods of Hinduism. They are Brahma, Vishnu and Shiva.

Trinity: Christian teaching that God is one but three persons

Universal Declaration of Human Rights: a very important document that was drawn up so everyone would know what they have a right to

Upanishads: a collection of religious texts in Hinduism

values: attitudes or ideas that a person or society consider to be important

Vedas: Hindu sacred writings

Vishnu: the Hindu God of preservation; one of the three Gods that make up the *Trimurti*

wellbeing: feeling healthy, comfortable and happy

world hunger: hunger on a global level. It is related to food insecurity and malnutrition. Food insecurity is when there is no reliable access to food in an area or country. Malnutrition occurs when people do not take in the necessary nutrients. People become undernourished when they do not have enough to eat.

worship: to show devotion or love to a God or deity

Writings: one section of the Jewish sacred text the Tanakh. The Writings are made up of songs and poems like the psalms or praises to God, the proverbs or wise sayings and the stories that were used to teach people.

xenophobia: dislike and prejudice against people from other countries

zakat: the third of the Five Pillars of Islam, requiring Muslims to give to charity